MW00994207

FREE Study Skills DVD Offer

Dear Customer,

Thank you for your purchase from Mometrix! We consider it an honor and privilege that you have purchased our product and want to ensure your satisfaction.

As a way of showing our appreciation and to help us better serve you, we have developed a Study Skills DVD that we would like to give you for <u>FREE</u>. **This DVD covers our "best practices" for studying for your exam, from using our study materials to preparing for the day of the test.**

All that we ask is that you email us your feedback that would describe your experience so far with our product. Good, bad or indifferent, we want to know what you think!

To get your **FREE Study Skills DVD**, email <u>freedvd@mometrix.com</u> with "FREE STUDY SKILLS DVD" in the subject line and the following information in the body of the email:

    a. The name of the product you purchased.

    b. Your product rating on a scale of 1-5, with 5 being the highest rating.

    c. Your feedback. It can be long, short, or anything in-between, just your impressions and experience so far with our product. Good feedback might include how our study material met your needs and will highlight features of the product that you found helpful.

    d. Your full name and shipping address where you would like us to send your free DVD.

If you have any questions or concerns, please don't hesitate to contact me directly.

Thanks again!

Sincerely,

Jay Willis
Vice President
<u>jay.willis@mometrix.com</u>
1-800-673-8175

SLLA

SECRETS

Study Guide
Your Key to Exam Success

SLLA Test Review for the
School Leaders Licensure Assessment

Published by
Mometrix Test Preparation
SLLA Exam Secrets Test Prep Team

Copyright © 2017 by Mometrix Media LLC

All rights reserved. This product, or parts thereof, may not be reproduced, stored in a retrieval system, or transmitted in any form or by any means—electronic, mechanical, photocopy, recording, scanning, or other—except for brief quotations in critical reviews or articles, without the prior written permission of the publisher.

Written and edited by the SLLA Exam Secrets Test Prep Staff

Printed in the United States of America

This paper meets the requirements of ANSI/NISO Z39.48-1992 (Permanence of Paper).

Mometrix offers volume discount pricing to institutions. For more information or a price quote, please contact our sales department at sales@mometrix.com or 888-248-1219.

Mometrix Media LLC is not affiliated with or endorsed by any official testing organization. All organizational and test names are trademarks of their respective owners.

ISBN 13: 978-1-62733-924-7
ISBN 10: 1-62733-924-8

Dear Future Exam Success Story:

Congratulations on your purchase of our study guide. Our goal in writing our study guide was to cover the content on the test, as well as provide insight into typical test taking mistakes and how to overcome them.

Standardized tests are a key component of being successful, which only increases the importance of doing well in the high-pressure high-stakes environment of test day. How well you do on this test will have a significant impact on your future, and we have the research and practical advice to help you execute on test day.

The product you're reading now is designed to exploit weaknesses in the test itself, and help you avoid the most common errors test takers frequently make.

How to use this study guide

We don't want to waste your time. Our study guide is fast-paced and fluff-free. We suggest going through it a number of times, as repetition is an important part of learning new information and concepts.

First, read through the study guide completely to get a feel for the content and organization. Read the general success strategies first, and then proceed to the content sections. Each tip has been carefully selected for its effectiveness.

Second, read through the study guide again, and take notes in the margins and highlight those sections where you may have a particular weakness.

Finally, bring the manual with you on test day and study it before the exam begins.

Your success is our success

We would be delighted to hear about your success. Send us an email and tell us your story. Thanks for your business and we wish you continued success.

Sincerely,

Mometrix Test Preparation Team

Need more help? Check out our flashcards at: http://MometrixFlashcards.com/SLLA

TABLE OF CONTENTS

Top 20 Test Taking Tips

1. Carefully follow all the test registration procedures
2. Know the test directions, duration, topics, question types, how many questions
3. Setup a flexible study schedule at least 3-4 weeks before test day
4. Study during the time of day you are most alert, relaxed, and stress free
5. Maximize your learning style; visual learner use visual study aids, auditory learner use auditory study aids
6. Focus on your weakest knowledge base
7. Find a study partner to review with and help clarify questions
8. Practice, practice, practice
9. Get a good night's sleep; don't try to cram the night before the test
10. Eat a well balanced meal
11. Know the exact physical location of the testing site; drive the route to the site prior to test day
12. Bring a set of ear plugs; the testing center could be noisy
13. Wear comfortable, loose fitting, layered clothing to the testing center; prepare for it to be either cold or hot during the test
14. Bring at least 2 current forms of ID to the testing center
15. Arrive to the test early; be prepared to wait and be patient
16. Eliminate the obviously wrong answer choices, then guess the first remaining choice
17. Pace yourself; don't rush, but keep working and move on if you get stuck
18. Maintain a positive attitude even if the test is going poorly
19. Keep your first answer unless you are positive it is wrong
20. Check your work, don't make a careless mistake

Copyright © Mometrix Media. You have been licensed one copy of this document for personal use only. Any other reproduction or redistribution is strictly prohibited. All rights reserved.

Copyright © Mometrix Media. You have been licensed one copy of this document for personal use only. Any other reproduction or redistribution is strictly prohibited. All rights reserved.

Visions and Goals

School vision

A school leader's vision should: (1) afford meaning in employee lives, (2) set excellence standards, (3) motivate employees and enlist their commitment, (4) transition between present and future, and (5) go beyond current school conditions. Some researchers define visions by types of changes they entail. For example, first-order changes involve school improvements, as when schools adopt new reading programs. Related to such changes are first-order visions, also defined as program visions. Second-order changes are changes that require the school's responsibilities, relationships, rules, and roles to be reorganized. These kinds of changes mean that the school leader must envision not only how new practices or programs will work, but moreover how new groups of accountability systems, relationships, and expectations will coherently combine to form a whole. This requires the school leader to have system vision. For example, a high school's reorganization to schedule class periods requires major changes regarding teacher instructional planning needs, numbers and kinds of course offerings, accommodation of extracurricular activities, etc. Hence program vision and system vision reflect distinct kinds of district and school changes.

School visions not only depict the future, they inspire employees to realize them. Experts have noted the bonding effects of visions shared by leaders and followers through their common values, goals, and commitment to the cause of meeting those goals. School leaders frequently develop visions personally, but recognize that other people will implement them. The same is true for collaboratively-developed visions. Differences between the two involve their respective pros and cons: leaders' personally-developed visions have advantages of coherence, clarity, and potentially quick implementation; while disadvantages are that leaders may be expected to accomplish them independently, and that employees may resist them. Collaboratively developed visions have advantages of prompting group responsibility and being more appropriate to district contexts, and disadvantages of a lengthier development process less amenable to meeting urgent demands for rapid action and change. In either case, visions require a sense of ownership. Experts find that visions, whether leader-initiated or collaboratively developed, are more likely to be implemented successfully by employees when they are shared.

While on a smaller, more specific level, school leaders logically align their school goals with the school vision they have developed and establish school policies to reflect those goals and vision. Their development of school visions and goals on a larger, broader level must reflect national policies. This drive has placed ever-increasing emphasis upon the administration and the reporting of high-stakes national and state standardized testing to measure, monitor, and remediate student academic achievement. Educator activities in preparing students to succeed on these objective performance measures and meet national educational standards are similarly emphasized. From the federal level, state standardized tests reflect the national standards. Similarly local school districts' standardized assessments reflect state standards, school systems reflect district standards, and individual schools replicate system standards. As such, while school leaders have personal visions and goals for their individual schools, these goals are still necessarily aligned with federal policies to keep the largest overall educational goals consistent with national vision.

Copyright © Mometrix Media. You have been licensed one copy of this document for personal use only. Any other reproduction or redistribution is strictly prohibited. All rights reserved.

School leaders can assess and self-assess knowledge by asking how they make sure their school purpose, vision, and goals inform the processes of instruction and learning. Respondents may know that school leadership utilizes a systematic approach so that all persons involved are important to the functions and processes of the school. Stakeholders assume ownership by pursuing a vision and purpose that they share with all others involved. Commitment to the shared vision and purpose also supports them in enforcing the current school policies, finding and taking advantage of professional development opportunities, and encouraging students to participate actively in their processes of lifelong learning. School leaders may also ask how they use a process for making sure that the school purpose and vision are kept up to date and in alignment with the school expectations for educational effectiveness and student learning. They and other involved stakeholders should know regarding this question that the school district will periodically (e.g., every three years) review the school's vision and conduct a reevaluation of how the school goals are currently reflecting the school purpose and vision.

School-wide expectations

School leaders use college and career preparation and state academic standards to adopt school standards. Using these standards and collected data, they decide which standards will support their students' success most strategically and have the most long-term value in each discipline, and develop curriculum maps to inform educator curriculum and instruction design and planning. In alignment with college preparation, school leaders provide school-wide guidance in adopting scholarship practices and character expectations. They develop transition plans and timelines for new standards adoption as needed. They develop processes for reviewing the curriculum maps of skills and content they have created to ensure reflection of and alignment with essential standards of concepts, content, and skills across grade levels. They support teachers to plan strategic assessments in alignment with the curriculum maps and review teacher plans, giving feedback as needed. They may also arrange for educators to review one another's plans to assure they are rigorous, relevant, and aligned with goals. Finally, school leaders supervise teacher selection and/or creation, and alignment with curriculum, of quality interim assessments.

Data collection and analysis

School leaders should use not only test scores, but multiple sources of data (e.g., information obtained from students, teachers, parents, and members of the community) to monitor how their schools are realizing their missions, and to intervene for school improvement. Leaders can encourage students, teachers, and parents as members of the school community to analyzing the data to identify opportunities for school improvement, dangers to school functioning, and school weaknesses and strengths. Leaders should inspect the data according to student groups, student cohorts, grade levels, and by teachers within grade levels; across school years; by subject matter; according to the results of both formative and state-mandated, standardized summative assessments; and according to student, teacher, and parent respondent categories. By analyzing different layers among the data, school leaders can understand these in more depth to gain insight into various possible problems and improvements. To focus their efforts at school improvement, leaders need to identify the most important, specific problems that exist.

School leaders should first initiate collection and analysis of school data. Then they can formulate three or four summary statements based on their data analyses. These

Copyright © Mometrix Media. You have been licensed one copy of this document for personal use only. Any other reproduction or redistribution is strictly prohibited. All rights reserved.

statements should assemble diverse data components to provide a detailed perspective of specific school problems that have strategic impacts, and where these problems are focused. Leaders should form summary statements based on what they have learned from studying the data. They should review each of their statements regarding how severe each problem is, and how feasible it is to address each problem. The statements will become the bases for setting strategic school goals. To pursue these goals, leaders must consider both their local context and scientific evidence for decision-making about improvement strategies. What is effective and under what circumstances are determined best through research evidence obtained through experimental research designs. True change can be achieved through strategies using planned, visible monitoring and feedback processes combined with educator expertise, review of high-quality research, and clearly specifying improvement goals informed by data.

Data-based decision-making

The process of making decisions based on data collection and analysis for the purpose of school improvement is continual and evolving. School leaders examine data collected and develop school improvement strategies based on their analyses of those data. After schools have implemented these strategies, leaders and school staff must continue to monitor implementation by collecting additional data aligned with goals they have defined. Monitoring not only supports implementing school improvement strategies, it moreover furnishes critical feedback about the effectiveness of newly adopted strategies and whether they are likely to accomplish their intended effects. School leaders need to guide schools in making corrections and adjustments during the course of implementation. Continuous monitoring enables school leaders to assess whether their schools are improving continually, and to what degree. During this process, solutions to some problems may be achieved, while some new problems may also develop. By collecting and analyzing diverse data indices and building community in schools, leaders can help schools address weaknesses, build upon strengths, and identify and take advantages of opportunities to succeed.

The crucial role of a school's mission and goals is to guide school program and curriculum activities. Data-based decision-making processes begin with the school mission, which affords a summary of values of the school community, goals the school intends to attain, and the direction in which the school is going. School leaders should be engaged in a continual process of analyzing data they and others collect about school operations. By closely studying and basing their decisions on these data, leaders can establish strategic goals aligned with the school vision and mission. These goals should meet the most important defined indices of school effectiveness. By consistently connecting the school mission with data recorded, school leaders can monitor schools' progress toward realizing their goals on an ongoing basis. Data can be used for understanding and changing how resources are allocated for goals; how schools relate to families and communities; the character of the school climate and the teachers' professional community; the expertise of teachers and the quality of professional development provided to them; rigorous student content standards; and aligned, coherent curriculum and instruction.

Accountability in curriculum, instruction, and assessment

School leaders should not only hold teachers accountable to implement their agreed curriculum, they should also support teachers in doing so. Leaders should regularly review

Copyright © Mometrix Media. You have been licensed one copy of this document for personal use only. Any other reproduction or redistribution is strictly prohibited. All rights reserved.

the practice indices of relevant, rigorous and aligned curriculum, instruction, and assessment (e.g., learning objectives, classroom assessments, and data on student achievement). To reproduce and maintain effective practices, school leaders should share with others and celebrate outstanding examples of curriculum and student performance. They must make investments in high quality instructional resources and materials that are aligned with school curriculum and standards, and make sure that their teachers always have access to these tools. In the same way, they must make investments in assessment instruments of equally high quality that are aligned with the standardized tests used in their schools and with their school standards, and assure teacher access to and use of these assessments. By frequently visiting classrooms and providing teachers with feedback, school leaders can closely monitor how well teachers are implementing the curriculum, instruction, and assessment upon which they have mutually agreed.

SMART

"SMART" stands for Specific, Measurable, Achievable, Relevant, and Time-specific. This acronym is frequently employed for writing educational program objectives. "Specific" means the language of an objective should specifically state an issue, the group involved, and the program's time and place. "Measurable" means the objective should clearly establish what must change and quantify by how much. "Achievable" means the objective must be realistic about what the program can accomplish in terms of resources and time available, and the scope or scale of what to accomplish. "Relevant" means a specific objective relates to the goal it is designed to meet. And "time-specific" means that the time in which a program objective is expected to be achieved is clear. An example of a non-measurable objective for a family literacy program would be: "To raise awareness of ESL student parents' low literacy rates." This is vague and not quantified. An example of a corresponding measurable objective would be: "After a family literacy program is implemented in all district middle schools for eight weeks, participant attendance will increase by 10 percent and family surveys will show 50 percent more families using home reading strategies."

Measurable

"Measurable" means observable. In other words, goals and objectives that can be measured can be externally seen, heard, felt, or otherwise noticed by others. Only outwardly demonstrated behaviors can be measured. Therefore, goals written in language that reflects internal states cannot be measurable. For example, when writing goals for schools or students, using the verb "will"—e.g., "Student X will complete nine out of 10 written assignments within one school week," or "School X will demonstrate a 25 percent increase in passing student test scores by the end of the next semester"—represents measurable goals because it is possible to determine whether these actions took place or not. However, the use of verbs such as "hopes," "dreams," "aspires," "plans," "wishes," "indicates," "thinks," "would like (to)" or qualifiers like "maybe" represent non-measurable goals because they indicate internal states, thoughts, or feelings rather than external behaviors. Contrast a goal saying "Student X will attend college after graduation from high school," which is measurable, with one saying "Student X wants to attend college after graduation from high school," which is not measurable.

Copyright © Mometrix Media. You have been licensed one copy of this document for personal use only. Any other reproduction or redistribution is strictly prohibited. All rights reserved.

Political policies to support equitable and excellent education

To support the outcome of learning for every student, educational leaders consistently function both to support local, state, and federal laws, regulations, statutes, and policies; and also to influence these. School leaders serve as advocates for continually increasing the support for equity and excellence in education. Educational leaders also work to improve the public's comprehension of local, state, and federal policies, regulations, laws, and statutes and the things they require of citizens for compliance and active participation. One way in which they accomplish this improvement is to employ effective communication skills for interacting with the most important makers of decisions in both their own local communities and also in wider political arenas. In addition, school leaders collect data regarding the educational performance of students, teachers, and schools. They communicate these data timely and clearly to policymakers and other political decision-makers. This communication includes specific information about their local educational settings for the purposes of informing progressive political debate and working to improve educational policies.

Focus questions

School leaders might ask, "How do we build and increase stakeholder commitment to and understanding of our school vision statement?" School personnel and stakeholders alike can respond. For example, they can indicate their knowledge that schools call meetings of staff and community members for developing a school vision statement, the school board considers public comments, and approves a final vision statement. They can say all stakeholders and school staff may engage in creating the vision statement through the process of meetings, approval, and publication of the vision statement campus-wide in multiple locations, on the school website, and in the student handbook. School leaders might also ask, "How do we systematically develop, maintain, and utilize profile information about our school, the students, and their performance?" Stakeholders and staff may say the school district keeps a yearly statistical profile, shares these with all stakeholders, and provides parents access to the profile at conferences, on the school website, and in the school office. They may also know the school encourages students to engage in this process by composing essays about the school vision's meaning to them.

Surveying various school stakeholders

School leaders may survey key stakeholders by presenting them with a series of statements with which the respondents indicate how much they agree or disagree. For example, they might select a number on a Likert-type scale indicating "agree strongly," "agree somewhat," "agree slightly," "neither agree nor disagree," "disagree slightly," "disagree somewhat," or "disagree strongly." They could offer all stakeholders surveys on leadership practice, school practice, and school climate. Regarding school vision, mission, and goals, an example of a statement about leadership practice could be, "The school leaders clearly communicate high expectations for student learning." For school practice, a statement could be, "I know what the student performance expectations are at our school." For school climate, a statement might be, "Our school challenges its students to meet high expectations." Regarding teaching and learning, a leadership practice survey statement for teachers could be: "Our school's administrator has established a school-wide, formal process for making instructional improvement plans." A school practice survey statement for parents could be: "If my child

Copyright © Mometrix Media. You have been licensed one copy of this document for personal use only. Any other reproduction or redistribution is strictly prohibited. All rights reserved.

needs extra help, he can get it at our school." A school climate survey statement for teachers might be: "At our school, feedback and collaboration are valued."

Diverse families and communities

Studies show that families generally care about their children's success and have similar high aspirations for them regardless of their culture, ethnicity, race, or income. Researchers have indicated a need for further investigation into whether the high aspirations of low-income and minority families positively influence their children's academic performance, and into the effectiveness of family involvement programs for enhancing student achievement. Diverse families also commonly share active involvement in their children's educations, though types and degrees of involvement with low-income families may be affected by economic stressors and limited means. School staff and families report inconsistently regarding degrees of school outreach and family involvement, for unclear reasons. Obstacles to minority or low-income family educational involvement identified by research include lack of knowledge and understanding of American education processes; discrimination and exclusion issues; cultural perceptions regarding family educational roles; language differences; and context variables like transportation, child care, and time limitations. Studies also find schools can frequently help overcome these obstacles. Some intervention strategies seem to hold promise for reinforcing school-family-community relationships in low-income and/or minority populations. Some studies suggest the necessity of addressing complex school-family-community interactions rather than any single factor for closing achievement gaps.

Based on study findings, researchers recommend school leader demonstrations of ongoing, active support to build school-family-community relationships with diverse populations. Leaders should honor family concerns, hopes, and dreams for their children. They should adopt formal policies at school and district levels promoting family engagement, particularly focusing on diverse student families. School leaders must acknowledge both the diversity and commonality among all students and families. They should furnish supportive services and resources to aid immigrant family understanding of how American schools function, and of what is expected of both students and families. Leaders should support and enhance the abilities of their school staff for interacting effectively with families. They are advised to prioritize school outreach, taking needed additional measures to enable family involvement both at home and at school. Experts also advise school leaders to realize that building trust with diverse families takes time.

Based on the findings of their studies, researchers recommend that school leaders should offer resources and training to diverse families to enable them to support early literacy development in their children. They advise school leaders to assist minority families to learn and apply specific strategies for monitoring and communication that will support their children's learning. In addition, they say that school leaders should support and encourage students in becoming and staying involved in a variety of school-sponsored and community-sponsored after-school and extracurricular activities, which will enhance their access to enrichment experiences beyond academic instruction. Researchers also recommend that school leaders should assist low-income families in getting the services and supports that they require in order to assure their own safety, security, health, and nutrition so they will be better equipped to provide for, take care of, advocate for, and participate actively in the education of their children.

Copyright © Mometrix Media. You have been licensed one copy of this document for personal use only. Any other reproduction or redistribution is strictly prohibited. All rights reserved.

Learning communities, as well as wider communities, can shape, organize, plan, and implement their collective ideas through the structure afforded them by collaborative partnerships, whereby they can design comprehensive strategies that support and strengthen families and students. Some dimensions of the collaborative partnership-building process include recognizing opportunities for change, developing a vision of change over the long term, mobilizing people and resources to effect change, recruiting involvement and support from non-traditional and diverse partners, selecting an effective structure for the group, building trust among the members, and developing opportunities for collaborative partners to learn. School leaders often initiate collaborative efforts. But even when others, such as parents, school employees, local policymakers, or other community members initiate it, school leaders can still follow through by meeting with them; with superintendents when new private or public funding becomes available for comprehensive services; and with health and human service providers to develop strategies connected to schools for child care, violence prevention, job preparation, adult education, health care, etc. Leaders should recruit non-traditional community leaders and families as well as more usual participants.

Collaborative partnerships among schools and communities

Collaborative partnerships among school and community members may make shared decisions via group consensus, majority rule, or committee decision-making. For group consensus decisions, input from each group member is needed, and each member must agree that he or she understands, supports, and will implement the collective decision. An advantage of this is that the thorough discussion of all alternatives, enabling that all voices are heard, and commitment fostered by this approach makes it ideal for collaborative partnerships. A disadvantage is that it can be a time-consuming process, not always amenable to time limits. A quicker approach is majority rule, wherein the largest number of votes determines the choice. Despite its time-saving advantage, its disadvantage is that participant commitment to collaborating can be damaged when only one faction wins. Hence this method is recommended for decisions regarding more minor concerns. A third approach, decision-making by committee, also expedites progress. But similarly to majority rule, all group members may not agree with committee decisions. If the group often overrides committee choices, the committee members may feel the time and effort they invest are not worthwhile.

Consensus decisions

According to a model of decision-making by consensus (Baron, in *Principal Leadership,* February 2008), consensus decisions are made when a decision has an effect on the whole group. A group reaches consensus when every member can accept a committee, group, or individual recommendation; support implementing it; and agree not to interfere with implementing it. Once the initiator(s) explains the recommendation, faculty members ask questions to clarify their understanding. They then give feedback, including concerns and affirmations. The person(s) making the recommendation listens closely to feedback and respond with how they did or would address concerns. This process does not instantly change faculty collaboration; however, faculty meeting culture can be changed by having teachers pair up and brainstorm all unproductive aspects of meetings and identifying their single most frustrating factor. Meeting leaders and facilitators record these, asking each pair to identify one agreement to prevent these most frustrating procedures and behaviors. Then they ask teachers and administrators to form a small work group for reviewing and

Copyright © Mometrix Media. You have been licensed one copy of this document for personal use only. Any other reproduction or redistribution is strictly prohibited. All rights reserved.

synthesizing the agreements to propose at the next meeting, using the same consensus model to address proposals. If consensus seems impossible, many schools apply a rule of 80 percent agreement, with disagreeing members promising to support and not obstruct implementation.

Key stakeholders in education

Students are key stakeholders in their own educations. At stake for them is their individual success throughout school, and the opportunities open to them in their future lives thereafter. Parents are key stakeholders in their children's educations. Opportunities they want for their children, children's success, and their own pride in children's accomplishments are at stake for them. School personnel are key stakeholders: their job satisfaction, pride in student success, and professional effectiveness are at stake. School district staff members, also key stakeholders, have expectations for accountability and Adequate Yearly Progress (AYP) at stake. School board members are key stakeholders for whom accountability, realizing district missions, and media coverage received are at stake. All taxpayers whose taxes support public schools are key stakeholders: receiving valuable returns on their investments in schools via paying school taxes is at stake for them. Members of the business community are key stakeholders as well. Community economies, and their access to hiring school graduates with the skills they need in employees, are at stake. Other community members are also key education stakeholders. Real estate property values, how "livable" their communities are, and community pride are things at stake for them.

While internal stakeholders are more able to influence positive school changes, they are unable to maintain these changes alone over time. "Mission drift," priority shifts, and staff attrition can influence organizational functioning, so one year's improved results diminish the following year. External stakeholders informed of school academic improvement goals can help maintain district focus on these over time, mitigate the influences of employee turnover, and prevent mission drift by concentrating on school improvements aligned with their district's purpose or mission, i.e., "mission-oriented change." To engage external stakeholders, school leaders and staffs must transcend traditional efforts like fundraising, social events, volunteering, homework help, and parent training. To promote continuing collaboration to enhance student learning, (1) school leaders and staff must take the initiative to furnish stakeholders data and other information for productive partnerships promoting student achievement. (2) Collaborative activities must be aligned directly with school student achievement goals. (3) All members can play meaningful parts; school leaders and staff must clearly explain these; and genuine, cooperative endeavors are necessary. (4) Schools must provide accurate, clear, relevant achievement data and share information transparently. (5) All participants must share a common vision and values regarding student achievement.

Communicating appropriately with important stakeholders

According to research from the Statewide Longitudinal Data Systems (SLDS) grant program from the National Center for Education Statistics, school leaders must communicate effectively with legislators, other state agencies, post-secondary education leaders, program offices, school district officials, and other important stakeholders during the processes of designing, developing, and implementing systems. They recommend: identifying a variety of key stakeholders and reaching out to them early; establishing realistic expectations;

Copyright © Mometrix Media. You have been licensed one copy of this document for personal use only. Any other reproduction or redistribution is strictly prohibited. All rights reserved.

leveraging or forming groups to spearhead outreach endeavors; being inclusive, yet focused, with appropriate timing; making and following clearly and carefully conceived and defined outreach plans; designating significant persons as "point people" and "ambassadors"; viewing communication as partly an activity for managing change; recognizing differences among groups of stakeholders and customizing one's style accordingly; listening and responding to input from stakeholders; organizing meetings around products or questions that are very specific; garnering and maintaining stakeholder support by implementing some early successes; and crediting stakeholders with their help in designing and enhancing systems.

The Institute of Education Sciences' National Center for Education Statistics has a Statewide Longitudinal Data Systems (SLDS) Grant Program which has conducted research into best practices in education. This includes studying aspects of school leadership's communication with important stakeholders such as other state agencies, program offices, school district leaders, leaders of post-secondary educational programs and institutions, legislators, and others. In these studies, the researchers have identified not only a series of best practices to follow for the most effective stakeholder communication, but also several undesirable practices which school leaders should avoid when communicating with key stakeholders. For example, they warn school leaders not to ignore the political environment in which they are interacting. They say that when communicating with the majority of stakeholder audiences, school leaders should avoid becoming overly technical in their speech. They caution school leaders against engaging in open forums on a large scale. They advise school leaders against failing to follow through on promises they make. They say school leaders should not assume that everybody is in agreement about system goals. And perhaps most importantly, they tell school leaders, "Do not NOT communicate."

Improving communication skills for school leaders and school leadership team members

Researchers have found three strategies for effective communication skills. (1) Paraphrasing: after listening to what a colleague or employee has reported, repeat what you perceive as the most salient part of it in your own words. This shows that you were paying attention; that you understood what the other person was saying; and allows the other person to confirm, correct, or clarify your perception if he or she feels it necessary. (2) Checking perceptions: after listening to what another person has communicated, reflect the emotion(s) you perceive the other person was feeling about the subject of the communication. For example, one might say, "From what I heard you say, it is frustrating when you cannot obtain all of the information that you need to do your job." Or, "I have the impression that you feel your co-workers are not supporting your efforts." (3) Asking clarification questions: obtain a more observable, clearer view of what has been communicated as the other person questions to clarify it. For example, one might ask, "Do you mean that teachers are less able to plan suitable interventions because they do not have enough time for shared planning?"

In addition to paraphrasing others' communicative content, checking on others' emotions as one perceived them, and asking questions to clarify the meaning of others' communications, there are three additional communication strategies that researchers have found effective for school leaders. (1) Summarizing: when nearing the end of a conversation, it is helpful to restate concisely what you think you heard the other person say to verify whether this is what he or she intended to express. For example, one might say, "To sum up what you have

Copyright © Mometrix Media. You have been licensed one copy of this document for personal use only. Any other reproduction or redistribution is strictly prohibited. All rights reserved.

said, for the next PTA newsletter, John and Marcia will write an update on the progress made by this leadership team." (2) Asking relevant questions: to continue and expand an ongoing discussion in order to establish and learn more information related to the subject, ask questions about the topic being discussed. For example, one might ask, "If we believe that our writing curriculum is effective, what data or evidence do we have that can prove that?" (3) Attentive, active listening: leaders should show others they are engaged in a discussion by acknowledging what they say through nonverbal cues, e.g., leaning toward the speaker, making eye contact, nodding appropriately, etc.

Delegating and distributing responsibilities

For effective school management, school leaders must attend to such diverse factors as analyzing assessment data, addressing high-level issues regarding student discipline, supervising food service, planning the budget, etc. Because of the range and variety of tasks for which they are responsible, school leaders would be overwhelmed and unable to complete any task fully or successfully if they did not delegate duties effectively. A single person cannot manage an entire school. Therefore, school leaders must distribute responsibilities among employees. First they should evaluate all of the existing duties and assign them levels of priority. The most important leadership responsibilities are those the school leaders should retain for themselves; they can then divide the remaining duties among teams composed of school staff members and/or individual staff members. Leaders should pay attention to matching duties to staff member qualifications. For example, data analysis would be appropriately assigned to math teachers, writing reports could be delegated to English teachers, etc.

School leaders not only solve the problem of managing an entire school when they delegate various duties to employees. By distributing tasks effectively, they also create greater investment in the school's success by teachers and other staff members. The greater the role teachers and others play in school management, the greater their insights become about the necessities of maintaining school operations. This comprehension informs greater feelings of involvement in the success of the school. This involvement in turn enhances their sense of commitment to the school's success. Many state departments of education include in their evaluations of school leaders the component of "distributive leadership," i.e., how effectively the school leader assigns duties to staff members, as one criterion for judging a school leader's success. After delegating tasks to employees, school leaders must follow up with them consistently. This involves scheduling regular meeting times with employees, developing protocols for employees to report back to school leaders on progress or problems with their assigned duties, creating progress records for employees to complete regularly, and/or having committees keep and deliver meeting minutes to school leaders.

Effective instructional leadership

Among the first models of instructional leadership was one proposed by Thomas Sergiovanni (1983). In this model, he identified five forces of leadership: technical, human, educational, symbolic, and cultural. The technical force concerns administrative management practices, for example leadership theory, organizational development, planning, and time management. The human force includes instructional leadership elements of interpersonal interactions, such as the leader's roles in communicating with faculty and staff, motivating them, and ensuring they fulfill their job roles and responsibilities. The educational force entails the school leader's instructional roles, i.e.,

- 12 -

Copyright © Mometrix Media. You have been licensed one copy of this document for personal use only. Any other reproduction or redistribution is strictly prohibited. All rights reserved.

implementing curriculum, learning, and teaching. The symbolic force in instructional leadership, while difficult to define and comprehend, involves the school leader's capacity for embodying a symbol of what is purposive and important in the school. The cultural force, while similarly difficult to explain and understand, involves the school leader's skill for articulating the school organization's beliefs and values across time.

Skills, behaviors, or tasks important to success of school leaders

In a large-scale study of school leaders in Illinois (reported in McEwan, 2000), researchers found a number of behaviors, skills, or tasks that were recognized as most crucial to successful school leadership. These were: modeling high professional standards for faculty and staff; setting high expectations for both the students and the staff; establishing a vision, mission, and goals for their school and maintaining these over time; evaluating the performance of school staff; keeping a visible presence in the school; establishing an orderly and safe school environment; maintaining positive interpersonal relationships with faculty, students, staff, and all members of the learning community; developing school improvement plans; setting up systems for internal school communications; adhering to legally mandated programs of education; and interviewing candidates for teaching positions. In literature review meta-analyses, some researchers report that strong school leaders demonstrate the following behaviors: they effect discipline and order, are dynamic and forceful leaders, marshal needed resources, create atmospheres of high expectations, show commitment to academic goals, serve as instructional leaders, consult with others effectively, evaluate their outcomes, and use time efficiently.

Shared vision and goals

Accompanying the facts that teaching is challenging and difficult, and schools are complex settings, is the fact that many schools lack a shared, clear sense of purpose centered on student learning. This lack results in loss of teacher motivation, program fragmentation, and failure of school improvement endeavors. Educational work, including the design, planning, and implementation of curriculum, instruction, and programs can become uncoordinated, undirected, and depleted when there is no clear sense of direction informing them. A vision arising from values, dreams, and hopes is a picture of what the school should and can become. A mission, more precise than the vision, may proceed from the vision and typically articulates what the school is trying to achieve and for whom. To implement these consistently, school leaders can form teams with members of all major school groups. Together they can study the significance of vision and planning in organizational success, and contact associations that use workshops, conferences, and staff development to help schools develop their visions.

Implementing vision, mission, and goals

School leaders must develop educationally centered and clear visions, as well as clearly defined mission statements to help realize those visions, to enable their schools to succeed. They should work together with school employees and members of the community to achieve consensus about what beliefs, goals, and learning they find most important. To implement their school vision, mission, and goals consistently, school leaders and their staffs can learn more about the various elements of school visions through observation of other leaders and staffs as they develop their visions and missions; review other schools' mission statements to discover how they articulate their school values, dreams, and

Copyright © Mometrix Media. You have been licensed one copy of this document for personal use only. Any other reproduction or redistribution is strictly prohibited. All rights reserved.

concepts and how they address student learning; collaboratively develop and post mission or belief statements in all classrooms; watch organizational leadership videos of other leaders discussing their school visions; and observe how other school teams address shared visions, including what they mean to achieve, how they recruit new members, and how they recognize team members' contributions and celebrate successes.

To enable their schools to be successful, school leaders must not only collaborate with school staff and community members to develop a school vision, mission, and goals, they moreover must implement these consistently. During implementation, some pitfalls to avoid include the following: vision development by an isolated team, because those who were omitted will not support it. Shared visions necessitate contribution and conversation that includes all key stakeholders in the learning community. Taking excessive time to develop visions without acting on them lowers employee motivation. Experts advise beginning with actions to achieve small changes, and then developing formal mission statements. Also, simply developing and having shared visions are insufficient; school leaders must additionally articulate and communicate these consistently and regularly. Student learning must be a primary part of any school vision. Educators should not expect shared school visions to improve student performance immediately; during the introduction of innovations, student performance typically levels or decreases before eventually increasing as new systems stabilize.

A common obstacle to establishing or changing a school vision and/or mission statement is the natural human fear of change and the unknown. When school leaders propose a new vision or mission statement, staff will see it as an obvious sign of impending change. School leaders can address their fears if they anticipate the kinds of interior conversations their employees entertain prior to, during, and after a new school vision or mission is developed. Employees are likely to ask themselves questions like the following: why do we need a new vision (or mission)? Do I believe in it? Will I be able to accept it? Will I be able to support it? What will this new vision demand from me personally? How will my life change as a result of this new vision? With the new vision in place, will I be able to keep doing what I have always done or not? Why or why not? Do I believe that my school is able to accomplish this new vision? Do I believe I can help realize this new vision? As employees ask such questions, school leaders can help them cope with changes by listening to their feelings and thoughts, and validating them.

Barrier to developing a strong school vision

School leaders are often commanded by central or regional office supervisors to deliver a school vision by a due date. In these cases, one individual or a small group hastily create a statement without other stakeholders' input or recognition by other school staff. Such closed approaches prohibit inspiration, collective buy-in, or follow-through. Staff will mistrust the vision (or mission) and ultimately ignore it. It will compare to their previous experiences of temporary whirlwinds of activity, followed by putting school visions, missions, and improvement plans on the shelf, proverbially out of sight and out of mind. Staff members who were not involved in such plans have no motivation to commit to them. School leaders can prevent this kind of barrier by enlisting the engagement of all faculty members to develop a fresh, new, relevant and meaningful vision statement. When all members commonly share an understanding of a collective vision, their aggregated talents and strength have more chance of being fulfilled. Researchers have observed that schools

Copyright © Mometrix Media. You have been licensed one copy of this document for personal use only. Any other reproduction or redistribution is strictly prohibited. All rights reserved.

succeeding best at improving student academic achievement also share core values, informing their clarity of purpose.

Essential elements in developing goals

When school leaders and teachers collaborate to develop goals that will enable them to realize their school mission and/or carry out their school improvement plan (SIP), two essential elements are clarity and specificity: they must be clear in articulating what they want to accomplish and how, and they must be specific in stating all components and steps exactly. As they develop each goal and every action step designed to realize each goal, school leaders and other educators should pose the following five sets of questions to themselves, and then answer them: (1) why? Why does this goal or step have to be accomplished? (2) Who? Who is responsible for this goal or step? Who will participate in it? Who will be affected by it? Who are the stakeholders and the audience? (3) What? What do we need to do? (What we need to do should be directly related to question 1, the purpose.) (4) When? When will this be done? When will we know we have completed it? When will be able to measure our progress? (5) How? How will we measure our progress? How will we know whether what we did succeeded or not?

Action step or activity for meeting an instructional goal

Suppose 25 percent of 9th-grade ESL, ELL, and LEP students have failed Algebra I last year, and many LEP students communicate struggling with new terminology and vocabulary in Algebra I. The school leader and faculty set a goal that this year, 9th-graders with LEP will pass the state standardized test in Algebra I at a rate of 80 percent by the end of the school year instead of the current 75 percent rate. They can then develop an action step to achieve this goal: teachers will use graphic organizers and foldables in lessons to help LEP students learn new algebra terminology. This meets the SMART framework: specific by clearly identifying expectations—to learn new algebra terminology better—and identifying two specific strategies (graphic organizers and foldables). It is Measurable: teachers can use their lesson plans, team minutes, and/or checklists for measuring whether, how, and how much they apply these strategies. It is Achievable: Algebra I team teachers experienced in using the strategies agree to show other team members how. It is Relevant: educators identified 25 percent of LEP students failing Algebra I, and LEP students express difficulty learning new vocabulary. It has a Time frame: teachers will incorporate the strategies when introducing new terms.

Using data in instructional planning and decision making

Numerous recent research studies demonstrate that student achievement can be improved through the judicious use of data for making instructional decisions. For educators to make instructional decisions that are well informed, they cannot know all that is needed from the results of just one assessment. Therefore, researchers emphasize the importance of using multiple sources to obtain data. In addition, schools in general gather huge quantities of data about student performance, behavior, and attendance; perceptual data via focus groups and surveys; and administrative data as well. Researchers state that the quantity of information is of secondary importance to the significance of how these data are utilized. For example, with training from the Southwest Educational Development Laboratory (SEDL) staff, a school district in Louisiana applied Response to Intervention (RTI) in 2010-2011 for literacy instruction and school improvement with diverse student needs. SEDL

Copyright © Mometrix Media. You have been licensed one copy of this document for personal use only. Any other reproduction or redistribution is strictly prohibited. All rights reserved.

assisted teachers in including the ongoing data collection and analysis needed in RTI. From analyzing student work samples, teachers identified concepts and skills with which individual students were struggling and needed additional explicit instruction.

According to research findings, experts recommend that schools and their leaders make data collection and analysis important parts of a continuous cycle of improving education. As components of this recommendation, school leaders should have their staffs collect, organize, and report a variety of different types of data about their students' learning. They should interpret the import of these data, and from their interpretations they should develop hypotheses regarding how they can improve and how their students learn. In order to test their hypotheses and to enhance their students' learning, educators should then modify their instruction accordingly. Experts also recommend that educators should teach their students to analyze the data about their own performance, and to establish learning goals for themselves. To implement this recommendation, educators must explain their expectations to students, and explain the criteria they will use for assessing their performance. They must give their students feedback that is constructive, well-organized, specific, and timely; and tools to help them learn from such constructive feedback. And educators must then use their students' resulting data analyses to direct the modifications they make to their instruction.

Using data to develop school culture, instruction, and accountability

In establishing a clear vision for using data, school leaders should first form school-wide data teams to support continuing data application; define crucial concepts of teaching and learning; create written plans articulating roles, responsibilities, and activities; and provide ongoing leadership regarding data. Second, school leaders should also furnish school staff with supports encouraging a school culture driven by data. They can accomplish this by assigning a facilitator based at the school who meets regularly with teacher teams to talk about the data. They can also devote and structure time for school staff to collaborate. An additional support is regularly offering professional development focused on this area. And third, school leaders should develop and maintain a data system at the district level. To achieve this, school leaders should get a diverse range of stakeholders involved in choosing a data system. They should clearly communicate data system requirements relative to the needs of its users. They should collaboratively decide whether to purchase or build their data system. This will vary by school district. School leaders and stakeholders should also plan and stage how they will implement their new district-wide data system.

Analyzing different categories of data to identify school trends

In the 2009-2010 school year, a Texas school district worked with the Southwest Educational Development Laboratory (SEDL) to examine district-wide data from its elementary, middle, and high schools. They analyzed the data by grade levels, campuses, and student groups in three main categories: (1) demographic data including student population, attendance, participation, and least restrictive environment for students with disabilities; (2) student learning data including the Texas Assessment of Knowledge and Skills (TAKS) in English Language Arts (ELA) reading and mathematics, ELA reading and math Adequate Yearly Progress (AYP), and STAR Reading Assessment and Texas Proficiency Reading Inventory data collected at the beginning and end of the year; (3) disciplinary data including referrals, suspensions, and alternative education program. They identified three trends: (1) elementary AYP was consistently met, yet concerns were that

Copyright © Mometrix Media. You have been licensed one copy of this document for personal use only. Any other reproduction or redistribution is strictly prohibited. All rights reserved.

test scores were slightly lower or flat, especially for reading in some grades. (2) High school AYP was not met in math for two years consecutively. (3) Teacher reports and office referral data analysis identified students consistently showing behavior problems. The district used the analysis to target improvements in elementary reading, high school math, and behavior in all grades.

School leader activities that show responsibilities in planning, monitoring, and assessment

Regardless of individually expressed school visions and multiple specific goals, all school visions and goals generally should always include improvement in instruction, and accordingly in student learning. School leaders are responsible for initiating, collaborating on, supervising the implementation of, documenting the application of, and evaluating short-term and long-term data-driven instructional plans that inform faculty teaching practices. They are responsible for supervising faculty's instruction to improve those classroom practices. School leaders should make classroom visits at a suggested minimum of 10 hours weekly and document these visits. They should initiate, supervise, and participate in forming and implementing a school (and/or district) improvement plan, and compose agendas for meetings they will hold for collaboratively developing this improvement plan. They should offer, listen to, and discuss strategies to effect change, improve instruction and learning, and support the school vision. School leaders are also responsible for reviewing and analyzing faculty and staff's instruction and assessment practices and the data they and others collect about these, and adjusting teaching and testing practices according to what the data indicate. They must also effectively observe and evaluate staff, following legal and contractual requirements and schedules.

Helping teaching staffs align instructional programs with school vision and goals

It is a responsibility of school leaders to help their faculty and staff align school curriculum, instruction, and assessment with the school's vision and goals, as well as with essential academic learning standards and requirements. They implement research-based teaching and learning strategies and materials. They thoroughly understand their assessment system, including what different tests measure and how. As evidence of these responsibilities, school leaders schedule regular staff meetings for collaborative curriculum and instruction planning. They make regular walkthroughs or "learning walks" and classroom visits as informal observation of program implementation and teaching and learning processes. They embed professional development for administrators, faculty, and staff, and document this training. They design calendars for monthly professional development opportunities. School leaders also help procure or develop appropriate formative assessments for faculty to use respectively in each subject area and grade level. They procure (or develop) and assign pre-, mid-, and post-learning summative assessments. They analyze student data and accordingly articulate which specific student improvements are needed. They collaborate in making an assessment plan for all subject areas, and articulate this plan to all staff.

Incorporating technology resources

School leaders can guide the development of a school vision that they will provide with ways to acquire contemporary information and technology skills that will enable them to lead productive, responsible, and healthy lives as adults in any world location. They can

Copyright © Mometrix Media. You have been licensed one copy of this document for personal use only. Any other reproduction or redistribution is strictly prohibited. All rights reserved.

guide the development of a school mission to construct and sustain educational technology programs that not only meet the highest quality of administrative and teaching goals and objectives, but also have the support of a cost-efficient, reliable, secure technology infrastructure. School leaders should ensure that their school's instructional and information technology plans are aligned with district and state goals. These goals should prepare students for their futures by integrating 21st-century information technology into instruction, learning, administration, and support functions. This is so important today to assure that students will have the ability to compete globally upon graduation, not only through technology skills per se, but also through expanded learning capacities afforded by educational technology.

By using 21st-century learning technologies, teachers can give students new ways in which they can actively engage and interact with learning objects. They can offer more authentic learning experiences to students, which afford them a renewed interest in learning and greater capacities to learn in more varied ways. They can help students understand instructional content in new ways. Teachers can also communicate perspectives about learning content to students that support such new comprehension. In order to accomplish these things, school leaders must assure that they and their faculty know how to choose the applicable technology tools to facilitate, guide, and direct student learning. School leaders must provide professional development to train teachers in how to make appropriate selections and applications of instructional technologies that will fulfill the learning objectives they have designated for their students. Only when technology is used in view of its potential functions, and to achieve what it is designed to accomplish, will instructional design succeed. School leaders must collaborate with faculty and staff and supply them with training to determine what does and does not work, and then apply the former and eliminate the latter. Technology is an essential support to meeting standards for continuous educational improvement today.

School resources

Four types of resources necessary to school are human resources, material resources, physical resources, and financial resources. Human resources are employees. In schools, these can include teachers, therapists, educational specialists, teachers' aides, paraprofessionals, school support team members, administrators, office and clerical workers, cafeteria staff, custodial staff, and other support staff members. Material resources include learning materials like books, other printed information materials including sheet music; computer hardware and software; concrete manipulative objects; in pre-K and kindergarten classrooms, toys; athletic equipment and supplies; art supplies and materials; maps, globes; for high schools, chemistry laboratory equipment and supplies, etc. Physical resources include classrooms, desks, chairs, window blinds; library equipment and fixtures; office equipment and supplies; for custodial staff cleaning equipment, cleaning products, trash receptacles; cafeteria foods, kitchen equipment, trays, utensils, etc.; for auditoriums and drama productions, audio equipment, stages, curtains, scrims, backdrops, scenery fixtures, etc.; for music departments, musical instruments, music stands, etc.; and more. Financial resources are funds and money that schools have available to spend on school operations, facilities, programs, and activities.

School leaders are responsible for overseeing that human, material, physical, and financial resources exist in sufficient supply and are used appropriately and efficiently for the purposes of realizing the legal requirements of school programs and supporting students in

Copyright © Mometrix Media. You have been licensed one copy of this document for personal use only. Any other reproduction or redistribution is strictly prohibited. All rights reserved.

attaining academic standards and demonstrating expected learning results school-wide. For example, a school must hire and retain enough qualified teachers of each subject to enable optimal teacher-student ratios. Research shows larger class sizes decrease student learning and achievement: school leaders must hire teachers in numbers proportionate to student populations. To meet school visions and goals, which should be aligned with governmental learning standards, school leaders must establish criteria for quantities and types of material learning resources (e.g., books, computers, manipulatives, subject equipment and supplies, etc.) sufficient for all students to have what they need for optimum learning. To assure a safe and comfortable environment enabling students to learn and teachers to teach, leaders must ensure adequate classroom space, furniture, temperature control, lighting, and other physical resources. School leaders must allocate available funds and plan and supervise budgets to procure and maintain all of the other resources.

Progress monitoring

According to the Interstate School Leaders Licensure Consortium (ISLLC), an essential task for school leaders is to develop accountability systems for monitoring and assessing their students' progress. Studies find effective school leaders assure systematic procedures to monitor student progress at both classroom and school-wide levels. Teachers typically monitor student progress by regularly (monthly, biweekly, or weekly) administering probes. Probes are brief measures, easy to administer, which obtain samples of the whole range of skills in each subject every student needs to learn by the end of the school year—not just skills needed to satisfy monthly or weekly learning objectives. Unlike mastery measures, progress monitoring probes indicate not only whether students have learned skills included in a lesson or unit, but additionally whether students are learning at rates enabling them to meet annual learning goals. Teachers plot graphs between baseline and initial student performance and end-of-year goals; observe progress patterns; and adjust their instruction accordingly, e.g., reteaching, intensifying instruction to 1:1 or in small groups, etc. School leaders can support teachers by making data-based instructional decisions toward ongoing improvement a part of school culture.

According to research, school improvement is best achieved and monitored by collecting and analyzing student progress data, and then taking actions accordingly. Some ways school leaders can promote relevant school-wide discussions about student progress and data include forming and supervising teams to collect and organize data into teacher-friendly formats. School leaders can establish collaborative subject area and/or grade-level meetings to discuss current and cumulative student progress data and their instructional implications regularly with faculty. They can explicitly present the idea of student progress monitoring to school staff, emphasizing how important it is to respond to monitoring results by changing their instruction as needed. They can explain to teachers that, just as they have long conducted formative assessments, monitoring student progress is not some new innovation, but a development of similar long-standing educational practices. They can help faculty procure professional development and resources they need to use student progress monitoring best. Effective strategies for fulfilling student needs include integrating progress monitoring with data-based instruction and collaborative structures.

Copyright © Mometrix Media. You have been licensed one copy of this document for personal use only. Any other reproduction or redistribution is strictly prohibited. All rights reserved.

Teaching and Learning

Grading policy and high expectations

At one school, three teachers learned of "no zeroes" grading policies at a summer staff development conference and proposed a plan for an extra-help focus team and training workshop. The school leader agreed, bringing a school improvement consultant for additional implementation training, and having one department pilot the program. Students could not receive a zero-grade for any assignment; if their work did not receive 70 percent, first teachers discussed it with them, set a new due date, and assigned them to attend the extra-help program. If they did not complete the assignment by the new due date or receive 70 percent or more, teachers contacted the parents and set another due date. The next level, if needed, was an administrator-teacher-student conference, additional parent contact, and Saturday extra-help program attendance. The next level was another administrator-teacher-student conference to design an action plan for completing the assignment. The final level was "crisis intervention" to decide other actions, e.g., suspension or alternative school placement. Most students only reached the second level in the first year. Teachers had flexibility in crediting late assignments and necessary policy modifications. Results included significantly fewer missed assignments, 57 percent fewer D grades, 72 percent fewer F grades, and a 68 percent decrease in students assigned to extra help.

Fostering a shared teacher understanding of excellence in instruction

According to an education expert (Blankstein, 2011), one activity that can develop shared teacher understanding of excellence is conducting "instructional learning walks" in a way that is relevant rather than simply required. The steps in this activity follow: first, teachers brainstorm to produce a list of things that indicate high instructional quality. They recall lessons they have observed or taught that succeeded highly in how students participated and the results obtained. They determine how they knew it succeeded, what students and teachers did to contribute to success, and chief lesson elements (e.g., teacher and student behaviors) contributing to success. They list teacher and student actions and behaviors that evidence quality instruction. Second, teachers share lists in small groups or teams, combining and editing them into a comprehensive list until they have three to five indicators in each category of teacher and student behaviors. Third, they differentiate indices of instructional quality vs. indices of instructional strategies or design—e.g., "focused student discussion" as a quality indicator, and "cooperative learning" as a corresponding strategy. The author observes that determining what to do is easy, while getting everybody to do it is more challenging, but possible through such activities.

Racial and ethnic disparities found in student motivation and academic performance

In studying suburban schools with excellent reputations for placing graduates into prestigious colleges, researchers nevertheless found significant achievement gaps for racial and ethnic minority students. For example, in Minority Student Achievement Network (MSAN) districts, compared to white and Asian students, African-American and Hispanic students had lower grade-point averages and reported less lesson comprehension. Additionally, they spent similar amounts of time doing homework, yet had lower rates of completing homework. Researchers concluded that lower grades and less homework

Copyright © Mometrix Media. You have been licensed one copy of this document for personal use only. Any other reproduction or redistribution is strictly prohibited. All rights reserved.

completion were not explained by student motivation or effort, but rather by differences in home supports and skill gaps. Asian students were found to complete more homework and get higher grades than other nonwhite students because they spent more time on studying and homework.

Researchers have found that African-American and Hispanic students in reputedly excellent suburban public schools not only achieved lower grade-point averages and reported understanding lesson material less than white and Asian students, they also found this was not due to lesser effort, but to fewer home resources, supports, and gaps in skills. Another significant finding of the research is that, when investigators questioned students about what motivated them to study, white students reported that teacher demands had the strongest influences to motivate them, about equally as much as teacher encouragement. But conversely, Hispanic and particularly African-American students reported that teacher encouragement, not teacher demands, was the most motivational factor for them to study more. Moreover, the researchers found that measures of student family socioeconomic status did not explain this difference. They concluded the differential motivational influence of teacher behaviors was "truly a racial difference." They also observed the implications of this difference that teacher-student relationships are even more important in achievement motivation for black and Hispanic students.

The Tripod Project is an example of a research-based initiative targeting achievement gaps between racial and economic minority students and others. Its name refers to three "legs" of education success: content, pedagogy, and relationships. It also identifies five tasks found by scholarship among diverse disciplines to promote cooperation and collaboration. A researcher (Ferguson, 2002) explains these tasks in terms of five stages of social and intellectual engagement in elementary and secondary school classrooms: (1) students will more likely succeed when they begin the year feeling trust in the teacher and interest in the class, as opposed to mistrust and disinterest. (2) Students will more likely succeed with a balance of student autonomy and teacher control, rather than too much or too little of either. (3) Goal-orientation and ambition in learning, not ambivalence, will enable student success. (4) Students will more likely succeed if they industriously work to pursue learning goals instead of being disengaged by boredom or discouraged by difficulty. (5) Students will feel and be well-prepared for future school and life when teachers help them consolidate their new learning.

Achievement gaps

Researchers (cf. Barton, 2004) find that underlying achievement gaps contain both school and non-school variables. Moreover, conditions inside and outside of schools interact to enhance learning. For example, high-socioeconomic communities whose families value learning more often have stronger schools, better teachers, and better parent-teacher relationships; low-socioeconomic communities are more likely to have schools lacking as many resources, and hence are less likely to attract the best-qualified teachers. While studies have established that actions like increasing instructional time and intensity, tutoring, extra attention, and superior teacher training and experience in early school years can mitigate disadvantages for young children who were not read to at home, research has not determined by how much. Researchers do know that, unfortunately, poor and minority students who most need such attention receive fewer such interventions. Barton identifies 14 factors correlated with student achievement. Factors both before and outside school include: birth weight, lead toxicity, hunger and nutrition, reading to young children,

Copyright © Mometrix Media. You have been licensed one copy of this document for personal use only. Any other reproduction or redistribution is strictly prohibited. All rights reserved.

watching TV, parent availability, student mobility, and parent participation. Factors in school include: curricular rigor, teacher preparation, teacher attendance and experience, class size, technology assistance in instruction, and school safety.

Research over the past two decades finds that student achievement gaps are produced by both home, community, and school variables. Thus school leaders must decide which factors they will lead their staff and colleagues in focusing upon. Despite documented underachievement among minority and low-socioeconomic status (SES) students, some school leaders (cf. Haycock, 2002) point out that there have also been thousands of high-minority and high-poverty schools achieving in their states' upper thirds in one or more combinations of grade and subject. This fact serves as an incentive for other schools to rise to that challenge instead of blaming underachievement on students or students' families. Researchers (cf. Singham, 2003) also note that, despite strong correlations between SES and school achievement, studies show even stronger effects of the school curriculum and resources available to students upon school performance. Because of the variation among research findings about causes of achievement gaps, school leaders are especially responsible to directing community efforts to investigate how instructional and learning opportunity distributions at their schools influence achievement gaps.

Experts find that school leaders must assume responsibility for designing purposeful action strategies aimed at eradicating inequitable instructional practices, and at establishing and maintaining school-wide or system-wide instructional improvement processes. Some educational researchers (cf. Williams, 1996, 2001, 2003) have observed that implementing measures to reduce class sizes, site-based management, parent involvement seminars, and other specific strategies or programs may improve short-term student performance slightly, but do little for long-term cumulative improvement because attempting "quick fixes" (Snell, 2003) via single intervention programs is a "fragmented" approach. Instead, they believe school leaders must focus on wider, more coherent sets of solutions aimed at bettering teaching and learning over longer time periods. School climates that cultivate good teaching accessible by every student can address achievement gaps. This indicates the critical role of school leaders in creating school- and district-wide agendas for improving instruction, and giving teachers the resources they need to realize it. They must also be responsible to model, through their regular communications with them, ongoing senses of agency and urgency in teachers, students, parents, policymakers, and community members to face and combat equity problems.

Professional development plans

School leaders should conduct needs assessments and use these data to begin with the greatest need area. They should provide teachers with conference materials, professional journals, and books for reading current educational research. Recommendations are to focus on one or two professional development topics each year, to schedule follow-up sessions, and to connect all follow-up sessions to the original topics. Leaders should give teachers a variety of activities. They should determine how many professional development (PD) hours are necessary to attain school goals, record individual hours, and spread hours across the school year. After-school PD sessions should be limited to one hour each, and summer sessions limited to one week. Leaders should deliver all school trainings scheduled to all staff members, and give equal opportunities for all staff members to participate in PD activities. They are advised to plan for plenty of classroom-based practice, including time

Copyright © Mometrix Media. You have been licensed one copy of this document for personal use only. Any other reproduction or redistribution is strictly prohibited. All rights reserved.

for reflection and feedback. School leaders should also provide teachers with scaffolding (temporary, as-needed, gradually faded support) for PD instruction.

(1) Effective professional development (PD) must be student-centered, not teacher-centered. Teachers should learn new instructional techniques and strategies not for their own sake, but for helping students to learn better. (2) Teachers must be actively involved in the learning process for PD to be effective. School leaders play a critical role in building learning communities in their schools, which are required to accomplish school reform. (3) While PD can occur outside of the school building, it still must be school-based and job-embedded by emerging from and contributing to everyday classroom practice, and by teachers' perceiving it as part of their daily work. Master teacher mentoring, coaching, and teacher peer observation in classrooms can facilitate this. (4) Teachers must collaboratively problem-solve. This promotes professional and community respect, and mitigates the isolation that classroom teachers often experience. (5) PD must be supported and ongoing. Repetition and classroom follow-up are required to bring longitudinal instructional change. (6) Teachers require theoretical understanding—both of theory underlying practice, and of how to apply theory to practice. (7) PD must be part of a comprehensive, systematic reform process with district-level support. (8) In providing PD, school leaders should avoid fads or topics unrelated or lacking supportive research to student learning.

Recommending instructional practices to teachers

Insistence on more intensive evaluation and supervision of teachers has been deemed ineffective by researchers. More frequent teacher evaluations would only increase student learning under two conditions: (1) educators knew how to enhance student learning but had lacked sufficient motivation to do it, and (2) school leaders possessed expertise and time for classroom observation to improve professional teacher practices.

Numerous studies support the efficacy of professional learning communities (PLCs) as a collaborative model for improving student learning outcomes. PLCs allow school leaders and teachers to meet regularly to collectively inquire and discover ways to help more students learn at higher levels. Rather than the traditional top-down model which regards school leaders as disseminators of one size fits all pedagogical knowledge, the PLC model is both dynamic and more efficient. Within the PLC model, current student data initiates a bottom-up inquiry process and teams of experts with diverse vantage points collaboratively decide which strategies to employ towards student improvement. PLCs empower administrators to efficiently and effectively facilitate quality teaching under a large variety of circumstances through regular professional and collegial dialogue.

Successful professional learning community

(1) School leaders and faculty embrace the concept that the school's purpose is high-level learning for all students. (2) Form collaborative staff teams who share responsibility and work interdependently to accomplish common and mutually accountable goals. (3) Assign teams to create viable and guaranteed curriculum for every unit, clarify essential learning for every student, agree to guidelines for pacing, and develop and commonly administer formative assessments for end-of-unit monitoring. (4) With the teams, use student learning information to identify students needing added support and time for proficiency; highly proficient students needing learning extension and enrichment; teachers who promote high student achievement levels, for examining and replicating their practices; teachers who

Copyright © Mometrix Media. You have been licensed one copy of this document for personal use only. Any other reproduction or redistribution is strictly prohibited. All rights reserved.

struggle with aiding student proficiency, for addressing their difficulties; and concepts and skills no teachers could help students attain at expected levels, for acquiring greater instructional effectiveness in these via networking, consultation with other team members, central office specialists, etc. (5) With teams, develop a coordinated intervention plan for systematically providing struggling students with diagnostic, timely, precise, directive additional support and time.

Standards for effective professional development

Four factors make professional development (PD) effective. (1) PD in vibrant learning communities. Regardless of their forms, learning communities value ongoing student and teacher learning, which promotes continuous classroom and school improvement; collaboration and problem-solving; cooperative and individual inquiry, experimentation, practice, and reflection. (2) Strong leaders, who facilitate and invite teacher participation, communicate PD's benefits to key stakeholders, and realize the value of high-quality PD. Leadership distribution should be flexible, not dictated by a single formula; and include school leaders, other administrators, teachers, district employees, higher education institutions, cultural organizations, and state education departments. (3) Sufficient resources—people, time, and money. Various sources, e.g., multiple stakeholder groups and organizations, should contribute resources. Teacher learning can be allotted more time through closely analyzing time uses in district calendars, school schedules, negotiated agreements, and other policy documents. Allocation coordination and investment return assessments also inform effective resource utilization. Adequate resources enable all teachers to learn, practice, and apply skill and knowledge informing instructional and practice effectiveness with students. (4) Rigorous data analysis. Schools and districts allot time for knowledgeable planners to analyze varied, disaggregated student data to pinpoint learning gaps, proficiency standards, and assessment and behavioral results, informing PD content selection.

Standards for professional development (PD) effectiveness include: (1) in-depth understanding of adult learning, and content and processes reflecting best workplace learning practices. PD matches individual teacher needs, goals, current expertise, and learning experiences; combines varied experiences; offers extended follow-up; uses information and communication technologies to expand and diversify content, and to extend access and participation, creating virtual professional learning communities. (2) Rigorous evaluations. PD planners assure sufficient resources for objective evaluations and reporting and distributing results. They identify types of evidence to collect as success indicators, matching goals and progress benchmarks, and when and how to collect and report data. Evaluation assesses PD's impacts on school organization and culture for supporting school improvement initiatives. PD sponsors timely communicate assessment results to key stakeholders. (3) PD deepens teacher skills and knowledge of content, pedagogy, and assessment. It assures teacher comprehension of content standards and how instruction meets them, and relationships among curriculum subjects. It enables teachers to learn use of research-based teaching strategies for student content standard mastery; learn and practice administration, analysis, interpretation, and reporting of varied classroom assessments; learning gap identification, and according instructional adjustments. (4) PD enables teachers to apply research to instructional decision-making.

Copyright © Mometrix Media. You have been licensed one copy of this document for personal use only. Any other reproduction or redistribution is strictly prohibited. All rights reserved.

Standards that school leaders could apply in opportunities they make available

(1) Collaboration: professional development (PD) enables teachers to collaborate as a means to the ends of enhanced student learning and school improvement, manage conflict constructively, and widen collaborative scope through communication technologies. (2) Diverse learning needs: PD develops teacher understanding of diverse student needs and learning styles to design and apply teaching and testing strategies for diverse student needs and state content standards, cultivating high teacher expectations and respect for all students. (3) Student learning environments: PD helps teachers establish safe, inclusive, supportive, caring, respectful learning environments for all students; develop and practice student ownership of creative conflict resolution and management routines; and enables teacher use of student behavior and discipline data to analyze and modify practices toward optimum learning environments. (4) Family involvement: PD helps teachers involve families and other community members in student education as active partners; develops teacher communication skills for developing partnerships, communicating content standard expectations for student mastery and local, state, and national assessment success; cultivates teacher understanding and respect for diverse backgrounds, and insight how these can be student learning foundations. PD also offers opportunities to teachers for mastering technology use as a means for making partnerships with family and community stronger.

Supporting teachers' professional development and growth

School leaders should work with district leaders to analyze their budgets and allocate the maximal funds for professional development (PD) resources to support teachers. They are responsible for assuring their faculty and staff participate in PD on- and off-site in high proportions. They must ensure that PD offerings are aligned with the targets and goals they have specified in their school work plans. They must furnish all their teachers with the resources they need to develop their teaching repertoires and content knowledge to develop excellence school-wide. School leaders should encourage structured observations, study groups, coaching, and other inquiry-oriented staff development approaches in order to support teachers in focusing on the interaction between teaching and testing practices and student learning and performance. School leaders should actively recruit and support instructional guides and school building-based coaches, supervising them directly, communicating with them often, and guiding them explicitly in terms of professional growth. They should encourage staff members showing exemplary engagement and success with school educational models to share their skills network-wide. They should also use observation, coaching, and evaluation to institutionalize and reinforce model practices.

Helping teachers apply teaching strategies for differentiating instruction

To help teachers address the needs of students with disabilities, ELLs, and others with diverse needs, school leaders should group students heterogeneously and flexibly, using ongoing assessments to adjust groupings, rather than tracking or ability grouping. While mainstreaming diverse-needs students as much as possible, they should ensure their school offers interventions, reading programs, summer school, tutors, and similar supplementary services for students with needs that regular education does not meet. Leaders should form multidisciplinary teams to recommend such school-wide supports based on student data. They can guide teachers to set the same long-term learning goals for all students while using tiered lessons and otherwise supplying multiple ways to achieve goals according to

Copyright © Mometrix Media. You have been licensed one copy of this document for personal use only. Any other reproduction or redistribution is strictly prohibited. All rights reserved.

student needs. Leaders should have teachers design tasks according to varied learning styles, furnish teachers with texts at different reading levels, and assure that all instructional practices include the participation and thinking of all students. They can ensure school communications accommodating cultural and language differences; equal student access to museums, universities, libraries and other social and cultural institutions; and see that performances and exhibitions represent all student work.

Providing teachers with assistance to incorporate technology into their instruction

School leaders should guide teachers in integrating technological literacy through all grade levels and subjects. They can have teachers assign students to conduct original research and produce presentations, performances, and products using technology; and to use social networking, design and presentation software, and other technologies to obtain and organize information and prepare to succeed in today's knowledge economy. They should require teachers to instruct students in legal and ethical issues around technology access and use. Leaders should dictate high quality standards for teachers to enforce in student work utilizing technology, and clearly distinguish between learning targets for technology skills vs. for content and thought quality in technology-assisted products. They must see that teachers use instructional technology such that it truly supports effective learning and teaching. Leaders can advise teachers to take advantage of technology innovations allowing information sources to transcend space and time to enable student assignments outside the school building and school day. They can lead teachers first to establish strong student concept comprehension, and thereafter to encourage students to use technology to magnify their researching and problem-solving skills. They must also lead teachers and students to utilize Internet technologies wisely, critically, ethically, and with integrity.

Demonstrating openness to change through collaboration with all school stakeholders

To be open to and accomplish change through collaborating with all stakeholders, school leaders must realize how family and student conditions influence learning. They identify community opinion leaders and the school's relationship with them. They communicate the school vision, mission, and priorities to their communities. They understand that students and school staff create impressions affecting school image, and how these are used to promote their school. In overseeing school operations, they use models of shared decision-making and leadership. They identify community, family, and business resources that can support their school. They understand how establishing and utilizing various networks, partnerships, and coalitions can benefit the school, and develop relationships inside and outside school. They actively engage their communities to advance school and student success. They also identify additional agencies that can help in connecting students with needed social, health, and human services to keep them focused on learning. And school leaders arrange opportunities for community and family members to be involved in wide ranges and varieties of school activities.

Organizations that enable shared power in partnerships

Vital to school success, partnerships of shared power find two important forums in Student Advisory Councils (SAC) and Parent-Teacher Associations (PTA). According to the National PTA, six basic factors are instrumental in encouraging families to become involved in their children's schools: (1) communication that occurs regularly and is reciprocal and

Copyright © Mometrix Media. You have been licensed one copy of this document for personal use only. Any other reproduction or redistribution is strictly prohibited. All rights reserved.

meaningful. (2) School leaders and other school staff support the parenting skills of their students' parents and guardians. (3) School leaders, faculty, and staff participate actively in students' learning, and they support and inform parents in also participating actively in their children's learning. (4) School leaders, faculty, and staff engage students' parents to become partners with them in making decisions for their schools. (5) School leaders encourage family and community members to volunteer at and for their schools. (6) School leaders actively engage in outreach efforts to various resources available in their communities, e.g., accessing community resources and function within the larger organization by serving as PTA officers and teacher representatives.

Changing perspectives through experience with community and school board

An example of how a school leader's perspective can change is when a school leader accepts a position at a school new to him (or her), and he (or she) is also not familiar with the community. By observing meetings of the school board, the new school leader will gain a better understanding about things such as how diverse that particular county is overall. He may discover that the elementary, middle, or high school where he is now working differs greatly from another elementary, middle, or high school a few blocks away from there, and that both schools are also extremely different from another school a few miles farther away. Despite striking differences among various local schools, the school board is one factor uniting all district schools. Because they are empowered to provide strategic policy and planning for the whole school system, school boards organize diverse schools within the system and give them a common framework. By realizing that school board decisions must involve what is best for the larger community, not only his individual school community, the school leader gains better insight into and respect for the task of managing a whole school district.

Remaining open-minded about issues

Some school leaders say a constant challenge is remembering that, whatever they think or believe about an issue, their viewpoint is simply a viewpoint or belief and not a research-based fact, law, or truth. One school leader (Robinson, 2014) quotes a Buddhist philosophy that the world, including each of us, is "not what it appears to be" in an absolute sense. Therefore, the way we see a situation or issue is not the truth; none of us owns the truth. This informs school leaders' attitudes: when they express their views as leaders, they must also humbly acknowledge these are not fact or law, but simply their views. In America's individualistic culture, many people believe what they know or think is the truth. Some school leaders point out that, to be authentic educational leaders, they must remember however they see things may not necessarily be how they are; they may not know as much as they think they do, and must accept this possibility. These leaders find too many individuals in our culture preoccupied with defending their own "truth" to listen to one another. They remind us it is not a negative approach to be open to others' opinions, but a positive step toward being authentic educational leaders.

Distributing responsibility and benefits among members of the learning community

Increased demands and mechanisms for accountability in education today not only impose more tasks on educators, they also give parents and other community stakeholders more voice in education, as exemplified by school councils controlled by students' parents. In this environment, an essential group of leadership practices includes those that empower other

Copyright © Mometrix Media. You have been licensed one copy of this document for personal use only. Any other reproduction or redistribution is strictly prohibited. All rights reserved.

people to make important decisions. Neither school leaders nor their superintendents can execute leadership functions alone. Successful leaders rely on leadership contributions from many other members of their learning communities, and they develop these. Their administrative co-workers and key teachers are sources of such leadership. Parent leaders are also critical to school success in terms of site-based management. In addition to people, leadership on an organization-wide level includes influence from sources like tasks or actions that achieve organizational functions. Concepts of democratic, collaborative, participative, and shared leadership overlap with the concept of distributive leadership, which may take a holistic or additive form. Additive forms of distributed leadership disperse tasks across organizational members regardless of member interactions, i.e., everybody is a leader; holistic forms emphasize interdependent leadership, i.e., the work of all leaders adds up to more than the sum of its parts.

Involving students in school improvement processes

School leaders can involve students in school improvement processes as planners and as teachers. As planners, students may be involved in designing new buildings, developing classroom behavioral guidelines, and/or choosing textbooks. Student planning may affect anyone from the whole student body to the individual student planner, or anything in between. Experts say any of these may have meaning; what are important are these activities' applications and conditions. For example, in some school programs, students relate school coursework to their life goals, researching their dream careers, examining high school graduation requirements, and selecting courses to take. Identifying lifelong learning goals invites teachers to meet individual student learning ambitions, clearly defines academic assistance paths, allows students to share dreams with supportive adults, and enables schools to adjust course offerings to meet student interests. At some schools, students made building-wide surveys, testified before education committees in state legislatures, planned school-wide forums, and participated in school leader hiring. As teachers, some students have developed programs wherein students taught classroom technology use to teachers, exchanging this knowledge for learning about curriculum topics from teachers. This promotes teacher perspective on technology, and student literacy in interest areas as well as required content, and relevant engagement.

Students can be involved in school improvement processes as partners in professional development, and as decision-makers. For example, some schools have developed learning communities including administrators, teachers, students, and parents participating in professional development sessions of guided critical reflection. These teams experienced transformations not only in their own expectations, but also those of the entire school. Students participated in collecting and analyzing data, culminating in the learning community's identification of the next school year's focus on differentiated instruction. Experts find students' experience and knowledge about teaching and learning are often more realistic than adults' because they live these processes daily. Some schools have involved students in learning communities using trained staff, guided deliberation, checking in constantly, and reflection during and after the process, including student insights with those of other team members in school improvement plans. As decision-makers, students in some schools have been engaged in forming, developing, and implementing district-wide policies and policy changes with impacts on schools citywide and on the city as a whole, including attendance, truancy, lockout policies, and cell phone policies; and some city school committees have added student representatives.

Copyright © Mometrix Media. You have been licensed one copy of this document for personal use only. Any other reproduction or redistribution is strictly prohibited. All rights reserved.

Allocating and prioritizing resources

Before prioritizing how resources are allocated, school leaders must map the resources available to the school and the current and projected school activities. This will enable them to make relevant recommendations for resource applications. Formally involving stakeholder collaboration can further connections between school resources and community resources to support students, schools, families, and communities. Community resources include families, health and human services agencies, religious organizations, justice and police organizations, youth development, economic development, unions, businesses, governing entities, higher education institutions, and enrichment and recreation programs and activities. School leaders should direct collaborations to focus on clarifying which resources are currently accessible, the way resources are organized to function together, and which procedures exist for amplifying resource utility. Collaborative teams can conduct self-study surveys to fuel discussions of current program and process functioning; analyses of activity priorities; and decisions to prioritize, eliminate or emphasize, reassign, and schedule certain resources among activities and programs.

Resources whose status can be collaboratively examined

School leaders can involve stakeholders in collaborations to examine which resources they have or need in terms of programs, services, groups, persons, activities, and funds that can make their school stronger. For example, they can ascertain whether they currently have, lack, need, or need to increase active partnerships in instructional resources like pre-K readiness programs; tutoring, mentoring, and homework hotlines; school reform initiatives; career academy programs; technology and media; and adult education, literacy, ESL, and citizenship classes. In school management and governance, they can assess the status of resources among advisory entities, shared leadership, and their PTA (or PTSA). Among financial resources, they can evaluate the status of donations, fundraising activities and programs, grant programs, funded projects, and adopt-a-school programs. In school-based services and programs to alleviate obstacles to learning, they can study what their school and community have, need, or need more of among home involvement programs and activities; pre-service and in-service staff development; transition programs; crisis prevention and response programs; and student and family assistance services and programs.

Distributed leadership

Contrasting with leadership hierarchies, distributed leadership limits the potential error from decisions made by a single leader with limited information; it represents more accurately an organization's everyday divisions of labor. It allows organizations to benefit more from the abilities of a larger number of its members; enables members to make more use of their full ranges of individual strengths; and affords members a better appreciation of how their behaviors affect the organization as a whole, and of their organizational interdependence. According to experts, when groups and individuals holding different organizational positions can contribute to leadership functions in activities where they are most influential, this represents an advantage. Others point out the significance of reciprocal accountability, as when school leaders are accountable for performance to superintendents, yet superintendents are also accountable to the needs and input of school leaders. Distributed leadership is viewed as offering more ways for organization members to learn from each other in a teamwork context. More decision-making participation can

Copyright © Mometrix Media. You have been licensed one copy of this document for personal use only. Any other reproduction or redistribution is strictly prohibited. All rights reserved.

result in more commitment to strategies and goals, more experiences of on-the-job leadership development, more self-determination, superior environmental and organizational responsiveness, reinforcement of leadership influence through overlapping actions, and holistic solutions less possible individually.

Giving teachers safe environments for expressing their beliefs

Because all demands on today's school leaders are virtually impossible to satisfy, teachers have longer tenures in schools than administrators. Teachers cannot advance their professional responsibilities and challenges without becoming administrators, and thus need other ways to extend their influence and apply and share the experience and knowledge they amass over time. Because teachers can collectively contribute more varied expertise than a school leader can alone, it is important for teachers to also demonstrate leadership. A safe environment for risk-taking and creative thinking is necessary for teacher leaders to develop. School leaders encourage their confidence by not criticizing their expression of ideas that may initially seem unusual. For instance, school leaders can ask at staff meetings what elements, similar to those in their classrooms, teachers identify as making the school's professional environment safe for new ideas. They can schedule regular, brief times during meetings for proposing different, original ideas, regardless how offbeat. Leaders must also commit to cultivating teacher leaders, proactively helping them acquire leadership skills, e.g., facilitating meetings, analyzing data, etc. They must overcome fear of teachers undermining their own authority; a significant paradox is that the more leaders share power, the more authority they acquire.

Pitfall that teachers can present to the development of teacher leaders

Australian educators note that in their country, they call a certain phenomenon "tall poppy syndrome," i.e., individuals who raise their heads above the others' risk having them cut. This expression refers to teachers who resist assuming leadership roles, and/or interfere with their colleagues' assuming them. For example, a teacher who has been recognized by their national professional teaching standards board might avoid sharing news of this honor with co-workers. School leaders can help to offset this problem by establishing school cultures that value and acknowledge teachers who go beyond their traditional roles and duties and take the initiative to assume leadership projects, roles, and responsibilities. Another way that school leaders can help teachers develop into teacher leaders is to offer them opportunities to learn leadership skills, which are typically not included in most teacher preparation programs. For example, they need to learn skills for facilitation, collaboration, instructional improvement, assessment design, and curriculum planning. While some teachers may independently pursue such skills through professional development training, university courses, and/or district-wide offerings, school leaders can facilitate their learning by regularly offering them opportunities within and outside their schools.

Teacher creativity and risk-taking

Educational experts observe that while the traditional view of school leaders has been authoritarian, this kind of leadership is controlling, coercive, and manipulative and ultimately counterproductive because it affords teachers no freedom and leads to their job dissatisfaction. Research has found that school leaders who used control tactics were not respected by or popular with their employees, and were viewed as manipulative. On the

Copyright © Mometrix Media. You have been licensed one copy of this document for personal use only. Any other reproduction or redistribution is strictly prohibited. All rights reserved.

other hand, school leaders who value teachers' opinions and give them freedom to take risks with curriculum design and other areas of their work are found to empower teachers. Teachers can be creative, and can apply teaching methods that reflect their individual personalities. Teachers whose school leaders afford them this freedom attribute their classroom success to their empowerment by school leaders. Educational researchers have identified school leaders as those who must encourage teachers to take risks in order to meet their students' needs, and to access teachers' strengths for reorganizing schools as a part of educational reform.

Controlling behaviors

20th-century studies show many school leaders used control tactics with teachers which were viewed as stressful, forceful, punitive, unilateral, and reactive. They manipulated work factors (both inside and outside classrooms), resources, advancement opportunities, and support. Some threatened teachers with sanctions to force compliance; unfairly awarded benefits and favors to teachers who submitted to political pressure; harassed some teachers into resigning; exploited their authority; and created false leadership, decision-making, and participatory opportunities. They also used submission to please some parents who wielded money and power to obtain things for their children, making decisions that violated educational standards; ingratiation, promoting illogical or irrelevant programs and activities to please the community; and inconsistency, contradicting and changing policies and decisions according to conflicting external pressures, including from board members and superintendents. The resulting lack of teacher control and autonomy undermined teacher leadership. Conversely, school leaders who trust their staff's abilities have been defined (McGregor, 1960) as Theory Y leaders. They believe that more intellectual potential can be realized in most schools, that problem-solving ability is distributed widely among learning community members, that people collaborating for relevant goals exercise self-direction that individuals learn to embrace and pursue responsibility that rewards through achievement generate commitment, and that work is as natural as play and rest.

Communicating effectively

An experienced elementary school leader (Cullen, 2012), speaking from direct experience, advises others that (1) the least effective ways to communicate in schools are at assemblies and over the PA system. She estimates only 10 percent of people will actually hear and comprehend these messages. She finds the most effective ways to communicate are face-to-face or with small groups of people taking notes; if they do not take notes, follow-up emails are required. (2) Like students, teachers must be taught and shown, not simply told, or they will not learn what their leaders say. They also need assistance, support, and opportunities to try; encouragement; being listened to, having questions answered; and cheering, applause, and celebration. (3) Supporting one's statements and ideas with sound, excellent, and current research lends them greater validity and credibility. (4) Always allow and encourage faculty and staff to try any new practice they ask permission to do, and support the results, whatever they are. (5) Listen to all school staff members: custodians, information technology specialists, bookkeepers, administrative secretaries, etc. are all experts in their own areas who know things the school leaders do not. School leaders should listen to them, appreciate them, and welcome their help.

According to the experience of an elementary school leader (Cullen, 2012), a school leader must (1) be aware. To be aware, he or she must be where students and staff are. Staying in

Copyright © Mometrix Media. You have been licensed one copy of this document for personal use only. Any other reproduction or redistribution is strictly prohibited. All rights reserved.

the office means school leaders miss many daily occurrences. Simply walking around inside and outside school and into classrooms affords awareness of daily events, challenges, and successes. Leaders cannot improve conditions without knowing what needs improvement. Being told by others is no substitute for seeing it for oneself. (2) After asking (or telling) staff something, follow up to make those communications meaningful. Asking teachers to watch a video or read a book but never asking about it later indicates it was unimportant. Employees see what is important by what leaders focus on, which is what improves. (3) As in the familiar saying that repeating something and expecting different results is a definition of insanity, leaders should feel free to change their minds and not repeat practices unless they are exceptionally effective. Changing one's mind to improve practices develops school personnel into growing, flexible, progressive teams. (4) Kindness, courtesy, and graciousness to all people makes them happy, productive, and motivated to work with leaders. (5) A sense of humor eases work and life.

Giving teachers effective feedback

(1) Rather than spending the day in their offices, school leaders must make time for teachers by visiting their classrooms regularly and knowing what they are teaching. Even in larger schools, they should visit each classroom monthly, giving feedback following each visit. They should also schedule quarterly conferences with teachers if necessary to hear their concerns. (2) School leaders should inform teachers of their expectations first, and then give related feedback: teachers are more receptive to feedback when it is not unexpected. (3) School leaders should encourage teachers to establish goals and then give them related feedback that will help them achieve those goals, as opposed to arbitrary feedback. (4) School leaders should give feedback immediately, not weeks or months later, for it to be effective. This need not always be in scheduled meetings or lengthy reports; passing on classroom visit notes they took or sending brief emails, along with invitations to schedule meetings for further discussion if desired, can suffice. (5) School leaders should identify teachers' strengths before communicating criticisms, and format the latter by asking them for solutions. (6) School leaders must create positive environments open to receiving balanced feedback to make it effective.

Collaborative data

Educational research shows that collaboration and data use have a reciprocal relationship: using data promotes constructive collaborations, and data initiatives tend to succeed more when teachers can work and learn collaboratively. Moreover, collaborative data use gives more opportunities for educators to share ideas and interact across disciplines, and to assume and interact with various roles within educational hierarchies. Four areas revealed through research into forming collaborative data teams are: (1) calibration, i.e., the process of exploring learning definitions and standards; (2) focus on student data; (3) educator engagement; and (4) data use supported by technology. Calibration dually entails continuing modification and standardization. It enables educators to reach consensus about learning definitions, standards, and goals. Reciprocally, inquiry-based approaches help construct common focus and vocabulary. Stakeholders can explore what students should learn and how to know learning has occurred through calibration processes. Building-level activities like multiple teachers grading the same student work with a common rubric furnish concrete processes for identifying strength, weakness, and inconsistency areas. System- and district-wide calibration can eliminate teacher conflicts, reinforce shared

Copyright © Mometrix Media. You have been licensed one copy of this document for personal use only. Any other reproduction or redistribution is strictly prohibited. All rights reserved.

educational visions, better connect policy with classroom realities, and help educators identify which accountability assessment information they find most useful.

Investigation into collaborative school data teams finds areas of calibration, focus on student data, educator engagement, and technology supporting data use. Thoroughly studying student data, including how well students were fulfilling time-limited and specific learning objectives, afforded studied districts in-depth information they desired. Researchers found teachers could find a wide variety of student data useful. Of these, a few common types include student profiles from permanent records, e.g., demographics, assessment histories, and pertinent family information; summative assessments, e.g., state standardized tests; and formative assessments. Summative data politically support long-term strategic information plans, help leaders and teachers identify specific remedial student groups, identify strengths and needs in educator practices, and aid capacity-building. Student profiles offer less detail, but afford teachers broader information across areas, aiding teams. Educator engagement is important because data initiatives based solely on mandates are less sustainable or likely to cause widespread instructional change, and for mitigating faculty mistrust in external accountability pressures. Active faculty involvement in constructing and implementing data initiatives allows inquiry and deep reflection that overt mandates do not—applying data toward faster, more effective school improvement.

Research into how collaborative data teams are formed and used in schools yields four areas: calibration, focus on student data, educator engagement, and technology to support data application. Widespread school data use has historically often been impeded by insufficient access data—not because data did not exist, but because they were typically stored inaccessibly for most educators. However, more recent user-friendly technology has solved this dilemma. Scholars point out that while technology is necessary to support data initiatives, it is not enough on its own and should not be viewed as the entire answer to school data use. Teacher use of data technology systems is faster and more productive when teams are employed, and appropriate support and leadership are needed for system effectiveness. Studies found differential outcomes from districts using similar student data systems due to their differing implementations: a district with very proactive implementation featuring regular training of school leaders, advising and coaching in building leadership ability and skills with system data use from an expert, and vigorous promotion realized significantly better results in data use capacity than another district with fewer opportunities and less training and promotion. Technology data systems and collaborative data teams supported one another reciprocally.

Classroom visits, observations, and constructive feedback

To make their instructional practices stronger, many school leaders work with teachers in building school communities that use regular collaboration that focus on school development. They find it important to have strong conversations to avoid divisions between administrators and faculty, and to promote the mutual professional growth of both. Some apply the *Framework for Teaching* (Danielson, 2007) in establishing shared language for their professional conversations and development. School leaders conduct regular classroom visits and make observations, have their assistant principals do the same, and share their feedback with teachers. Some leaders call brief daily morning meetings to discuss observations, feedback, and what supports they plan for each day. When schedules on some days preclude team meetings, some leaders have simple tracking systems in their school's office to support administrator work with teachers as backup. These leaders make

Copyright © Mometrix Media. You have been licensed one copy of this document for personal use only. Any other reproduction or redistribution is strictly prohibited. All rights reserved.

being in classrooms daily their priority. Teachers feel the benefit of being able to implement immediately the feedback they receive from leaders and/or subject-specific coaches leaders have assigned. They also report the benefits of visiting and observing other teachers' classrooms to learn from their strategies and skills.

Successful school leaders often collaborate with teachers in forming instructional steps pursuant to leaders' observations and feedback. They may also assign instructional coaches to support teachers, who are informed of the next steps leaders and teachers have collaboratively established, and can help teachers implement them. Some teachers report that, when their subject departments are implementing new curriculum, department teachers must develop some components in common. They find their schools' weekly professional development day enables them to address collectively such patterns. Another advantage of leader observation and feedback and teacher sharing of best practices is critical thinking regarding strengths and development need areas. One teacher reported that, during a feedback conversation, he and the school leader reviewed his ratings for each part of Danielson's *Framework for Teaching* (2007). He focused on the section Using Assessment in Instruction. He had observed during his lesson that on one quiz, students needed more time. He highlighted specific questions and assigned student pairs to areas where they needed support. He commented about the resulting lesson and that he would not have devised this solution without his leader's observation. From its success, he began deliberately applying this strategy the following day.

Experts note it is not enough for school leaders to complete a checklist when visiting classrooms; they must use observations to improve the quality of teachers' instruction to further students' success. School leaders influence school culture by designing and overseeing operations of processes, routines, and procedures—i.e., structures—they align with their and their school's core values. These structures must be observable, i.e., behaviors or practices that can be described and documented; concrete, i.e., not just abstract concepts but real things; and supported by evidence, i.e., real artifacts reflecting how the structures operate. In the observation and feedback process, leaders must establish common definitions among both administrators and faculty; communicate teaching priorities, both in their observation forms and via professional development; and give teachers feedback, both collectively through statistics, and individually through conversations and written communications. Every semester, leaders should follow a continuous cycle of walkthroughs resulting in formative feedback, formal observations resulting in both formative and summative feedback, walkthrough observations with formative feedback, formal observations with formative and summative feedback, and clarification of expectations. They must schedule observation times and places, and supervising planning and instruction must be included in their normal routine.

Curriculum design

Designing rigorous and relevant curriculum is not intended to add different or new instructional goals; rather, it is a structure applied to goals already existing for instruction and assessment. This structure incorporates not only teachers' instructional skills, but also challenges school leaders and faculty to view how they think about and evaluate the ways students acquire knowledge. To become successful in their future lives in today's society, students must know how to use disciplined inquiry methods to construct knowledge, with the end of producing outcomes meaningful beyond just school success. To achieve these outcomes, schools must give students foundations for the complex intellectual activity

Copyright © Mometrix Media. You have been licensed one copy of this document for personal use only. Any other reproduction or redistribution is strictly prohibited. All rights reserved.

involved. In addition to constructing knowledge, students must access their previous knowledge, acquire in-depth comprehension of issues or topics, and develop ideas and express them for problem-solving purposes. As adults, students will encounter complicated problems that are frequently unique or novel. They will need to apply what they have learned using specific intellectual skills, which curricular rigor helps them attain.

Rigorous curriculum

Relative to secondary school improvement, rigor in curriculum has been defined variously among extant research studies. However, according to the National High School Alliance (2006), when interpreted most basically, it can be viewed as a complex of principles, ideas, and strategies that enable students to be prepared well for college, careers, and civic activities. Elevated expectations for every student, accompanied by the provision of supports via extensions of learning opportunities and the establishment of intervention programs for students with lower performance levels, are included in rigorous high school curricula. In addition to curricula, the definition of rigor can encompass the quality of content and instruction, the course requirements, and the strategies used by educators to support students' achievement. While researchers offer various definitions, one aspect they commonly agree to is that a high school curriculum's rigor is among the leading indices that a student will attain high school graduation and a degree from a college or university. Schools should also offer curriculum that is relevant, i.e., related to students' lives, communities, and cultures; to developing 21st-century skills including technical and career education; and sufficient preparation for higher education, including partnerships with colleges and universities; and for employment, including community-based and project-based learning.

Standards-based instruction and differentiated instruction

According to differentiated instruction expert Carol Ann Tomlinson (2000), educators need not feel that accountability mandates for standards-based instruction must interfere with individualized learning for students with diverse needs. She asserts that the two only conflict when educators apply standards such that they disregard the principles of effective curriculum and instruction that they already know. Furthermore, differentiation is not a teaching strategy but a philosophy. This philosophy's beliefs include these: students vary in learning readiness, styles, interests, life circumstances and experiences even when they are the same age. Student variations significantly affect their learning needs, paces, and what teacher supports and others' supports they require for successful learning. When supportive adults push students slightly past the point where they can work unassisted, students learn optimally. When students can connect curriculum with their life experiences and interests, they learn best. Natural learning opportunities also enable the best learning. When schools and classroom teachers create a sense of community wherein students feel respected and important, students become more effective learners. Schools' main task is to maximize each student's capacity.

To evaluate how standards-based instructional approaches affect non-average students (e.g., gifted or academically challenged students with abilities outside of typical achievement norms), educators must examine the particular standards assigned and their standards-based practices. They should consider such factors as: whether the standards reflect the skills, comprehension, and knowledge that experts in their respective disciplines value most; whether educators are reflecting the standards in their curriculum, or using the

Copyright © Mometrix Media. You have been licensed one copy of this document for personal use only. Any other reproduction or redistribution is strictly prohibited. All rights reserved.

standards as a curriculum; whether they are rushing to address mandated standards, or if they have found methods for integrating them into the curriculum to allow students enough time to make sense of the skills and ideas they entail; whether the school's focus on standards energizes students and classes, or quashes inquiry, discovery, creativity, and joy in learning; whether the standards make learning less enticing and relevant to students, or more so; and whether the school's use of the standards helps the faculty remember that they are working with human beings—or instead makes them forget that they are.

In one school district, science teachers outlined a framework for K-12 in their field covering the essential principles, concepts, facts, and skills. Then they took their state's mandated science standards and mapped these for K-12. They discovered that these state standards reflected science facts and skills fairly well, but did poorly at making science principles and concepts explicit. By comparing their own framework with that of the state standards, the teachers filled in information gaps, and structured their curriculum for coherence and manageability. This helped all science teachers envision the expanse over time for K-12 science instruction, conceptually organize their teaching, and instruct keeping in mind the essential principles of science. As a result, they were able to develop a district-wide science curriculum that made more sense to students as well as to teachers. This curriculum helped students to think scientifically. It satisfied the standards mandated by their state, while also decreasing the teachers' feelings that they had to rush to cover all the information in disconnected ways to meet those standards.

A high school Algebra II teacher had a class with some students missing prerequisite skills, others learning independently without her, and some learning as fast as she could instruct them. To help all students pass the standards test and also acquire a solid grasp of mathematics, she began each textbook chapter by outlining specific concepts, skills, and understandings to master for each curriculum portion; guided students in connecting the material to their past learning; and assigned parts of every week for whole-class instruction, teacher-led instruction, and small-group activities. Sometimes she worked with groups having advanced skills in certain areas to propel their thinking, assist with multiple-alternative problem-solving, and help them apply learning to real-life, complex problems; other times with students needing guidance to apply learning, or additional instruction; other times forming student teams with varying degrees of readiness, assigning goals to solve problems as effectively as possible. She maximized each student's model for problem-solving and explaining solution reasoning by randomly calling on them to present and defend team approaches. Teams frequently evolved into collaborative study groups addressing everybody's questions, including regular after-school meetings. Students' standards test scores improved, as well as their understanding and enjoyment of algebra.

Required school leader knowledge regarding curriculum and instruction

While school leaders need not be experts on all subject matter in their school's core curriculum, they do need to understand the main concepts that are being taught. They should be able to discern whether teachers are instructing students in core curriculum they are expected to learn. They must grasp what in career, technical, and elective curriculum students need to learn. Leaders must be familiar with national and state standards in academic and elective courses for helping faculty identify which standards take priority, and which areas students should learn more in-depth. They should be able to distinguish between college-preparatory and regular curriculum. Experts advise school leaders to eliminate course leveling and have faculty teach key post-secondary preparatory material to

Copyright © Mometrix Media. You have been licensed one copy of this document for personal use only. Any other reproduction or redistribution is strictly prohibited. All rights reserved.

most students. School leaders should understand the essential nature of literacy across curriculum, and detect if teachers are promoting student literacy skills in all subjects. They should be familiar with standards students must meet, and discern whether assessments appropriately measure these. Leaders must also have enough knowledge regarding assessment to guide teacher teams in developing standardized tests and grading guides, and in measuring not only student performance but also their own instructional efficacy.

School leaders must recognize whether their teachers effectively apply instructional strategies. They should possess working knowledge of student-centered, research-based instruction, e.g., cooperative learning, project-based learning, the Socratic Method, research study methods, integration of academic and technical studies, and integration of technology. They must also understand conditions allowing teachers to apply such methods. School leaders should be experienced in techniques whereby they can predict how long it will take teachers to learn new methods, and help them do this. As they implement new teaching approaches, they should know how to network the teachers learning them. School leaders also must have an understanding of how much time is required for effective planning, which is necessary for producing a good quality of teaching. For example, when teachers are expected to teach academic content at higher levels to larger numbers of students, these teachers must have enough time to design methods for activating students' existing knowledge and experience, and relating the new learning material to this previous learning.

Identifying best teaching practices

School leaders should have sufficient knowledge about learning and teaching to recognize which teachers are increasing student performance most. They should be able to analyze what these teachers do to enable students to learn more in their classrooms. Leaders should arrange for such outstanding teachers to model their lessons for other teachers to observe to learn from their examples. School leaders should also comprehend what conditions in classrooms and schools cultivate cultures of higher expectations, and mentor and otherwise help teachers to expect more from their students. School leaders should have an ability to restructure school organizations to enable teacher teams to find ways of making knowledge more relevant to students. Leaders may organize small learning communities wherein teacher teams collaboratively instruct student groups. Such reorganization is especially helpful in low-performing schools because it demonstrates belief in the possibility of teaching more students at higher levels, makes openings for developing new leaders, and motivates new teachers. Leaders can assign department chairs, interdisciplinary leaders, or team leaders to teacher teams, and continually confer with them to maintain focus on curriculum, instruction, and student progress.

Curriculum alignment

In curriculum alignment, a school's educational programs, teaching methods, instructional materials, and assessment instruments are coordinated with local and state academic standards, as well as with each other. Curriculum alignment occurs in various parts at school, district, and state levels and enhances student achievement. Horizontal alignment refers to teaching the same content across all classrooms on the same grade level, as well as teaching content aligned with state and/or district learning standards and assessments. Vertical alignment refers to teaching material that advances through progressive grade levels, with scaffolding in each grade to prepare students for the next. Federal and state educational agencies work to improve education quality and academic achievement and

Copyright © Mometrix Media. You have been licensed one copy of this document for personal use only. Any other reproduction or redistribution is strictly prohibited. All rights reserved.

limit achievement gaps caused by socioeconomic, racial, and gender differences by standardizing education through curriculum alignment. School leaders can ensure this by mapping curriculum based on state standards to align content and skills across grade levels, and applying their own student data to ascertain which of the standards have the most lasting value and strategic impact for their students' success within and across subjects.

Supporting teachers in planning and implementing instruction and assessment

To support teachers in planning their instruction, school leaders provide targeted professional development and schedule enough time for teachers to write lesson plans, project plans, and other instructional plans. School leaders create curriculum maps to align their school curriculum with national or state standards and then give teachers their support for developing targeted assessment plans in alignment with those curriculum maps. They then review the teachers' instructional and assessment plans and give them feedback as needed. They may also arrange for the teachers to review one another's plans and supply each other with mutual critiques regarding their alignment, relevance, and academic rigor. School leaders also supervise teachers in selecting and/or developing formative or interim assessments that align with the school curriculum and meet criteria for high quality. In addition, school leaders should not only hold teachers accountable for implementing the curricula that they have all agreed to, they should also support their teachers in fulfilling those accountability expectations at the same time.

On a regular basis, school leaders should review and analyze the learning objectives that their teachers are setting and pursuing in their classrooms. They should examine and analyze the assessments teachers are giving students, the data they and their staff are collecting on their students' achievement and progress, and other indices of instructional practice. They should use their analyses of these elements to make an overall assessment of the curriculum, instruction, and assessment content and practices at their school in how well these align with state and national standards; whether they align with one another, within and across grade levels and across the curriculum; whether the instructional design, content, and implementation closely reflect the curriculum design and plan, and the assessments accurately measure curricular and instructional content; how rigorous these are academically; and how relevant to student learning and school goals. School leaders make investments to assure teachers access to instructional resources and materials and assessment instruments of high quality, aligned with their school curriculum and standards. Wherever they discover exemplary curricular rigor, relevance, alignment, and student achievement, school leaders should celebrate and share these to acknowledge teachers and students and facilitate reproducing effective practices.

Potential issues in instructing teachers to use assessments

Generally, formative assessments are process-oriented and summative assessments are product-oriented. However, within that broad definition, teachers often have multiple definitions of formative assessment not necessarily compatible with research definitions like that from the Council of Chief State School Officers (CCSSO). Teachers may define formative assessment as common formative assessments their school or district uses, summative assessments applied formatively, benchmark assessments, or a group of strategies for student engagement. When teachers' definitions differ from the research-based definitions, school leaders can help them think critically about these differences. They can also support all teachers in developing common understanding of the research-based

Copyright © Mometrix Media. You have been licensed one copy of this document for personal use only. Any other reproduction or redistribution is strictly prohibited. All rights reserved.

definition and its components. Another possible issue is that implementing formative assessment differs from overall program adoption, wherein teachers are given procedures to follow and materials to use. By comparison, the formative assessment process, whereby teachers learn through practicing, reflecting, and revising, can feel unclear, uneven, and/or messy. Leaders can respond by reassuring teachers this is normal; support their understanding that formative assessment appears differently by grade level, classroom, content area, and teaching methods; and provide teachers many reflection opportunities to help resolve such issues typical during early stages of change.

When a school leader offers a training course for implementing formative assessments in classrooms, such as that developed by the Council of Chief State School Officers (CCSSO), teachers may view formative assessment as simply another assessment they must include, in addition to all the assessments already used in their district or school. The danger is that, if teachers regard formative assessment as added onto existing ones, they will see it as yet another thing they must squeeze into an already loaded (or overloaded) teaching schedule. Consequently, they may neglect or resent it. School leaders must ensure that teachers instead understand formative assessment as an essential component of a comprehensive assessment system. They and the leadership teams they build can use the course information to clarify expectations of teachers to use various assessment types such as formative and summative classroom assessments, district assessments, state assessments, and benchmark assessments. They can also compare comprehensive assessment information to the Response to Intervention (RTI) model for alignment: RTI Tier I instruction incorporates formative assessment; classroom formative assessment data (while not contributing directly to the RTI decision-tree in the CCSSO model) are mainly to inform classroom teachers' instruction.

Formative assessment is highly aligned with standards-based instruction, derives from similar research sources, and thus has many elements in common with it. Therefore, when school leaders offer faculty a course such as that provided by the Council of Chief State School Officers (CCSSO), many teachers will recognize some material as familiar and object to it, saying "We already know this" or "this is just good teaching." To address these responses, school leaders should explicitly communicate connections between what they have already done at their school and the formative assessment practices they now want to implement. When school leaders explain how inquiry learning, using short-cycle data, standards-based instruction, etc. are connected to formative assessment practices they are instituting, this benefits teachers by enabling them to see the compatibility and coherence of these elements. School leaders should explain formative assessment is not "just good teaching," but moreover requires teacher-student collaboration in gathering and examining learning evidence to reveal next steps for each student's instruction. Leaders can also cite research showing educators "know" more than they "do" to show teachers the value of learning how to apply and integrate even familiar concepts into teaching practices.

In making assessment decisions, school leaders and teachers encounter conflicts among pressures, uses, and purposes for assessments that compete with one another. For example, teachers find constructed-response test items better for determining student comprehension, but selected-response and objective test items are externally mandated by government in large-scale standardized tests. Additional conflicts exist between auditing vs. learning; informal, ongoing formative assessments vs. formal, end-of-unit summative assessments; norm-referenced vs. criterion-referenced tests; testing according to absolute standards vs. value-added testing; traditional vs. alternative assessment; artificial

Copyright © Mometrix Media. You have been licensed one copy of this document for personal use only. Any other reproduction or redistribution is strictly prohibited. All rights reserved.

assessments vs. authentic assessments; speeded (or timed) test instruments vs. power testing instruments; standardized tests vs. classroom tests, etc. Because so many conflicts are inherent in the process of selecting and applying assessments, school leaders and teachers must thoroughly understand how the nature of an assessment is influenced by such diverse variables. When they understand all of the alternatives in assessment, trading off some advantages and disadvantages for others is unavoidable, and leaders must establish priorities to inform their own decisions and guide teachers' decisions regarding assessment.

Monitoring student progress

To know whether students are learning and can show proficiency in state standards, school leaders and teachers must integrate progress monitoring into classroom instruction. Knowing daily student status relative to content standards informs teaching. Educators need to collect student achievement data as indicators of progress toward school goals; to do this, they must first identify which data to collect. For example, if they want to know whether they are making progress toward meeting their Adequate Yearly Progress (AYP) criterion in reading, then they must collect data on individual students about their progress relative to objectives or indicators of their state's content standards for reading. School leaders must collaborate with faculty and staff, not only to show their support and involvement, but also to be informed themselves. They must also promote collaboration among staff members to stimulate their ownership of the standards, goals, and data and how they adjust their instruction accordingly. Staff should divide objectives and indicators among themselves in ways that are instructionally logical, with leaders providing guidance as needed.

To determine individual and group student progress toward school goals and state content standards, continuous data collection is important. Relying on quarterly assessments does not give frequent enough information for adjusting instruction; can make teachers see monitoring components as external, not integral to instruction; and does not advance faculty toward their ultimate goal of teaching and testing indicators and objectives for which they are responsible. School leaders and teachers must determine on an ongoing basis where students are related to the objectives at any time, and use this information to direct their instruction. School leaders should decide how often teachers should submit monitoring data they collect, and to whom. For example, a school leader may want teachers to submit data to their team leaders every two or three weeks so they can hold structured discussions of data at team meetings. School leaders are responsible for ensuring teachers submit data, and addressing it if any teachers do not. If their state assigns a scoring tool or rubric, school leaders must ensure teachers understand and can apply its criteria to predict probable student performance on state assessments. School leaders can also help faculty develop or select a spreadsheet, database, grid, or table as a data-recording template.

Included among reasons that school leaders should monitor student learning are: to assess group and/or individual student achievement, improve instruction, direct curricular development and revision, to graduate or certify students, diagnose learning problems, prevent some students from failing or disappearing unnoticed by the educational system, prove accountability, ascertain whether educators are meeting their standards, determine how their school compares nationally to other schools, and understand which programs are accomplishing results they desire. School leaders, as well as their districts and building faculty, must develop systems to collect information about instructional practices and

Copyright © Mometrix Media. You have been licensed one copy of this document for personal use only. Any other reproduction or redistribution is strictly prohibited. All rights reserved.

student progress at school and classroom levels. They should gather these data routinely and regularly analyze them, using the results to adjust teaching activities and methods. Some steps for applying data to enhance student learning include having teacher teams establish student achievement baselines for each goal area using school, district, and state test results, plus published and teacher-designed tests. Have teachers choose and apply instructional strategies in classrooms. Have teachers assess student work frequently to obtain ongoing and immediate feedback on their teaching strategies' effects, providing quicker improvement and continuing teacher motivation.

Monitoring instructional practices and school progress

School leaders need to collect data about which actual practices their teachers are using in classrooms, and to analyze their school's progress toward realizing their school goals. Experts advise starting by determining what their teachers want their students to be able to do and to know, and how their teachers are helping students to learn. Also, school leaders should consider what they and their faculties want all of their students to learn, according to each grade level, each course, and each instructional unit; how they will determine when every student has obtained the identified knowledge and skills; and what they will do to address early student difficulties for enhancing existing learning levels. Leaders and teachers can control conditions including classroom management philosophies and strategies, student-teacher and student-student relationships, student-teacher ratios, teaching strategies, teaching places and times, how instructional materials are organized, and assessments. Experts recommend using school assessment rubrics to evaluate beginning, current, and future status. Monitoring school development and change demands non-hierarchical, collegial teacher-supervisor relationships; focusing not on teacher conformity but teacher development; teacher collaboration to improve instruction; and leader support of continual teacher reflection.

Developing and examining the planning and design of curriculum and instruction

The educational environment today dictates that enabling every student's achievement defines the school's success. To attain this success goal, educators need to identify which students are at academic risk, and then modify their instructional methods to meet the needs of these students better. School leaders are instrumental in this process. First they must collaborate with faculty and staff in designing their school's curriculum and instructional programs. Then they must regularly review the curriculum and instructional programs—both to determine whether faculty and staff are implementing them correctly, and to determine whether their design is addressing all students' needs the way that they expected them to when they created them. If implementation is flawed, school leaders need to guide staff to include components they are omitting, change their teaching methods, etc. to bring implementation into alignment with the intentions of planning and design. If implementation is correct but not all students are having their educational needs met, leaders must collaborate with staff to identify unmet needs and which content and practices will address them.

Organizing teachers into data inquiry teams to determine what students need academically

School leaders should assign every teacher in their school to participate on data inquiry teams organized by grade levels and/or academic departments. They should instruct these

Copyright © Mometrix Media. You have been licensed one copy of this document for personal use only. Any other reproduction or redistribution is strictly prohibited. All rights reserved.

teams to work together regularly in analyzing the data they have gathered from the results of formative and summative assessments they have administered to their students. Leaders should direct their data inquiry teams to analyze the data at both the standard level and the individual item level, and analyze them according to individual students, classes, and subgroups of students. School leaders should then ask the data inquiry teams to develop action plans according to what their student data analyses have revealed, to implement these action plans, and provide support in implementing them. The data teams' action plans should cover all the steps that every teacher must take to increase student achievement levels, such as adjusting the curriculum, designing and providing academic interventions, and re-teaching material when needed. After teachers administer formative and interim assessments to students, school leaders can also have the data inquiry teams analyze the students' assessment results.

Meeting student needs through school cultures focusing on student data

To develop a school data culture, school leaders should clearly and consistently articulate a school vision regarding school-wide data use. They must additionally establish norms for teachers aligned with that vision, and organizational structures like data inquiry teams. Leaders should consistently model data-based decision-making and data application, and show their belief in data's effectiveness for enhancing instruction and learning. They model for teachers a commitment to collaboration without blame and shared outcome accountability. They empower teachers to analyze data collaboratively and make critical decisions accordingly. Leaders help teachers choose and apply suitable data collection technology with formats facilitating analysis, interpretation, and action. They participate in and provide teachers with continuing professional development to improve their abilities for analyzing and interpreting multiple data types. They require multiple sources of high-quality data on student performance, e.g., local, state, and national standardized tests; student work products; performance assessments; school progress reports; classroom observations; student presentations; and postgraduate performance indices like college admissions and success. Leaders use data on school culture and student character from sources like student motivation and engagement measures; school surveys; discipline, attrition, attendance, promotion, and graduation records; progress report sections covering character and scholarship habits; student presentations; and classroom observations.

Guiding teachers in using student data for meeting student needs

School leaders should guide teachers to analyze elementary and secondary student performance data because doing so will enable them to identify variables that motivate different students to achieve. Teachers can then apply this knowledge to their instruction to motivate students better, which will better meet their learning needs. Leaders should also guide teachers to explain clearly and explicitly to students their assessment criteria, and their expectations for student achievement in content knowledge and skills. Clearly understanding these requirements enables students to interpret their own performance data and set learning goals for themselves. Leaders should guide teachers to give students effective feedback, and strategies and tools like peer reviews and student-made assessment rubrics, to help students understand their strengths and specific improvement needs. Students can be more motivated by teachers' small-group instruction in goals students identified for themselves, and by teachers' re-teaching concepts identified as their weaknesses by many students. Leaders can also encourage teachers and students to

Copyright © Mometrix Media. You have been licensed one copy of this document for personal use only. Any other reproduction or redistribution is strictly prohibited. All rights reserved.

collaborate in generating reflective questions, graphs, and self-monitoring logs to direct data analysis and data-based performance improvement decisions.

Making the best use of student achievement data

Experts recommend that school leaders create and communicate a clear vision for school-wide use of student data, institute supports for the school's development of a data-driven culture, develop and sustain district-wide data systems, teach students to understand and use their own data for setting learning goals, and make data an essential component of a continuing instructional improvement cycle. To make data part of the improvement cycle, leaders must guide teachers to use data routinely and methodically to inform teaching decisions and meet student learning needs. This entails collecting data from multiple sources (e.g., state yearly assessments, district and school interim assessments, classroom achievement data, etc.), interpreting these to form hypotheses regarding strategies for increasing student performance, and testing those hypotheses through modifying instructional practices. Teachers should collaborate in all of these efforts. Establishing district-wide data systems enables aggregating data by content area, assignment type, or classroom to detect patterns. By interpreting data, leaders and teachers can identify individual student, as well as whole-class, strengths and needs. Hypothesizing about student learning influences informs instructional improvements, which in turn test the hypotheses, informing continuation, extension, or modification of those improvements or trying different ones.

Forming a school data team to support establishment of a clear school-wide data use vision

To institute effective data-based decision-making on a consistent and routine basis, school leaders need to create a strong school data culture. They can accomplish this by forming a school-wide data team composed of such stakeholders as teachers of different subjects and grade levels, classroom support professionals, an administrator, and a district-level staff member familiar with data. Such teams can collaborate with the overall school community. Data teams should not give expert advice, supervise data activities, or make staff accountable for data use; instead, they lead by modeling data use. Leaders should also guide data teams to clarify the school vision for data use, encourage staff to collaborate on improving teaching through data use, and regularly monitor school data use progress. Teams can define essential data-related education concepts, e.g., data, evidence, learning, achievement, collaboration, etc. Leaders should instruct data teams to develop a written plan relating data use to school goals, ensuring that goals are relevant and can be attained and measured. Staff responsibilities and roles, timelines, and specific data activities should be included in the plan, which may be a component in the school improvement plan and/or literacy, Title I, or other extant funding source plans.

Communicating to stakeholders about progress toward visions and goals

In some county school systems, leadership prepares and distributes, through the community, an annual report on the status of all schools in the district, including a letter from the superintendent; statements of the district's and school's core values, vision, and goals; colorful graphics; current student scores on required state standardized tests; special programs; percentages of staff qualifications; graduation highlights; the school calendar for the year; recognitions and news at each school; and contact numbers and website

Copyright © Mometrix Media. You have been licensed one copy of this document for personal use only. Any other reproduction or redistribution is strictly prohibited. All rights reserved.

addresses. School leaders each use regular school board meetings to report student achievement data and other school highlights. Local newspapers often report about board meetings, following up with superintendent or other district leader interviews. Students and parents may also receive performance results reports through individual school websites, letters to families, and school conferences. Superintendents, assessment directors, and other program directors may also present system-level attendance, graduation, and academic performance data. Superintendents offer data analysis articles to the community, sharing graphs and charts system-wide via e-mail; school leaders review these data in their meetings, and plan accordingly.

<u>Sharing interpretations of school data</u>
School leaders regularly engage in data-oriented discussions with stakeholders about their school improvement goals. They fuel these conversations with questions informing an inquiry, collaboration, and problem-solving process. A culture of sharing ownership of student success and using data productively is informed by clearly established norms which guide such conversations. School leaders and their teachers can produce displays of data which diverse stakeholders can easily understand and analyze. School leaders and teachers must make current school and student data accessible to stakeholders in a timely fashion, while the data is still meaningful and useful. School leaders should also support the collection and collective analysis of community engagement data from various sources, e.g., community partnerships and events, student and family satisfaction surveys, and school event community attendance statistics. School leaders should additionally support the collection and shared analysis of data regarding school organizational performance, derived from multiple sources such as patterns of applications, admissions, and enrollments; resources; fundraising; budget targets; and recruitment, retention, and satisfaction of school staff. School leaders can use the data they have collected for telling the stories of their schools, allocating resources, and leveraging educational reform.

Principles of classroom assessment

Despite multiple-choice tests, machine scoring, and other elements that make student performance assessment appear objective, assessment is still really based on the values, assumptions, and judgment of the professionals designing and scoring tests and rubrics, interpreting standardized test scores, giving grades, etc. Knowing this helps leaders understand the significance of theirs and their teachers' judgments to evaluating assessment quality and what the results mean. They must also remember the difference between measurement evidence and evaluation: the former entails conceptual understanding of descriptive statistics to interpret student strengths and weaknesses and make grading and admissions decisions, while the latter entails judging the value of data in application to specific contexts or uses. They should realize that assessment types influence student learning and motivation. They must know that all assessment incorporates error; that error is typically underestimated; and that reliability concerns scores, not tests. School leaders should also know that good assessment is fair and ethical as well as valid, enhances teaching, employs multiple methods, integrates technology appropriately, and is feasible and efficient.

Educational standard

Standards are learning goals. Standards are found on lists of educational competencies (concepts and contexts) that each student should attain by certain benchmarks (primarily

Copyright © Mometrix Media. You have been licensed one copy of this document for personal use only. Any other reproduction or redistribution is strictly prohibited. All rights reserved.

grade level). Standards are not curriculum. Standards do not instruct schools or teachers on how to teach their students. Day-to-day teaching decisions are left to the local school officials, while standards provide big picture guidance about what students should learn in order to be ready to successfully meet future learning opportunities. Modern standards typically focus on higher order thinking skills and suggest that students go beyond knowing "who" or "what" and towards "how" and "why." Modern standards coincide well with student-centered learning pedagogies (e.g., problem-based, project-based, discovery-based) that offer student opportunities for deeper thinking and greater creativity.

Standards-based curriculum vs. traditional curriculum

Modern standards (such as the Common Core) are centered on the development of higher-order thinking skills. A traditional classroom typically features students sitting in rows and columns of desks led by a teacher who disseminates required knowledge. Because one-size-fits-all teacher-centered instruction (with passive student participation) is not as effective with helping students develop higher-order thinking skills, standards-based classrooms tend to feature more student-centered pedagogies (e.g., collaborative problem solving, student discovery projects) with students actively participating in the learning process while teachers coach individual students. Higher-order thinking skills are developed as students verbalize their understanding with their learning partners. A standards-based classroom features more activities and fewer lectures. A standards-based classroom is focused on student learning rather than on covering a set list of topics. Standards-based classrooms rely upon the professionalism and training of teachers to adjust their instruction regularly to accommodate for the diversity of student and classroom learning characteristics.

Importance of formative assessment to standards-based student-centered learning

Summative assessments are the traditional fare of the classroom; they are closed form tests (or quizzes) on which students work individually and for which students receive some numerical score. These assessments provide a numerical measure of a student's progress towards some learning goal(s) but fall short of providing the teacher with feedback that might guide future classroom activities. Alternatively formative assessments (e.g., teacher observations, student reflections, group problems) are non-numerical open form appraisals of student progress. Though they do not provide quantitative data to represent student progress, they provide qualitative (sentence-based) feedback to guide classroom instruction. There is no one way to teach towards higher-order thinking skills, and student engagement with classroom materials is a key to success. As such, formative assessments are vitally important. They provide the guidance a teacher will need to tailor his or her classroom activities to a given class's unique characteristics. Formative assessment empowers a teacher to individualize curriculum towards students as they attempt to develop higher-order thinking skills. Without an established program of formative assessment, it is highly unlikely that any classroom will successfully empower students to develop the thinking skills called for by the standards.

Support needed to implement a standards-based curriculum

The success of any implementation of a standards-based curriculum is dependent upon classroom teachers, who will require the support of educational leaders. Transitioning teachers and students from a traditional teacher-centered classroom to the student-

Copyright © Mometrix Media. You have been licensed one copy of this document for personal use only. Any other reproduction or redistribution is strictly prohibited. All rights reserved.

centered classroom capable of fostering the development of higher-order thinking skills requires a stable pedagogical foundation developed through professional collaboration, fruitful discourse, and patient progress. No teacher or class will be successful in a transition directly from lecture-based instruction into high-ordered thinking. Rather, students and teachers must be gradually acclimated to new ways of classroom interaction. As an educational leader, you can facilitate a professional environment in which teachers can comfortably grow as educators. Teachers are generally receptive to a non-threatening collaborative process in which pedagogical goals are clearly communicated, specific strategies for student engagement are developed, and teachers have an opportunity to have their concerns addressed. As teachers gain experience with student-centered learning they will become more comfortable with the greater depth of learning required by the standards and will begin to better align their classrooms with the standards.

Reassuring concerned parents

Parents can become frustrated when they are unable to help their child with homework. In particular, their frustration may stem from a misunderstanding of modern classroom techniques for learning standard materials. They may say something like, "Why don't you just teach it the way I learned it?" As an educational leader you can both support your teachers and relieve parental frustrations, if such a question is ever brought to you. Regardless of the situation, always remain positive; any negativity will only fuel parental frustration. Encourage parents to speak with the teacher. Perhaps there is some misunderstanding of the intent of an assignment. You can encourage the parents to allow the student to do his or her own homework and ask questions of his or her teacher the next day. After all it is expected that the student will do the work, not a parent. Finally you might suggest the parent talk to family friends or relatives who may be more familiar with the material. Stress to the parent that education (for student, teacher, and parent) is not intended to be an individual endeavor. All parties should be encouraged to seek assistance when necessary.

Copyright © Mometrix Media. You have been licensed one copy of this document for personal use only. Any other reproduction or redistribution is strictly prohibited. All rights reserved.

Managing Organizational Systems & Safety

Teaching staff quality

Research into effective schools finds quality teaching staff a significant factor in enhancing student educational outcomes. Investigators studying how school leaders recruit, assign, develop, and retain their teachers have discovered four essential results. (1) Schools that are found more effective have the ability, when they experience vacancies in their teaching staffs, to attract and hire teachers who are also more effective from other schools. (2) Schools that are found more effective use more equitable methods of assigning new teachers among students. (3) At schools that have been found more effective at increasing student achievement previously, teachers subsequently employed there show more rapid improvement than teachers employed at other schools that are found to be less effective. (4) Schools that are found to be more effective are also found to have a greater ability to retain teachers of higher quality than other schools. Researchers interpret these findings as indicating not only how important personnel are to schools for bettering student outcomes, but possibly how important school personnel practices are as well.

Identifying strengths and weaknesses in teacher candidates in hiring practices

Multiple research studies show evidence that many school leaders can identify the most effective teachers, both among those applying for jobs and among those already employed at their schools. Particularly when they are hiring teachers with previous teaching experience, researchers find the average school leaders can tell which teachers are most effective. Some investigators note that, because the most effective teachers are likely to transfer to schools with the highest quality of faculty, it cannot be determined whether these schools' leaders are better at choosing good teachers, or good teachers are drawn to these schools. However, studies find strong evidence of the ability of school leaders to distinguish between the teachers on their existing faculties who were most and least effective in increasing student performance. They are not as well able to discern differences between teachers in the middle of the distribution for quality, though—which is to be expected due to the lesser contrast.

School facilities

Some common components of a school facility include the building and its electrical, mechanical, plumbing, security, fire preventions and suppression, and telecommunications systems; building fixtures; furniture; equipment; information technology; materials; and supplies. The school building and grounds include playgrounds, athletic fields, outdoor learning areas, parking lots, roads, and other vehicular access. In addition to physical elements, the school facility is moreover an integral part of the conditions enabling and contributing to learning. The experience that students, educators, and community members receive is influenced largely by the design of an individual school facility or campus. School facility design and management help impart to those attending, working, and visiting senses of safety, security, control, ownership, personalization, privacy, sociality, and (depending on the facility) congestion or roominess. School leaders should take these elements into consideration whenever possible while managing, planning, and/or designing school facilities. School facilities that are effective demonstrate responsiveness to changes in

Copyright © Mometrix Media. You have been licensed one copy of this document for personal use only. Any other reproduction or redistribution is strictly prohibited. All rights reserved.

educational delivery programs. They should at the least be accessible, secure, safe, comfortable, well-lighted, well-ventilated, and aesthetically pleasing.

Long-term educational planning can often uncover unmet needs in facility spaces. It is the goal of educational planning to review, clarify, or develop educational philosophies, visions, missions, curriculum, and instruction. Various school and community surveys and workshops may be included in educational planning to clarify or identify the district's vision and needs. Long-range educational planning can trigger district administrative responses in activities like financing decisions, demographic studies, community partnership opportunities, and new site acquisitions. Unmet facility needs are often addressed through developing comprehensive capital improvement plans resulting from long-range planning. Superintendents typically assign oversight of such programs by steering committees, with final decisions made by school boards. Committees retain financial consultants, educational consultants, design consultants, investment bankers, bond counsels, and public relationship consultants to define financing, budget, project scope, schedule, and legal issues among referendum-planning activities. For projects found feasible, they prepare and present public referendum packages to taxpayers in public hearings. Referendum passage enables more detailed facility planning, including contracting with architects, who subcontract with land surveyors; landscape architects; interior designers; and civil, electrical, and mechanical engineers. The facility programming and educational specifications process, followed by the design process and construction, can take two to three years.

Although planning, designing, and constructing school facilities last a few years, managing them lasts for their whole existence. The 21st century began with 28 percent of school buildings constructed before 1950; American school buildings' mean age was 42 years. Building materials, equipment, and furnishings last less than half as long, requiring continual maintenance, then replacement. Eventually, school buildings become obsolete. Historically, facility planning costs have had more attention than management costs. A recent trend has been a steady decline in the percentages of school operations budgets allocated for building management and maintenance. Consequently, at all educational levels, maintenance has been deferred, leading to a capital renewal crisis. School leaders have chief responsibility for daily school operations, including transportation, food, and custodial services. School leaders hire custodial personnel who monitor electrical, plumbing, and mechanical systems and perform building and grounds maintenance as well as cleaning the building. In recent decades, emergent environmental quality issues include controlling hazardous materials like radon and asbestos, conserving energy, and improving water and indoor air quality and acoustics (which may necessitate hiring facility consultants via districts). Leaders must also address building issues like government accessibility regulations, energy deregulation, and security issues like terrorism, violence, vandalism, and threats.

Communicating safety policies

School leaders must communicate all school safety policies that comply with federal, state, and local safety regulations for school physical plants. They must notify staff and parents in advance about any changes, including physical plant projects, which could affect the safety, health, and well-being of the students and staff. They must inform employees, students, and families of communicable disease exposure, biological or chemical exposure, or other unplanned events. To comply with physical plant safety regulations, school leaders must know all safety policies, including such elements as prohibiting weapons at school, areas for

Copyright © Mometrix Media. You have been licensed one copy of this document for personal use only. Any other reproduction or redistribution is strictly prohibited. All rights reserved.

picking up and dropping off students, etc. They must warn staff, students, and parents about spraying of pesticides, painting in the school, and other projects affecting the physical environment to enable protection for sensitive individuals. They need a plan in place for responding quickly to unexpected environmental exposures to limit unneeded time delays between exposure and treatment to optimize health. School leaders should involve employees, students, and families in developing and revising safety policies. To avoid openness to differing interpretations, they must ensure policies' clarity, explicitness, explanation, and dissemination. They should appoint school health and safety teams and clearly identify their reporting mechanisms.

School physical plant maintenance projects

When schools undergo projects such as asbestos removal, mold elimination, pesticide treatment, renovation, and painting, school leaders must not only keep students' hazardous substance exposure to a minimum, but moreover notify families of potential student exposure. This enables providing added protection for students with asthma, allergies, and other special health conditions making them more sensitive to hazardous materials. Accidental chemical spills on roads or highways near the school are also examples of unexpected and unusual environmental occurrences when school leaders should contact emergency departments for advice on how best to protect their students. School leaders and their staff members should also inform student families and public health professionals of any such exposure, including which substance(s) were involved, possible signs and symptoms to identify, and how to access any health care measures needed. School leaders should consider risk communication principles and goals to devise mechanisms for notification of environmental concerns. Adopting a plan facilitates prompt, appropriate response. Leaders must remember parents with limited English-language proficiency and literacy when communicating the plan. They should know which consultants their districts have available to help develop plans and investigate incidents.

Maintenance of school buildings and grounds

School leaders should develop comprehensive sets of procedures, and oversee their implementation, to conduct preventive maintenance of the school buildings and grounds to provide students and staff with safe, healthful environments inside the buildings and on the surrounding outside school grounds. Procedures should cover bathroom facilities, playgrounds, sports areas, and parking lots as well as classrooms, libraries, auditoriums, cafeterias, etc. Leaders should provide staff training in procedures. Buildings and grounds should have environmental safety reviews at least yearly. Walls, roofs, floors, subflooring, windows, HVAC systems, etc. need regular maintenance to decrease custodial effort and expense in preserving building cleanliness and improve energy efficiency and indoor air quality. Maintenance plans require procedures for keeping school grounds safe, including playground equipment and surfaces; and addressing weather-related indoor problems, e.g., wet floors on rainy or snowy days. Leaders should schedule regular equipment inspections and initiate repairs of anything not complying with U.S. Consumer Product Safety Commission guidelines. They must supervise custodial staff in keeping trash receptacles regularly emptied and covered, and toilet facilities safe, clean, functional, private, and well-supplied. School leaders should allocate budget for and have inspection and maintenance procedures and schedules developed by experienced maintenance supervisors.

Copyright © Mometrix Media. You have been licensed one copy of this document for personal use only. Any other reproduction or redistribution is strictly prohibited. All rights reserved.

School safety plans

Increasing social diversity and legally mandated inclusive education mean that schools today serve ever more children with impoverished homes, no homes, teenage parents, dysfunctional families, and special education needs—all with decreasing resources. Student gang activity, drug trafficking, and weapons possession all pose school challenges. School leaders must respond by developing and implementing safety plans to provide safe learning environments. Because education is compulsory, school leaders and staff are accordingly responsible to give students peaceful, secure, safe environments where they can learn. Every school and district must develop a school safety plan whose development is not only by school personnel, but involves participation by the whole community. The fact that the highest severity and numbers of school violence and crime incidents are in communities with the same statistics is not a coincidence. To counter these issues, school safety programs must be developed collaboratively, including participation by students, administrators, teachers, parents, mental health professionals, law enforcement officers, community and business leaders, and a broad variety of other community professionals serving youth. Schools exist for learning, not controlling violence and crime; their safety plans require engagement, support, and expertise contributed by various resources.

Effective school safety programs emphasize school climates building on individual student assets and strengths; enhancing protective factors, resiliency, and self-esteem; developing psychosocial skills; recognizing socially competent behavior; positive alternatives; and prevention. They offer students varied pro-social activities and relevant school engagement, both of which counter disorder and violence. Goals for school leaders include: leading their schools in making needs assessments, developing a school safety plan, and monitoring its implementation; developing a system for continuously tracking, reporting, and giving feedback on school crime and incidents, and furnishing concerned stakeholders with this information; designing the school environment to have safe patterns of traffic to, from, and inside the school; adopting crisis management and emergency evacuation procedures for their schools; and forming a school planning team or school safety council. They should include representatives of school staff, students, parents, and community members in the group. This team or council has the responsibility to make decisions and give advice about crime and violence cases with critical importance, evaluate school safety status on an ongoing basis, and propose school safety plan and/or school disciplinary code revisions as they see the need.

Once school leaders have developed school safety plans with the participation of school stakeholder and community members, they must review it to evaluate whether it is being implemented correctly and consistently, and whether its implementation is effective in promoting safety. Leaders should conduct formal reviews at least once a year of all school safety procedures and policies, and verify that any developing safety issues are sufficiently addressed by existing school emergency response procedures and crisis plans. They should review all communication systems within their school district and with community responders, including where and how they will inform parents in case of emergencies. Leaders should contact area hospitals, emergency responders, victims' assistance, and other community partners to review their emergency response plans, and discuss with them any short-term needs for their schools in the event they are currently experiencing a crisis. School leaders should also periodically conduct new needs assessments and, based on their findings, implement additional or revised professional development and crisis training to their employees.

Copyright © Mometrix Media. You have been licensed one copy of this document for personal use only. Any other reproduction or redistribution is strictly prohibited. All rights reserved.

In addition to regularly reviewing the school safety plan itself to ensure its implementation and effectiveness, school leaders can also institute procedures whereby they and their staff can review the safety of the school buildings, grounds, facilities, and equipment for compliance with the safety plan. They may employ a detailed checklist, for example, with "Yes or No" question items to check for every safety aspect of every part of the school. In reviewing buildings and grounds safety, this can cover ventilation, air quality; classrooms, art rooms, science labs, band rooms, family and consumer science rooms; bathrooms, auditoriums, multipurpose rooms, hallways, stairwells, exits, floors; kitchens, cafeterias; technical education spaces; custodial, housekeeping, and maintenance services; underground storage tanks; heating, furnace, and boiler rooms; air conditioning equipment; playgrounds; school buses; parking and traffic; emergency preparedness and crisis plans; and a checklist for off-site school-to-work safety. Reviewing the safety of athletic facilities and equipment can include checklist items for gymnasiums, swimming pools, weight training facilities, wall-climbing facilities; student athletes, coaches; cheerleading; track and field; baseball and softball, soccer, lacrosse, and field hockey; gymnastics, etc. Items include adequate lighting, seating; equipment and furnishings in good repair; absence of hazardous conditions like electrical, chemical, tripping objects; sharp edges, wet floors, obstacles; clearance; employee training and instruction, etc.

Among the district, superintendent and other administrative staff, school staff, student, and parent responsibilities, the school leader's responsibilities in school emergency planning include: selecting and assigning staff members to be members of the Building Response Team; acting as, or designating another employee to act as, the school emergency coordinator; assigning school emergency responsibilities to staff members according to requirements; making sure that the school building emergency plan is aligned with the school district vision and mission; monitoring the participation of all school staff in the required competencies and trainings; conducting drills, evaluating responses, and initiating necessary revisions of the plan according to the drill evaluation results; encouraging faculty to integrate school safety, emergency preparedness, and violence prevention into the curriculum; regularly keeping parents informed about the emergency notification system; arranging for the school to procure, maintain, and store emergency equipment and supplies; furnishing the local emergency manager and district superintendent with copies of the school emergency plan; supervising periodic safety checks of transportation vehicles and school facilities; and keeping the district superintendent informed about resources the school needs and actions they have taken.

Emergency management

The four phases of emergency management are Prevention (or Mitigation), Preparedness, Response, and Recovery. Effective school emergency plans must be based on all four of these phases; furnish the whole school community with direction; document all requirements for implementing and maintaining the plan; be printed, communicated to all school staff, and regularly practiced via exercises and drills, in addition to all staff's being trained in plan procedures yearly at a minimum; and be reviewed on an ongoing basis and revised as needed. The U.S. Department of Education recommends that all school emergency plans should reflect National Incident Management System principles; assure the safety of all school community members, including visitors, students, staff, and any of these having special needs and/or disabilities; reflect the four phases of emergency planning (see above); provide for addressing all possible hazards; include collaboration

Copyright © Mometrix Media. You have been licensed one copy of this document for personal use only. Any other reproduction or redistribution is strictly prohibited. All rights reserved.

with community partners for their development and maintenance; and have their development and reinforcement on the basis of the local characteristics and needs of the school district and its buildings and grounds.

School emergency response teams

(1) District response teams include superintendents or designees; elementary and secondary school leaders and assistant leaders; health and safety directors; buildings and grounds supervisors; emergency coordinators; transportation, food services, special education, and communications directors; school resource officer, school social worker, lead nurse, school psychologist, and teacher representatives. With community response agencies, they develop school emergency plans; conduct planning, training, and drills complying with state requirements; help build response teams; and assure planning continuity. They may also perform district-level response functions like finance, information, or behavioral health crisis interventions. (2) Building response teams include building administrators, teachers, buildings and grounds, health services, student support services, technology, food service, special education, school resource, and office support staff representatives. Trained in emergency response functions consistently with the district emergency plan, they develop and revise building emergency plans and procedures, train staff, conduct drills, document and evaluate drills, and respond to actual incidents. (3) Medical response teams, including school nurses; school psychologists and counselors; chemical health specialists; teachers and other staff trained in CPR, AED, and first aid with annual certification; all help in medical emergencies until responders arrive. (4) District-level recovery teams, led by superintendents or designees, develop and implement recovery plans to restore school infrastructure and learning environments after major emergencies.

NIMS and ICS

The U.S. Department of Homeland Security adopted the National Incident Management System (NIMS) for all federal, state, and local government agencies to use for responding to emergencies. Within the NIMS, the Incident Command System (ICS) is the organizational structure for managing emergency response. This system offers a coordinated, integrated structure for management, shared vocabulary, and flexibility for including fewer or more functions according to an individual emergency's scope. School emergencies require the same incident command functions that community emergencies do. School district and building response teams are organized to correspond with the incident command functions of the ICS. There are five main function areas of the CIS. (1) Command: this function is responsible overall for managing events and incidents, and directly responsible for public safety, information, and liaisons with community response agencies. (2) Operations: this function develops objectives, organizes resources, and directs resources and actions to provide responses to incidents. (3) Logistics: this function identifies the services and resources needed for supporting the needs of incident response. (4) Planning: this function collects and evaluates information, identifies issues, develops action plans, and gives recommendations for future actions. (5) Finance: this function manages the financial aspects of incidents, monitors incident response expenses, coordinates with insurance companies, and meets record-keeping needs.

Communicating with the media regarding school emergencies

For emergencies, district administration designates a public information officer (PIO) to manage all district and school communications with media. All media inquiries are referred to this district PIO. Districts are responsible, in coordination with community response agencies, for public statements. District administration also designates a district spokesperson and establishes a joint information center (JIC) away from the emergency area in partnership with all agencies involved as a single media contact point for message coordination. The PIO coaches and prepares the district spokesperson, coordinates with responding agencies for safe media photography and video within agency protocols and school privacy policies, prevents media representatives from interfering with emergency responders or endangering themselves, provides press releases and regular updates, corrects reports, dispels inaccurate rumors, and documents all media contacts. School leaders inform all staff and district administration of emergency incidents; direct all media inquiries to the district PIO; transmit all factual information to the district PIO; designate a site spokesperson upon district administration's direction; reviews emergency details, updates staff, and dispels rumors throughout the incident; notifies the PIO and district administration of any media presence in the building; and requests on-site assistance with media if needed.

Communicating with involved parties related to emergency and support personnel

In a medical emergency, school leaders should make sure somebody has called 911, and communicate any additional and/or updated information to emergency services operators. School leaders should obtain a medical emergency profile of the victim(s). They should contact the school emergency response team to respond. School leaders should make sure a staff member, student, or other person is available to meet first responders and direct them to the victim's location. They should provide first responders with information from the victim's medical emergency profile and any additional information about the victim's status, or make sure someone trustworthy they designate provides them this information. If necessary, the school leader should assign a school staff member to go to the hospital with the victim. The school leader should notify the victim's parents, legal guardians, or emergency contact person(s) of the emergency, and also inform district administration. They should initiate recovery procedures as applicable, including conducting a debriefing with students and/or staff. Additionally, they should document all staff actions during the emergency.

Ways in which school leaders document their communications

School leaders are responsible for initiating needs assessments to determine the safety needs of their school. After determining these, they must enlist the collaboration of school staff and community stakeholders to create a school safety plan. This plan covers the procedures all school members will follow for keeping their school as safe as possible. School leaders supervise how staff implement this safety plan. They monitor whether it is being implemented correctly and consistently, and whether its implementation is effective or not. They need to document their monitoring observations. Pursuant to this monitoring, they must give feedback to school staff and students about how the safety plan is being implemented, including commendations for effective implementation and corrections in the event of deficient implementation. School leaders should follow up their communication of such feedback by documenting it. If (or when) incidents disrupting school safety occur,

Copyright © Mometrix Media. You have been licensed one copy of this document for personal use only. Any other reproduction or redistribution is strictly prohibited. All rights reserved.

school leaders must document these, as well as documenting the resulting feedback they give to stakeholders. School leaders are also responsible for documenting or designating others (such as a school planning team or safety council they appoint) to document the emergency and crisis management procedures they adopt.

DDIS

Six functions, which are components of DDIS that school leaders can construct, are data acquisition, data reflection, program alignment, program design, formative feedback, and test preparation. School leaders and faculty collaborate to create cohesion among these functions, which enables applying data on student achievement to inform teaching and learning with useful classroom knowledge. Data acquisition entails processes of searching for, gathering, and organizing information for instructional and learning guidance. Chief among these data are student scores on standardized achievement tests. Additional data types needed include student records on placement, behavior, and other guidance counseling department information; community survey data; student demographics; teaching personnel and observation; classroom grades; budget information; curriculum information; school technological capacity; and school calendar and master schedule information. Data acquisition also encompasses data reporting and storage capacities. Local systems frequently build upon district and state accountability systems. When pertinent data are stored in different formats and locations, political issues regarding positional information access can impede streamlining data access. But specific student performance information needs have prompted many school leaders to create local customized data systems; and vendors offer varied products for storing and analyzing data.

Data reflection involves structured opportunities for school leaders and teachers to collaborate in interpreting student learning data to set instructional or learning improvement goals and associated action plans. They may do this as a school, or by subject or grade level. Program alignment—an essential part of program planning and evaluation—entails making instructional programs consistent with content and performance standards while also meeting student needs and enhancing learning. Subject or grade-level meetings and teacher and peer evaluations work to align curriculum with content standards, and classroom instruction with curriculum. Professional development, guidance, support programs, community outreach activities, and other non-curricular initiatives also ensure program alignment. So do school interactions with external agencies, as standardized curricula are frequently mandated and alignment tools provided by school districts. Program design involves school actions regarding perceptions of instructional needs, via adapting or designing curriculum, pedagogy, instructional strategies, and student service programs to enhance learning. It addresses identified issues through the policies, procedures, and programs a school designs or adopts. It includes individual student-level programs, group curriculum design, and grants and budgets to finance programs.

Formative feedback generates iterative, student-centered cycles of evaluation. These are designed for facilitating timely, continuing information flow, which can enhance not only student learning outcomes, but also the quality of school-wide instructional programs. Students are empowered to assume ownership of their learning through improved instruction, which is informed by the concept of formative feedback. Within a DDIS, a key function of formative feedback is bettering program design. It can include both teacher practice and student learning data; however, when teacher program implementation practices are considered, it becomes a DDIS component. It differs from data acquisition and

Copyright © Mometrix Media. You have been licensed one copy of this document for personal use only. Any other reproduction or redistribution is strictly prohibited. All rights reserved.

data reflection by specifically focusing on data collected about programs implemented in a school. Experts suggest that, as DDISs mature over time, these differences become less distinct. Test preparation involves activities to develop student performance improvement on district and state tests, and enhance student motivation. It can include teaching students about test formats, developing specific skills identified in standardized tests, addressing test subjects where data reveal student weaknesses, and informing students of behaviors (e.g., eating and sleeping well) that improve test scores. Test preparation extends program design, easing student response to growing testing pressure and time.

Programs that apply current technology appropriately for education

School leaders should certainly take advantage of current technologies for their numerous benefits. For example, technology makes learning both easier and more efficient by presenting it in multimodal and multisensory formats, affording greater repetition and accommodating diverse learning styles and abilities. Multimedia presentations also enrich learning. Technology enables students to communicate and network with and learn from peers, experts, and mentors worldwide. It offers them tools for self-monitoring, self-assessment, reflection, metacognition, learning at their own paces, and working more independently. This develops greater self-determination and self-efficacy, and frees more teacher time for more explicit, targeted, and differentiated instruction. Leaders can provide student access to online instruction, on- and off-school sites, and as separate offerings and/or integrated into other school programs. School-college partnerships, Advanced Placement courses, and International Baccalaureate (IB) Diploma Programs are also facilitated through technology. School leaders must have adequate resources to support these programs, and apply them effectively to realize school goals and purposes. School leaders and staff should participate in decisions for allocating resources toward best fulfilling their school vision and mission, and academic standards, for student achievement outcomes.

Factors instrumental in implementing school-wide technology adoption

Studies show that implementing educational technology requires professional development (PD), leadership, school structure and organization, and resources and support. To be effective, PD must be (1) intentional, carefully planned, with goals set; (2) continuous, because teaching is a constantly changing profession and teachers need frequent active, in-depth learning opportunities and daily classroom practice; and (3) systemic, thorough school- and system-wide teacher collaboration and knowledge-sharing as part of overall school culture. School leaders are (1) role models: leading by example through attending PD and learning and using new technologies with teachers, keeping current with research, and encouraging teachers' trying new things. (2) Learning organization leaders: establishing change conditions by setting high standards for learning, cooperating, and collaborating. (3) Motivators: prioritizing change, supporting and encouraging teachers' endeavors. (4) Resource providers: assuring teachers have necessary resources to accomplish change goals. (5) Facilitators: leading change initiatives; giving teachers learning opportunities; assuring movement of projects through every stage of implementing technology; and identifying factors that impede and promote integrating technology, resolving any problems they encounter. Resources include money, staff, and time; support includes external, community, and administrative support for technology and for participation.

Copyright © Mometrix Media. You have been licensed one copy of this document for personal use only. Any other reproduction or redistribution is strictly prohibited. All rights reserved.

AUP

Classroom Internet technology is accompanied by parent and educator fears of dangers, including children's encountering threatening people online, violence, and obscene or inappropriate images and words. An Internet Acceptable Use Policy (AUP) is a solution. According to the National Education Association, an AUP should have (1) a preamble, explaining the need for the AUP, its development process, goals, and the school conduct code's inclusion of online activity. (2) A definition section defines important terms and words the policy uses. (3) A policy statement indicates which computer services the AUP covers and conditions for student use, e.g., completing a computer responsibility class to understand AUP guidelines. (4) An acceptable uses section defines appropriate student computer network use, e.g., "for educational purposes," including definition(s) thereof. (5) An unacceptable uses section identifies specifically and clearly which student computer or network uses are unacceptable, e.g., off-limits websites (like term paper sellers, chat rooms, etc.); prohibited student information posting, transmission, or forwarding (e.g., profanity, sexually explicit content, violence, or harassing messages); and student behaviors restricted as destructive to network services. (6) A violations (or sanctions) section informs students how to report policy violations or question policy application—which may be according to the school's general disciplinary code.

Educators cannot develop a useful AUP in isolation. They must base it on a philosophy that strikes a balance between freedom and responsibility. For example, some school district AUPs first assert the American citizen's basic right to information access, but additionally require students who are legally minors (under the age of 18 years) to submit agreement and permission forms signed by their parents and themselves in order to be allowed independent use of electronic information and telecommunications resources. By including both elements, such AUPs demonstrate that students' intellectual freedom exists on the basis of their assuming responsibility to accept limitations in that freedom. Experts advise that educators, including school librarians, should be prepared to do the following: promote positive examples of Internet use by young people, develop a school AUP, furnish other school and library AUPs as examples, understand Internet website-blocking software programs and related censorship and safety issues, address incorrect perceptions of Internet pornography, become familiar with added Internet resources for librarians, and contact organizations devoted to electronic freedom of information.

Sources of revenue for many public schools

In many public schools (though of course this varies individually), most of their district revenues come from the federal government, their state government, and their city or municipality government. State governments are often the largest sources of funding, with city funds providing maybe a third of what states do, and perhaps half or more compared to state funds provided by federal government. A small percentage is typically contributed from other sources. State and city education departments often hold budget development sessions in the first quarter of the year (January-March), with their chief financial officers and staff basing district budgets on early projections, which are relatively finalized within the quarter. Districts typically determine overall school funding, plus individual school budgets, based on projected school enrollments for the coming school year. They then adjust funds further to account for anticipated expenses, such as employee salaries and benefits. District offices of achievement and accountability project enrollment in each grade of each district school. However, because enrollment projections are difficult, they submit

- 56 -

Copyright © Mometrix Media. You have been licensed one copy of this document for personal use only. Any other reproduction or redistribution is strictly prohibited. All rights reserved.

these to school leaders to comment on and revise. Committees of representatives from achievement and accountability, operations, finance, and student support offices establish final enrollment projections.

Planning school budgets

School district employees and school leaders can often predict fairly easily what staff salaries will be in the next school year; however, it is more problematic to estimate what employee benefits will cost, especially for health care as these have been steadily increasing recently. District office employees also have to estimate what insurance, utilities, debt payments, etc. will cost; and additionally reserve enough money for emergencies, such as unplanned furnace, boiler, or air conditioning repairs, etc. Some expenses are not reflected in school budgets, yet are vitally necessary to school operations; transportation, for example, can be the most important of these. Not only do regular school buses and drivers cost a lot, there are additional expenses for individual transportation plans included in special education student individualized education programs (IEPs), and for furnishing transportation to homeless students and others with special needs. Early in the year (e.g., February in some districts), school districts use their projected revenues and expenses to issue individual school budgets to school leaders. These display enrollment and revenue allocation numbers side-by-side for school leaders' easy reference. Leaders collaborate with their school community to identify upcoming school-year priorities and share information to prepare budgets.

Most public school districts make budget planning tools available early in the year and schedule training sessions to help school leaders and school community members plan their budgets. Data and human capital specialists in some district networks provide continuing budget planning support. School leaders submit school budgets, and generally must schedule school community meetings shortly thereafter (e.g., 10-14 days). In some districts, an advisory team member and school family council chairperson must complete feedback forms about the budget-planning process. District offices usually involve most of their departments in reviewing individual budgets submitted by school leaders, and contact school leaders directly to discuss any concerns or questions. If significant changes are indicated, school leaders must reconvene school family councils and school leadership teams to discuss these. In summer, district budget offices receive school enrollment updates and disseminate these to individual schools. Network team members or budget office employees contact school leaders if enrollments are substantially higher than projected so they can apply for budget advances to hire more staff during summer. End-of-September total student enrollments per school determine final budget allocations.

Efficient resource application when resources are not increasing or are decreasing

Economic constraints challenge school leaders in realizing improvement visions. Schools frequently react to diminishing resources by cutting services and programs, and/or putting off improvements. Leaders can identify expensive programs that do not increase student performance; consider alternative means for the same ends, e.g., substituting study groups for speakers and workshops as professional development; saving on office support, food service, and transportation via four-day school weeks; prioritize programs and practices most tied to school vision and mission; recruit local business leaders to support family and community advocacy; share professional development (PD) resources with other schools and/or districts; search for more volunteers to tutor, etc. Another result of economic

- 57 -

Copyright © Mometrix Media. You have been licensed one copy of this document for personal use only. Any other reproduction or redistribution is strictly prohibited. All rights reserved.

challenge is school leader turnover through career advancement and retirement. Leaders can address this by nurturing leadership capacities across employees to sustain realizing the vision. They should identify employee leaders, giving them opportunities to develop their leadership skills. Leader commitment and recommitment to vision includes discussing it with teachers, families, and community; working closely with new staff to familiarize them with school vision and culture; protecting staff from lower-priority projects detracting from the vision; extending capacity by rotating leadership duties; giving faculty processing and reflection time at ends of faculty meetings and PD sessions; and celebrating successes.

Professional development provided by school leaders and the quality of faculty members

Researchers find that school leaders can control the quality of their teaching staff on average through the provision of professional development and similar professional instructional skills development. It appears, according to earlier studies, that teachers can improve significantly in their work performance as they attain more teaching experience—and especially in the first few years of their teaching careers. While professional teacher development is an important component for ensuring and enhancing the quality of teachers at every school, investigators believe it may be especially beneficial for teachers in schools serving student populations whose majorities are low-income, minority, and low-achieving students. Schools with these kinds of student populations frequently encounter more difficulties with both recruiting and retaining teachers who are highly effective in their instructional practices. In addition, researchers offer the opinion that professional development in schools to enhance teacher skills while on the job can be both the most effective and the most feasible way for school leaders to elevate the overall quality of their faculties.

Evaluating teachers

One of a school leader's most important functions is to evaluate the teachers on his (or her) faculty. Some expert educators deem teacher evaluation the most important school leader task. Although experts believe all school leaders are motivated to conduct teacher evaluations well, they say this does not necessarily mean they do so. One of the biggest factors affecting whether they do so or not is time. They find school leaders who consistently assign priority to visiting classrooms regularly, monthly or more—even when visits are only brief walkthrough observations or evaluations—definitely have an advantage over those who do not. Leaders who only glimpse classrooms one or two times yearly are much less likely to have clear ideas about teachers' actual instructional skills or be able to give relevant feedback, enabling teachers to reflect about their own teaching skills and practices in more depth. Experts say evaluation must be a continuous process, not a series of isolated occasions. They also stress the importance of always giving objective, understandable, constructive feedback, and following up continuously to assure teachers are acting on their recommendations and reinforce positive steps they see teachers taking.

Considerations for classroom observations

Some school leaders say they observe classrooms to get a glimpse not of teaching but learning. They feel emphasizing learning, by both students and teachers, strengthens their schools. Some say the only way to prove teachers have taught anything is to prove learning has occurred. Experts on transforming schools into professional learning communities (cf.

Copyright © Mometrix Media. You have been licensed one copy of this document for personal use only. Any other reproduction or redistribution is strictly prohibited. All rights reserved.

DuFour) say three issues are the focus: what educators want students to learn, how they know students are learning, and what they do if they discover students are not learning. School leaders find these issues equally good for beginning teacher evaluations. Some note the quality of work teachers engage students in is an insufficiently addressed area. Evaluations seek student-centered classroom atmospheres conducive to learning, teacher creativity and flexibility, and students engaged in learning processes. School leaders evaluate lessons for logic; time-efficiency; connection to prior and future lessons; beginnings, middles with independent and guided work, and ends with student assessment and conclusions; on-task and off-task time; balanced convergent and divergent teacher questions; calling on students equitably; opportunities for students to share ideas and thoughts; student dialogue and collaboration; posted student work; technology integration; good student-teacher interactions; and student and teacher enthusiasm.

Developing leadership abilities and skills in staff members

There are four ways school leaders can cultivate leadership in their staff members: (1) they can help staff increase their knowledge and skills bases by asking them to participate in screening and interviewing job candidates, inviting employees to accompany them to district-level meetings, offering them work on projects outside their usual expertise areas, and asking employees to work with them when interacting with potentially troublesome parents. (2) Get employees involved in school leadership by asking them to serve on the school leadership team, asking them to lead faculty book study groups, inviting them to participate in school improvement projects, and inviting them to lead curriculum planning committees. (3) Give employees opportunities for observation and reflection by discussing with them why and how school leaders handled a situation in a certain way; and encouraging employees to keep journals to reflect on their observations of leaders they know, including what they find good, bad, or flawed in their practices and behaviors. (4) Support employees' participating in professional development by encouraging them to join professional organizations and engage with them, asking them to mentor new employees, and asking them to make informational presentations to other staff members to report on conferences and other professional development activities they attend.

Student mental health

According to the National Institute of Mental Health, approximately 10 percent of American minors are affected by impairing mental health disorders, raising their risk of dropping out or school failure. Some challenges confronting school leaders in promoting student mental health include: (1) inadequate research. Although most student problems are psychosocial or environmental and addressable by prevention and promotion, rather than psychopathological or internal, they routinely receive diagnoses of serious disorders indicating costly, sometimes inappropriate treatments. (2) Limited resources. With intensified accountability for academic outcomes in recent years, school counselor responsibilities have shifted from mental health to academic performance, widening gaps in professional support services. Moreover, counselor-student ratios are overly large. New support staffers receive little systematic in-service development. School districts spend very small budget percentages on salaries of mental health employees, who frequently serve multiple schools. (3) In addition to funding shortages, resources are distributed unevenly. (4) Finally, cultural traditions stigmatizing mental health issues in our society marginalize their priority in schools.

Copyright © Mometrix Media. You have been licensed one copy of this document for personal use only. Any other reproduction or redistribution is strictly prohibited. All rights reserved.

Three student mental health intervention domains are: (1) promoting both students' academic success and their healthy cognitive, emotional, and social development and development of resilience; protective factors; general wellness and assets; self-efficacy; integrity; responsibility; self-direction; self-evaluation; personal safety; safe behavior; effective physical functioning; health maintenance; social relationships; work relationships; creativity; careers; and life roles. (2) Identifying and addressing obstacles to student learning and achievement, which include psychosocial problems, educational problems, psychological disorders, and external stressors. (3) Providing emotional and social support to students, their families, and school staff. Three main areas of concern for school leaders about mental health-related learning obstacles are: (1) addressing external stressors, including perceived or objective demands, stresses, deficits, or crises in homes, neighborhoods, and schools; insufficient safety, food, clothing, and other basic resources; inadequate support systems; and violent or hostile conditions. (2) Addressing psychosocial and educational problems, e.g., attentional, linguistic, learning, school adjustment, life transition, attendance, dropout, family, interpersonal, social, behavioral, conduct, gang-related, delinquency, mood and affect, anxiety; neglect, abuse; substance abuse; physical status-related and sexual activity-related. (3) Serving, accommodating, and instructing students with disabilities and disorders, including ADHD; learning disabilities; depressive disorders; conduct disorders; post-traumatic stress disorder; eating disorders; school phobia; developmental disabilities, and emotional disturbances.

The National Association of Secondary School Principals (NASSP) recommends a number of actions by federal, state, and local governments; school boards; and superintendents to promote comprehensive school mental health programs. In addition, they recommend the following activities for school leaders to pursue: given applicable funding, school leaders should provide comprehensive staff development for school personnel and community service personnel working in schools. This includes training in the following: supports and techniques required for early identification of students having or at risk of mental disorders; how to use referral mechanisms to connect students with school and community intervention and treatment services; strategies for promoting positive environments school-wide; the operations, functions, and organization of school systems; and models of consultation, coordination, and collaboration in school settings. The NASSP also recommends that school leaders promote mental health in their schools through the following actions: creating effective school leadership teams; establishing high teacher and student performance expectations; modeling and encouraging positive professional and interpersonal teacher-student relationships; encouraging parents and community members' quality school involvement; reinforcing school curriculum, instruction, and assessment; promoting academic learning's extension through student activities and service programs; and fostering self-discipline and respect for others in students.

School leaders can support and oversee a variety of school functions to support mental health for students and families. (1) Assessments of students for first-level or initial screening for problems; assessments for diagnoses and planning interventions based on needs and strengths. (2) Referrals, triage, and monitoring and managing student mental health treatment. (3) Direct services and instruction. This includes instructional enhancement of wellness; advocacy; guidance counseling; skills development; school-wide programs promoting safe, caring environments; crisis intervention and assistance; psychological first aid; school-home liaisons; disability and difference accommodations and modifications; transition programs; follow-up programs; short-term and long-term remediation, treatment, and rehabilitation; and other primary prevention programs. (4)

Copyright © Mometrix Media. You have been licensed one copy of this document for personal use only. Any other reproduction or redistribution is strictly prohibited. All rights reserved.

Leadership, development, and coordination of school-owned resources, services, systems, and programs with the purpose of developing a multidimensional, comprehensive, integrated program and service continuum. (5) Providing supervision, consultation, and in-service instruction, oriented across disciplines. (6) Finally, improving the involvement and connections of home resources, community agencies, and other community resources.

School codes of conduct

Behavioral norms are reflected in the school climate. Behavioral guidelines are commonly outlined in a school's code of conduct, which state regulations generally require. Conduct codes provide rules governing the behavior of students, faculty, other school staff, and visitors to schools. State regulations typically require full copies of codes of conduct to be given to every teacher as soon as possible following adoption, as well as copies of any amendments; code of conduct summaries, in plain language, to be sent to all parents before the school year starts; given to all students, in age-appropriate language, in assemblies at the start of every school year. Teachers, students, and parents can review codes of conduct together to assure joint understanding and agreement, and to allow identification of any potential policy, procedure, or practice gaps. Schools and school leaders are responsible for reviewing their school's code of conduct every year and updating it as needed. When updating it, they take into account how effective the code's provisions have been, and how consistently and fairly these have been administered. Reviews also enable school leaders and personnel to determine whether new technologies have necessitated revisions.

Many state education departments and school districts regard codes of conduct as documents ideally suited to setting behavioral expectations for students and staff, especially concerning technology use and Internet safety on school grounds and at school functions. Typical regulations require schools to provide complete copies of codes of conduct to all teachers; and also make these available to students, parents, and other community members for review. Another typical regulation is that school districts post their complete code of conduct, any amendments, and annual updates on the district website (assuming one exists). School districts may form committees for reviewing codes of conduct and district responses to violations thereof. Such committees should include representative administrators, students, teachers, parents, PTA members, school safety staff, other school personnel, community members, and law enforcement officials. State education department experts recommend that code reviews be assisted by individuals with expertise in technology, who also thoroughly understand the technology use of the school's students, faculty, and other staff. This helps assure the code will address challenges inherent with emerging technology. Public hearings to inform and receive community feedback are usually required before boards of education adopt code updates.

Copyright © Mometrix Media. You have been licensed one copy of this document for personal use only. Any other reproduction or redistribution is strictly prohibited. All rights reserved.

Collaborating with Key Stakeholders

Providing social and emotional support and prevention services to students

School leaders will be more effective in improving the results achieved by students and schools when they are aware of the relationship between not only excellent instruction, but also comprehensive school health programs, which incorporate attending to the mental health needs of all students. Empirical research has shown that, over time, interventions that enhance the decision-making, emotional, and social skills of students have positive impacts upon their standardized test scores and school grades, indicating a strong relationship of mental, emotional, and social health support with academic achievement. Prevention programs that affect every student and the early identification of and intervention with students at risk are both equally critical. Some examples of programs for prevention and early identification and intervention include educating school staff, students, families, and community members about mental health issues; early screening programs for emotional and behavioral problems; programs for the prevention of school violence; social skills training programs; bullying prevention programs; conflict resolution training programs; and suicide prevention programs.

School-community collaboration in providing mental health services

Because most children spend the majority of their time in school, schools are ideal settings for regular school-family communication, positive development, prevention, and intervention. School environments and staff are familiar to parents. Studies show students are more likely to seek counseling services available in schools. Schools are the main (or only) mental health service providers to children in many U.S. states and communities. In addition, the continuum of care must integrate school mental health services with community services. Clinical psychiatric care and other services are not appropriate or feasible in schools. Community services providers must collaborate with school counselors, school psychologists, and school social workers to coordinate timely, smoothly connected processes for making sure children get the support they need. Research in the field of school mental health indicates that school staffs need to work together with policymakers, community providers, and families to establish an integrated, cohesive intervention continuum, which is equally able to address severe student problems and the universal needs of all students.

Economic benefits of meeting students' mental health needs

Among many significant negative outcomes of neglecting student mental health are higher risks and rates of school failure; suicide; substance abuse; unsafe sexual behaviors; social isolation; and long-range social problems like poor health, unemployment, and incarceration. Not supporting student mental health has not only negative impacts personally upon individuals and collectively upon society, but moreover serious negative economic consequences. For example, research from Columbia University Teachers College (2005) found every 18-year-old age cohort never finishing high school loses America an estimated $192 billion—1.6 percent of the gross domestic product—in tax revenue and income combined, while increasing each cohort's education one year would recover almost half that loss. In another example of economic impact, the Seattle Social Development

Copyright © Mometrix Media. You have been licensed one copy of this document for personal use only. Any other reproduction or redistribution is strictly prohibited. All rights reserved.

Project (2004), targeting grades 1-6, has saved an estimated $9,837 per student by preventing long-term social problems. Recommended public policy goals include better leadership and coordination between the Department of Education and Substance Abuse and Mental Health Services Administration (SAMHSA), student needs-based blended funding, better availability and access to good school MH services, funding and incentives to reduce shortages of highly-trained school MH providers, and focusing on evidence-based interventions and programs.

Advantages of integrating comprehensive educational services

Some education experts find that, while all students need both large and small group instruction, separating some students from classrooms causes isolated skill development and fragmentation. In contrast, when services are both comprehensive and integrated for all students, teachers must share their expertise with colleagues and students across their disciplines—e.g., specialties in Title I, bilingual, at-risk students and special education fields. Educators share resources and organize services according to individual student strengths, needs, and interests. An underlying principle of integrated comprehensive services is that the system, not the student, is the source of student failure. School leaders and teachers make preventing student failure and promoting student success their first goal. Rather than developing curriculum based on average or median student groups and then adapting it to individual students afterward, educators must begin with differentiated curriculum and instruction that are culturally appropriate and relevant. Staff design must be based on student needs, with staff valuing the importance of sharing their expertise with students and colleagues for reciprocal capacity-building. This requires reorganizing and merging funding and resources toward building system and teacher capacities to target preventing student difficulties.

Integrating programs and services to improve instruction and support for all students

Historically, many school planning committees and site councils performed their functions according to student population norms, operating under the assumption that students receiving special education, Title I, ESL, at-risk and other specialized services were supported by designees of federal and state mandates, hence not within the planning teams' purview; and they believed they were not responsible for designing or managing these students' programs. However, educational researchers point out that legal mandates not only guarantee student eligibility for special services but, in guaranteeing all students equal access to equal educations, they moreover require that all students receive the same rights and opportunities in educational systems. Therefore, school leaders must have members of school planning committees participate in developing their school vision and mission. Planning team members must be able to exchange feedback with fellow team members and with all stakeholders in the learning community and larger community. School leaders can enlist the activity of planning teams to make educational decisions, create supportive learning environments, and assure equality for all students and school staff.

Staff design

Teaching staff often lacks the design given to curriculum and instruction. Due to historical practices, habit, perception of equity issues, comfort levels, etc., students have been separated from peers in discriminatory ways, precluding staff collaboration to support their

Copyright © Mometrix Media. You have been licensed one copy of this document for personal use only. Any other reproduction or redistribution is strictly prohibited. All rights reserved.

educational needs. Instead, leaders can give staff opportunities to identify natural supports within the environment; assess smaller, integrated settings for appropriateness; assign staff to diverse student groups according to their expertise; and work with staff to design curriculum and instruction to meet diverse learner needs. Although educators can feel daunted by the range of individual student needs, experts point out that, while varied, these ranges are actually predictable and clear. Rather than reacting after students fail and are identified as eligible for special services, leaders can prevent failure through proactively designing staffing and supports. Team-teaching among general and special education staff often becomes "turn-taking," analogous to children's parallel play. This limits individual teachers' expertise, causes disconnected education for students, and maintains the status quo. Instead, leaders can engage teachers in sharing their expertise through truly collaborative processes, giving students and teachers continuous, systematic learning experiences and meeting needs for wider groups of students.

Roles of families in children's education

Families must be included in the collaborative process of designing student education. However, in addition to their being involved, school leaders need to define the roles of family members clearly, and establish guidelines for actions they and their staff take to foster family sharing of ownership in education. School leaders must also strategically implement family educational involvement by providing capacity for diverse family membership and participation in their designs. There are three dimensions of family roles in educations. (1) Families are their children's primary advocates. (2) As part of a school-based dialogue, families are advocates who can speak on the behalf of other families. (3) In developing a learning community, families afford utility and support. When school leaders and staff acknowledge, respect, and access all three roles and cultivate compassionate partnerships with families, families will naturally become connected with the learning and larger communities. However, if only an elite group of family volunteers participate, then other families may avoid participation out of a feeling of inequality. This indicates school leaders and staff must plan pragmatic, strategic involvement of all families, at the levels they are able, as often as possible.

Included among challenges to family school involvement are: parents' past negative experiences with school; difficulty for families with disparate backgrounds to interact; school activities that dictate to families instead of asking what they are already doing or what they want; cultural and language differences—e.g., some families' cultures dictate deferring to educators as authorities, which educators may misinterpret as disinterest; lack of opportunities, supports, and access caused by poverty; race and class issues, especially when a school's majority family race differs from its majority staff race; less affluent families' intimidation by more affluent families' resources and involvement; school leaders' lacking preparation and professional development for family interaction, and lacking time and resources on the job for trying innovative or new strategies. Included among facilitators are: leaders' broadly defining and thinking creatively about family involvement; encouraging family collaboration and shared leadership; family home outreach visits; welcoming school environments; school leaders' community visibility; having school staff constantly assess progress in family involvement and making data-based decisions; using state Title I and Smart Start funding to employ school parent facilitators to involve families; and planting seeds, starting small with already involved parents, allowing time for growth and as they share with others.

Copyright © Mometrix Media. You have been licensed one copy of this document for personal use only. Any other reproduction or redistribution is strictly prohibited. All rights reserved.

Federal mandate for school-family collaboration

Research has found that student achievement is predicted more accurately by family involvement than by family socioeconomic status or income. Before school, children's most influential motivators, role models, and teachers are their families. School attendance and testing participation, which enable districts to fulfill yearly progress goals, are more likely by students whose families are involved in their schooling. Students are more likely to continue their educations when their families have been involved. Children who perceive their parents as respecting and interacting regularly with school personnel tend to develop better relationships with teachers and learn more from them. When a student's parents are more involved, teachers have higher expectations of those students, and the students receive higher grades and test scores. Additionally, many studies find student attitudes toward work and career choices reflect their families' attitudes toward education and careers.

Sharing leadership with families and communities

Strong leadership must be both distributed widely and focused strategically. Individual school leaders have such increasing demands on their energy, resources, and time that sharing leadership approaches become necessities. This naturally results in greater community interaction. Many school leaders have learned to retain their leadership while sharing decision-making with staff, families, and community partners. They find that shared leadership increases their staff's satisfaction and commitment to school improvement initiatives. One thing that can really help school leaders to manage sharing leadership with community partners is to hire a community school coordinator, also known as a liaison or resource coordinator. This individual can help school leaders find partners within the community, maintain relationships with community partners once they have established them, and manage the efforts of multiple community partnerships so that staff members know what resources and supports each partner is sharing with their school and so that services are not duplicated. Coordinators can also expedite open communication among leaders, staff, and community partners.

Asset mapping

One important community engagement strategy for school leaders is to learn about the community first. Many leaders survey students, families, staff, and community members regarding specific needs or issues. Some engage various stakeholders through focus groups or full-day conferences. They prepare by collecting demographic data including homelessness, poverty, immunization rates, and more from school sources, local agencies, census reports, United Way publications, etc. Using these data, they can help communities establish realistic goals, and direct suitable resources to attain them. They also use data to determine baselines for tracking subsequent longitudinal progress, opening conversations with community members, and even developing a shared community school vision. Leaders can uncover untapped community resources, and learn of community needs and changes viewed through student perceptions. Some high school leaders integrate annual mapping by freshmen of community services and opportunities into social studies curriculum, distributing the data to all students, teachers, and families. This helps families find services, identifies service and support gaps, informs the school vision and community partners' implementation of it, and helps students realize how they can help their community.

Copyright © Mometrix Media. You have been licensed one copy of this document for personal use only. Any other reproduction or redistribution is strictly prohibited. All rights reserved.

Uniting the learning community and improving communication through cultural diversity

Successful school leaders view cultural diversity as not only a challenge but also a strength. Students, families, and school staff members increasingly include different races, cultures, languages, and lifestyles. School leaders must unite diverse members to achieve cohesive learning communities. Effective leaders emphasize discussing diversity honestly and openly rather than pretending not to notice it. Open conversations help school employees and families differentiate cultural facts from cultural assumptions, helping them focus on economic factors that can influence behavior. The better school staff understands family social, economic, and political realities, the better they can motivate students and communicate with community members. In one example, a Nebraska elementary school had Native American students who often arrived to school late; teachers felt their parents did not value education. However, through communication with families, the school leaders discovered these parents avoided forcing children to do things; according to their beliefs, doing so could prevent the children's bodies and spirits from bonding fully—an incomplete process in young children. The leader and faculty found ways to work within this belief system, like providing more thematic and hands-on learning to promote student enthusiasm, and giving parents home activities to keep students from falling behind.

Enlisting the collaboration of family and community members

Experts emphasize the importance to community engagement of leaders' telling their school's story to others. According to John Dewey, "communicating, with fullness and accuracy, some experience to another… and you will find your own attitude toward your experience changing." The Public Education Network maintains that public responsibility for education and sustainment of policy and practice can be achieved through public engagement combined with specific goals for school reform. Successful school leaders point out that, rather than getting preoccupied with educational rhetoric, they must always remember that they are working with real people, and therefore compassion and care take priority. They place emphasis on the need for all school leaders to learn how to communicate effectively, and to "tell our story well." They find that once they engage in this behavior consistently and their community members and parents become aware of it, they will be willing and motivated to participate and contribute a great deal.

Effective school leaders find that when they access facts and figures pertinent to their school's status, situation, and needs and share these strategically, and also honestly share stories from their schools that illustrate aspects of the processes of teaching and learning, they are able to motivate their audiences to take action on behalf of the school. These school leaders search for allies to help accomplish their vision and mission. They also develop teams who have the ability to communicate with a variety of constituencies, such as teachers' unions, civic groups, faith-based organizations, collaborative initiatives that address issues concerning education and youth, funds for public education, intermediary groups, and many more. Successful school leaders also ask their school, family, and other community partners to locate and share statistical data that support their cases. They then apply those data for informing the policies they develop, and for establishing baselines to which they can compare subsequent progress.

Copyright © Mometrix Media. You have been licensed one copy of this document for personal use only. Any other reproduction or redistribution is strictly prohibited. All rights reserved.

Holding community conversations to build financial and public support

One school leader finds the key to obtaining financial and public support for her school is community conversations. She talks with every available audience about her school and students, customizing messages for each group but with a common theme—everybody plays a part in shared responsibility for student success. With the business community, she shares real estate data to demonstrate that property values increase and consumers spend more money at local businesses when communities contain better schools. She also points to community families' returning to the school as students' tests scores have improved. She tells business community members that children develop pride, shared values, and success important to their future adulthood when they experience the physical presence and financial support of local business people. This convinces community members and families that the school is a good place for their financial contributions, and a "premier" school for their children requires more support. With families, this leader shares large increases in school academic performance indices over several years, and significant increases in Latino student scores the first year. Consequently, fewer students are bused into their community, and more local families attend her school.

Engaging community partners can help to equalize student opportunities in schools lacking sufficient resources, an increasingly common situation today. Even in affluent schools, decreasing budgets and academic curricula restricted in focus make it difficult to give students vital enrichment and learning activities, which motivate students to attend school. Field trips, intramural athletics, art and music programs, and even recess are reasons many students come to school and feel a sense of community there. School success becomes a struggle for many students due to home instability, unsafe neighborhoods, unaddressed physical and health problems, immigration issues, and poverty. While these are most evident in low-income communities, they pose problems in nearly every school. Community partners significantly assist schools with these concerns in three ways: (1) they aid student and family access to needed social, health and mental health services. (2) They give students safe leadership and experimentation opportunities; and adult guidance and positive role models in classrooms and communities that develop their academic and non-academic skills, contributing to their physical, intellectual, emotional, and social development. (3) They establish relationships that give students greater stores of social capital, enabling their successful interactions in the world beyond their own communities.

When school leaders want to attract community partnerships, it will help if they can stimulate community members to consider in greater depth what the purposes of education are, and how these purposes can best be accomplished in public schools. Successful school leaders find that, rather than only communicating tales of traditional student successes in school, it is more useful to tell stories as well about experiences that illuminate the different kinds of obstacles that students encounter in their educations and how they have to overcome them. Sharing both the successes and challenges of students can help prospective community partners to think in very different ways about teaching and learning. As an example, one school leader related a story of a student who failed a written biology test on mitosis. The teacher, believing that the student's written responses did not reflect her knowledge, asked her if there were other ways she could express what she knew. Trusting and feeling comfortable with the teacher, she later choreographed a dance clearly demonstrating full understanding of the subject. This story quickly illustrated for non-educators how teachers must measure success creatively, and how success takes different forms and times for some students.

Copyright © Mometrix Media. You have been licensed one copy of this document for personal use only. Any other reproduction or redistribution is strictly prohibited. All rights reserved.

Defining relationships with community partners

Once they have established partnerships with community members, many school leaders formalize these relationships, defining them in written documents of their shared vision for student success. To define school-community partnerships further, school leaders may write a memorandum of understanding (MOU). These documents can make the goals and expectations in the partnership clearer. In general, the MOU will contain the following components: (1) the vision and mission that the school and the partner share; (2) the expectations and responsibilities of the school and the community partner; (3) the person (or persons) responsible for the management and oversight of any programs that may be offered in the school by the partner; (4) plans for the school leaders and community partners to convene regular meetings to review their progress and identify any areas needing improvement; (5) the responsibilities of the school and the partner for evaluation and monitoring; (6) the kinds of training that school personnel, partner staff, and volunteers should be given, and who is responsible to provide the training; and (7) procedures to incorporate the partner into school activities, and school staff into the partner's program, to enable better joint responsibility and mutual understanding.

Communicating with the media to engage the public in education

When schools engage the public, they increase local capacity for continuing dialogues regarding education, and generate political motivation to transform educators' good ideas into actual change and sustain it. School leaders have historically acted internally, depending mainly on relationships with central office and school board members for resource building and remaining isolated from their communities. However, more school leaders are recognizing that they need more public support to meet more stringent state standards and further comprehensive student-centered agendas. Public schools are supported by taxpayers, many of whom have no children in school and thus know little of school needs. They typically underestimate the value of initiatives to pass levies and bond issues. By communicating with the media, school leaders can raise community awareness and engage the public, enabling citizen investment in local school endeavors through community partnerships, relationships with families, and attracting volunteers. In addition to enhancing public perceptions of school reform efforts, research finds public engagement strengthens local safety and security, reinforces community pride, raises citizen and student participation in school and community service, and revitalizes communities.

Most school leaders have not been trained in public engagement or media communication; neither of these things are viewed as important parts of their jobs. Some leaders do not feel comfortable with introducing sales-oriented aspects into their educational activities. Some do not feel adequately equipped with the skills required for effectively engaging the public. And some school leaders are averse to getting involved in public situations and conversations that might require them to defend their work and/or answer questions. Community political issues can become explosive, and school leaders who are successful often avoid involvement to prevent resulting negative school images. Even when such images are groundless, they can last indefinitely. Though understandable, this attitude deprives them of increasing public support for their schools. Another public challenge is that more than half of Americans do not have children attending public schools. Consequently, as voters they seldom approve school improvement referenda as these are

- 68 -

Copyright © Mometrix Media. You have been licensed one copy of this document for personal use only. Any other reproduction or redistribution is strictly prohibited. All rights reserved.

not personally relevant to them. It is a major challenge to find ways taxpayers can feel connected to local schools.

A school's vision should reflect its surrounding community's diverse needs. School leaders can learn about their communities by asking them for input regarding what they want and what they can contribute to the school. They can publicize their desire to talk with families and others from the community through the media. Leaders can also share their leadership with teachers, alumni, and families, who are the best school spokespersons. They can also get significant support and leadership from local public education foundations. School leaders can access these resources through good communications strategies. They can form a school public relations committee with representatives of students, families, staff, and community partners who can generate positive press about the school and quickly address events with negative influences. Some school PR representatives also write letters to the editors of local newspapers, as well as informally sharing positive school information with neighbors and friends. Leaders can share school success, enhance school image, discover community wishes, procure community support and help, and nurture understanding through a few succinct and well-placed stories positively reflecting the school vision and message in the media.

Collaborative and non-collaborative approaches to educational program evaluation

In evaluating educational programs, early approaches were either collaborative or non-collaborative. Collaborative approaches have strongly involved stakeholders throughout the evaluation process to ensure that the results of the evaluations were valid. Some early examples included stakeholder-based evaluation (SBE) and practical participatory evaluation (PPE). Non-collaborative approaches have involved stakeholders mainly as sources of data, which served the purpose of obtaining information about educational program functions and effects that were valid. However, researchers have observed since then that it is not always possible to distinguish clearly between collaborative and non-collaborative program evaluations. Investigators of the methodology underlying stakeholder evaluations have noted that, although it has become increasingly common to use qualitative evaluation methods wherein stakeholder roles are emphasized, less attention has been given to actual stakeholder positions, and to specifically what is evaluated. Researchers find it important to identify characteristics of various stakeholder groups, both how they interrelate and influence one another, and their respective independent identities.

Variables included in evaluations involving stakeholder roles and positions

When researchers examine educational program evaluations, they find that evaluators often use level models wherein the results of development and training interventions are divided into interrelated parts or levels. Some examples of level models include the CIPP (Context, Input, Process, and Product) Evaluation Framework model (Stufflebeam, 1983); the Antecedent-Transaction-Outcome approach (Stake, 1967); the four-levels approach of participant reaction, participant learning, participant behavior, and desired results (Kirkpatrick, 1998); and a five-level approach modifying the latter, including participant reaction, participant learning, organizational support and change, participant use of new knowledge, and student learning outcomes (Guskey, 2000). These models are considered positivist in nature, and quantitative, instrumental, and unitary in their approach. Critics have found them, in their sequential assumptions and levels, insufficient to explain specific

Copyright © Mometrix Media. You have been licensed one copy of this document for personal use only. Any other reproduction or redistribution is strictly prohibited. All rights reserved.

outcomes in specific context by not offering adequate details about their underlying theories or mechanisms. As an alternative, others have proposed constructivist program evaluation models.

Constructivist approach to educational program evaluation

As a response to finding positivist approaches to program evaluation models limited in analyzing complex social processes where stakeholders are involved, some have proposed a constructivist approach to program evaluation as an alternative (cf. Guba and Lincoln, 1989). In this approach, evaluators formulate questions in advance to ask, which take into account the perspectives of the variety of stakeholders involved in the evaluations as an evaluation guide. This method enables evaluators to explore the individual realities constructed by all participants in the research. Researchers then synthesize these various realities with other data they have obtained to reach a consensus. Incorporating the perspectives of the investigators is also enabled by this methodology. It therefore allows all participants to influence and learn from the process, and to share reflective and subjective reflections. Through comparison and contrast, this evaluation method stresses results that are jointly constructed instead of individually constructed as in other models.

According to researchers, a constructivist model of educational program evaluation, which enables multiple stakeholder perspectives in the joint construction of reality as the evaluation outcome, consists of two phases: discovery and assimilation. In the discovery phase, the evaluator wants to describe the context and what is being evaluated. In the assimilation phase, the evaluator wants to integrate the new information discovered into the construction that already exists. In using the constructivist evaluation approach, evaluators must do the following: (1) identify who stakeholders are; (2) discover stakeholder concerns, issues, and assertions; (3) supply a method and context for collecting and analyzing stakeholder feedback; (4) reach a consensus among and within the various stakeholder groups; (5) if consensus is elusive, have an agenda for negotiating among stakeholders; (6) gather and disseminate information to inform the negotiation; (7) establish a forum wherein negotiation can transpire; (8) create a report to deliver to stakeholders; (9) review any issues, concerns, or assertions that have not been resolved.

Prioritizing community engagement

According to the U.S. Department of Education's Reform Support Network (2014), which involved 11 states in turnaround initiatives, state education agencies (SEAs) can figure significantly in advancing community engagement by building upon their current functions as accountability system and resource providers. This includes such specific strategies as: stipulating measurable short- and long-term community engagement goals and strategies in district and school improvement plans and grant applications; including engagement goals and indices in ongoing school improvement results monitoring; encouraging districts to finance community engagement infrastructures using state-administered federal school improvement funds; using needs assessments and monitoring of district ability to identify and respond to openings for state support; investing in SEAs via community liaisons, state liaison directors, and other personnel; local and state partnerships, and state-developed resources and tools; better coordinating state social services agencies with school districts to reinforce family support services in school communities; coordinating communications and collaborations with school districts regarding turnaround goals, resources, and strategies, e.g., establishing central councils including parents, community leaders, elected

Copyright © Mometrix Media. You have been licensed one copy of this document for personal use only. Any other reproduction or redistribution is strictly prohibited. All rights reserved.

officials, non-profit directors, faith leaders, and school leaders; and requiring more active SEA community engagement through creating statewide districts for managing turnaround schools directly.

Fostering community engagement in school reform

The U.S. Department of Education (ED) has found that, to engage their communities in school reform, the schools, districts, or state education departments must inform them. ED research identifies both traditional communication forms, like advertising, mailers, newsletters and flyers, and virtual communication like blog posts and e-mails. It has also found many different events, including courses, workshops, welcome sessions, picnics, barbecues, summer programs, open houses, neighborhood walks, etc. not only communicate information to communities, but additionally enable community members, families, school staffs and turnaround staffs to get acquainted. School leaders and coordinators use strategies enhancing the effectiveness of known outreach techniques, e.g., openly conveying accurate information, enabling ample feedback, holding events in safe and welcoming locations, taking technology access and parental literacy into account, offering materials in different languages, using messaging consistently, and concentrating on early outreach. They also eliminated obstacles to participating by providing child care and transportation, and holding evening meetings within housing projects in dangerous neighborhoods.

Actively listening to community feedback and responding to it

Research by the U.S. Department of Education finds that school leadership achieves more effective community engagement and communication when they inquire of community members, including parents; listen to the feedback they offer; and respond to their concerns and questions via conversations, surveys, focus groups, and public forums. By listening carefully to community feedback, school leaders can determine whether community members have understood and responded to information provided through outreach events and accompanying materials; and identify better methods of connecting with families and community members, informing them, and taking advantage of their assets by listening. School leaders and staff members who not only listen, but moreover promptly and consistently respond to community members' concerns, report their approach sheds light on community opinions and strengthens community trust. For example, informed by community feedback, discussions, and meetings, a school board approved replacing middle and high schools with a charter middle school, a grade 6-12 arts school, a high-tech early college high school, an international studies school, a regional athletic and activities program uniting all four new schools in extracurricular activities, and a regional bus system, to address priorities identified by the community.

Offering community members meaningful opportunities for participation

Leaders have engaged communities in school reform by: (1) involving families in academic improvement by providing strategies for home support of student learning and for student advocacy through regular meetings, training sessions, family education classes, and formal parent empowerment programs featuring family engagement courses. (2) Involving parents as organizers. Some schools have established programs to train parents as community organizers, including not only community organizing and leadership development trainings, but also professional development courses for parent leadership teams and school-based

- 71 -

Copyright © Mometrix Media. You have been licensed one copy of this document for personal use only. Any other reproduction or redistribution is strictly prohibited. All rights reserved.

parent coordinators. (3) Involving community partners in supporting students and families. Schools have developed community partnerships to bring housing, career, medical, mental health, and professional development resources, free wellness centers, after-school homework help, tutoring, etc. to families and schools. Measures showing the impacts of community engagement strategies include: increased parent attendance to seminars, workshops, school events, and community school improvement meetings; increased community attendance and participation at school improvement meetings; more family-to-school outreach; parents' becoming school improvement advocates and organizers; parents and community members' serving on school and advisory councils, actively creating policies, programs, and practices; fewer school behavior problems; and increased student enrollment, attendance, satisfaction, and achievement.

Transforming community members into leaders and advocates

When school leaders have informed family and community well, gotten them involved and invested in school improvement, many family and other community members have found that what they have learned and the programs they have helped to develop have inspired them to become local school champions who lead others and take action on the schools' behalf. They then volunteer to speak to parents, answer their questions, and build community relationships at schools newly established as part of the reform initiatives in which they participated. In some school reform initiatives, essential elements in developing infrastructure for community engagement in improving low-performing schools include working with outside organizations, establishing central councils, and employing professional community organizers. Central councils increase collaboration. School leaders work closely with local advocacy organizations on forming committees to inform school board decisions about school improvement plans. One-way communication, like sending home informative letters without ways for recipients to respond, or holding open meetings attended only by members with strong views instead of representative community samples, are replaced by more reciprocal conversations and participation.

Strategies to increase family and community school engagement and support

In some school improvement initiatives, school leaders recognize that families and other community members are frequently disoriented by widespread changes in their schools' organization and operations, including wholesale replacement of school staff. They address this sense of disruption through making early engagement their priority. For example, they start building bridges to communities in advance of assigning a school to their school improvement program and the management organization that administers the reform initiative. Over time, they extend the community relationships they establish. School management organizations also concentrate on parents, elected officials, local community leaders, and faith leaders to build family school support and involvement through continuing community and family engagement strategies. In some school systems, leaders improve low-performance schools by furthering community and family engagement by funding family and community outreach coordinators for every school to instruct school staff in how to engage with parents, and educating parents in the skills and knowledge for supporting their children's learning at home and advocating effectively for them.

Copyright © Mometrix Media. You have been licensed one copy of this document for personal use only. Any other reproduction or redistribution is strictly prohibited. All rights reserved.

Improving student enrollment, engagement, and achievement by engaging communities

Some school system leaders have initiated collaborations with local advocacy groups to help them organize comprehensive efforts to engage their communities in their school improvement plans. Their belief that community engagement would stimulate greater student enrollment, engagement, and ultimately higher student academic achievement was proven when this collaboration established a committee, which provided information to the school board to help it make decisions regarding the school improvement plans. The board approved a number of school improvement plans which were found to be very successful not only in increasing student enrollment, attendance, and achievement and decreasing student behavioral problems in school, but also in increasing the attendance and involvement of parents and other community members in meetings, events, policies, procedures, organizing, and advocacy. Other school system leaders have established policies and structures in their central offices that have served to support and encourage the engagement of parents and other community members in each individual school, as well as system-wide.

Connecting community members with school activities, programs, and improvement efforts

Some school systems provide summer programs wherein parents learn about the school culture and academic offerings; require parents to contribute volunteer time each school year; hold workshops instructing parents in academically supporting their children and preparing them for college; and employ parent and community engagement directors to supervise teams in charge of community relations, parent participation, and student recruitment. In other schools, leaders have not only initially concentrated on forming community partnerships to address student needs and on augmenting parental participation, but subsequently realized that hiring staff members who had strong community connections and were dedicated would additionally engage parental and community support. Therefore, they hired community engagement coordinators who devised new plans that included considering different, more authentic strategies for engaging parents and community members; redefining their improvement initiative by launching a branding campaign; and furnishing parents with support and tools to engage them and help them become partners with and advocates for their schools.

Evolution of the roles of school leaders

Historically, school leaders and others may have viewed the role of the school leader as simply being school managers. However, in today's educational and social contexts, their roles have become increasingly challenging and complex. School leaders must combine the ideals of supporting children's physical, intellectual, emotional, and social needs with the demands of high-stakes accountability mandated by government laws. In order to establish effective learning communities where all students and adults alike can fulfill their greatest potentials, school leaders must have and demonstrate a combination of skills, vision, and courage in advocating for and leading such learning communities. School leaders not only need to support instruction through each action that they take, delegate, or authorize in their schools and through efficiently and judiciously utilizing every resource that is available to them, but moreover, their jobs entail more than these operational roles. They must also acquire and examine data from multiple school and community sources and

- 73 -

Copyright © Mometrix Media. You have been licensed one copy of this document for personal use only. Any other reproduction or redistribution is strictly prohibited. All rights reserved.

analyze these data to identify current trends; gaps in achievement, services, and resources; and insights into teaching, learning, and community processes. They must develop and sustain shared school community visions that will prepare students for a society that is continually changing.

Colleges, universities, and the government sharing accountability with school leaders

According to the National Association of Elementary School Principals (NAESP), to support school leaders in their roles of leading through being informed of community characteristics, attributes, needs, and trends, colleges and universities can share leadership and accountability with them by redesigning their school leader and teacher preparation programs to reflect NAESP's Leading Learning Communities standards. These standards focus on preparation programs that equip school leaders and teachers to prepare students for success in the 21st century. The federal government can share leadership and accountability with school leaders by developing federal programs that assist school districts in supporting school leaders by providing them with professional development resources, including mentoring aimed at strengthening school leaders' capacities for serving all students. The federal government should also hold school districts accountable for producing these results through such programs. The U.S. government can also support a national system of voluntary advanced certification for school leaders. This certification process should incorporate Leading Learning Communities standards and additional benchmarks, reward school leaders for effectiveness, establish improvement targets for all school leaders, and supply professional development guidance.

Considering today's increased demands for school accountability, such accountability should be accompanied by increased resources for achieving it. For example, schools and school leaders should be able to collect various types of data in order to document and analyze school status and progress. This analysis allows schools and school leaders to build the capacities they will need for realizing the goals upon which they have agreed. State governments' education departments can support school leaders and share leadership and accountability with them by strengthening and refining existing methods and resources for collecting data, which will assist school leaders in their jobs. State education departments can also share accountability and leadership with their local school leaders by building networks of school leaders and creating more learning opportunities for school leaders. For example, state education department officials can establish electronic Listservs, online networks, organize conferences for school leaders, and initiate mentoring and coaching programs for school leaders.

School districts supporting the leaders of individual schools

School leaders need resources and time for developing the skills and knowledge for making schools perform highly. They also need resources for their own effective performance as instructional leaders in their schools. School districts can help by building individual leaders' ability for providing instructional leadership. Districts can supply funding, other support, and flexibility to enable alternative arrangements for leadership. In order for school leaders to be effective instructional leaders, they must share school management functions with others. School districts need to improve working conditions for school leaders by supplying them with financial support for serving their student populations well, and by allowing them autonomy regarding budgeting and hiring to allow them to establish and sustain school programs to meet school goals. School districts, as well as state

Copyright © Mometrix Media. You have been licensed one copy of this document for personal use only. Any other reproduction or redistribution is strictly prohibited. All rights reserved.

education departments, can improve pay structures and salaries as incentives for school leaders to meet standards. They can also offer advanced training, international exchanges, and sabbaticals as rewards for effective leadership. Additionally, school districts should fairly assess school leaders by considering not just students' standardized test scores, but a range of measurements, reflecting existing knowledge of elements defining the "whole school leader" and effectiveness in the profession of school leadership.

Involving diverse populations in school improvement by identifying their leaders

School leaders need to know their communities to involve them in school improvement. By conversing with people who lead community colleges, local churches, social service agencies, chambers of commerce, and cultural foundations; owners of established local businesses; and members of the city council, school leaders can start to identify community leaders. They can also find equally influential, albeit less visible, community leaders in housing project directors, block captains, local grocers, and grandparents. Knowledgeable about neighborhood issues, these individuals can help inform school leaders in designing school events and meetings. They can also inform them about what motivates community members to engage with schools. School leaders should identify their community's civic, political, cultural, social, and religious organizations that work with low-income and minority residents and parents; and business leaders; community advocates; and parents whom culturally and linguistically diverse populations respect and find credible. They can create contact lists with current information about organizations and leaders and which issues are most important to them, regularly meet with as many community groups and leaders as possible to discuss potential collaborations, regularly follow through with them regarding next steps, and share information.

Engaging parents and other community members from diverse populations

It is important to communicate regularly with parents to engage them in school life; however, all too frequently, parental contact only entails student academic or behavioral problems. School leaders need to communicate with families and other community members more often and ask them to influence school directions. But challenges in diverse neighborhoods include time constraints against school activities, like working multiple jobs and caring full-time for students' younger siblings, language barriers, and family avoidance of public schools out of their own past negative experiences with them. School leaders can use outreach strategies: having volunteers call, personally inviting parents to school events; parent phone hotlines with classroom phones so parents can speak directly with teachers; visiting shelters to converse with homeless parents; door-to-door neighborhood walks, accompanied by several teachers of different grades, giving informational handouts, conversing with parents; weekly or monthly school newsletters; promoting school and community events using local TV and newspapers; making videos for parents about homework help, volunteering as teachers' aides, etc.; home visits; sending home district calendars in community languages; and distributing parent folders with school mission, goals, policies, volunteer activities, tips, etc.

School leaders can start by collaborating with staff to revisit school goals, determine how parent and community involvement can further them, and collectively define public engagement. Leaders should give all staff members (not just teachers) opportunities to learn more about language and culture barriers impeding parental engagement; invite business owners, parents, and community leaders as cultural experts to staff meetings to

Copyright © Mometrix Media. You have been licensed one copy of this document for personal use only. Any other reproduction or redistribution is strictly prohibited. All rights reserved.

discuss how varying cultural perspectives influence parental roles in children's educations; share strategies and tips; and identify other help and training that staff may need. They can collaboratively develop overall community engagement plans through such discussions, including parent and community outreach plans, understanding community cultures and attitudes toward public schools, collaborating with parents to understand children's best learning modes, and involving parents and community members in daily school life. Leaders can offer resource materials and informal workshops on how the school system functions; budget, curriculum, learning, etc.; characteristics of good schools; volunteering at school; and creating home learning environments for children. They can also create school family resource centers with flexible schedules for informal parent and community meetings, gatherings, workshops; furnish transportation if possible; repeat workshops to accommodate more attendees; and hold them in community centers, restaurants, churches and other accessible, comfortable locations.

When parents and other community members understand the school improvement endeavors of school leaders and staff, the results of their activities are more likely to last longer. In contrast, when schools do not involve all community members in decisions about public education, many community members respond with confrontations, mistrust, or apathy because they were not included in the decisions. Their opinions, needs, and desires were not considered, and there were no opportunities offered or efforts made to enlist their participation, which would create a sense of ownership. Research finds fewer students drop out, more students attend, and student performance improves when parents and community members are engaged in schools. School leaders, teachers, and superintendents realize that students' school success can be profoundly affected by parental involvement and interest in their learning. Community members can collaborate with school leaders and teachers about how to enhance student achievement, and/or help with school events. Parents help their children with homework. Both may help community groups build support for neighborhood schools, chaperone field trips, and/or volunteer as classroom aides.

Bridging divides between diverse family and community members and their schools

Parents who speak different languages or have no formal education often lack understanding about public school systems, making them less likely to reach out to schools. Some parents' cultural backgrounds have taught them that teachers and school administrators are authority figures they should not question. School leaders can have multilingual staff translate at PTA meetings, parent trainings and workshops, home visits, and school events; hire liaisons with strong community ties to promote school staff's cultural understanding; help less literate parents support children in non-literate ways, like asking children about school events and assignments; interview family and community members about their beliefs concerning family and school roles in children's lives and how children learn; and invite families to share cultural traditions with school staff. They can also designate school parent rooms for meeting with teachers and other parents; borrowing resource materials; and accessing posted information on library hours, jobs, social services, school volunteering, community events, videos of parent workshops for those who missed them, etc. Validating and honoring family and community members who support schools serves to create welcoming, acknowledging, inclusive climates; encourages and maintains their meaningful involvement; and thanks them.

Copyright © Mometrix Media. You have been licensed one copy of this document for personal use only. Any other reproduction or redistribution is strictly prohibited. All rights reserved.

School leaders may realize the many salutary results of parental and community engagement in schools, yet still feel challenged in accomplishing it—particularly with culturally and linguistically diverse neighborhoods, low-income neighborhoods, and parents who lack formal education. School leaders and teachers working in these areas often feel frustrated and disappointed about trying to involve parents and public. This is not, however, because these parents do not care about the futures of their children. They want what is best for them, to be instrumental in their children's learning and futures, and to work with educators. The source of educators' difficulty in accomplishing this may be school attitudes: many educators expect families and others to become involved independently. Posting fliers at the school when parents rarely visit, or sending them home with students who stuff them in their backpacks and forget about them are ineffectual methods. Experts call on educators to rethink their approaches; they will need to make much greater, more organized efforts to involve parents. In the long term, the outcomes are worth the additional efforts.

In order to succeed in getting parents and community members who are harder to reach involved in their schools' activities and decisions they make that affect schools, educators need to develop and/or reinforce relationships with leaders in their community. To establish rapport, build trust, and develop these relationships, school leaders need to attain a stronger understanding of the language and cultural barriers that can interfere with the best intentions of both educators and parents and community members, and with the educators' best attempts. When school leaders develop their own cultural awareness and help their staff members do the same, they must then incorporate this awareness into all the things they do in the interest of engaging culturally diverse parents and other community members. They must make commitments and be sure to follow through on them. Educators must become knowledgeable, not only about cultural differences, but moreover about how these differences influence community perspectives regarding educational issues. Local social services counselors, ministers, and others familiar with their neighborhoods can be sources to whom educators may turn for help.

When school leaders spearhead interagency collaborations, they can build comprehensive support systems for students and families who are at risk. They can also extend all service professionals' knowledge about student and family needs. By coordinating multiple services from various agencies, they can decrease the fragmentation so common among these agencies and services. School leaders should avail themselves of all community resources, including health and social service agencies, local businesses, universities, other educational institutions, and other community organizations. Partnerships involving collaboration among parents, community agencies, and businesses enable exchanging student and family information, developing shared educational and service visions and missions, pooling funds for common purposes, and offering multiple services within schools. Schools and social service providers must be culturally and linguistically sensitive and responsive. Misunderstanding and distrust between families and social services can result from varying cultural practices and beliefs, plus power interaction histories. Organizations can alleviate these by giving more control and input to community members, hiring staff members who reflect community diversity, training staff to work with diverse groups, and changing harmful or ineffectual practices and policies.

Copyright © Mometrix Media. You have been licensed one copy of this document for personal use only. Any other reproduction or redistribution is strictly prohibited. All rights reserved.

Aspects of family and community involvement and differences historically and today

School leaders' jobs traditionally have required knowledge about student learning and how to plan, design, and implement curriculum, instruction, and assessment. In the past these were primarily what were expected of school leaders. Today, however, they are also expected to acquire expertise in parent, family, and community engagement. The increasing drive for accountability has placed schools under greater public scrutiny than before. Although educators have always found parent involvement important, various schools have responded in a range of ways. Some view it as critical and design comprehensive plans for outreach, while others only accord it afterthought status. Variations occur at these two extremes and everything in between. School success now depends as much on parent and community engagement as on planning lessons, instructional methods, and assessment. Historically, U.S. minority populations were mostly found in large cities and border states. Today, demographics have changed; schools nationwide are more diverse racially and ethnically. This requires not only critical thinking, but moreover action to engage diverse communities in decisions influencing public schools.

Role of school leaders relative to community health and human services

Viewing school leadership in the context of the community, children's chances in life are seen as unlikely to improve unless their homes, blocks, neighborhoods, schools, local clinics, etc. act collectively. It becomes important for school leaders to create successful partnerships with homes and communities, mobilizing parents, social service agencies, and neighborhoods in genuine collaborations to help children and their families. As such, school leaders need the same skills as community organizers. They must advocate for their schools as providers not only of educational services, but of child-centered and family-centered social services. School leaders can offer leadership for revitalizing communities by forming partnerships with health and human service agencies, churches, and youth agencies. While at-risk students frequently receive services from various agencies, such services are often fragmented rather than coordinated, with service providers and agencies unaware of what others are doing or of information about student needs. School leaders can help effect these collaborations by making their schools central locations for multiple agencies.

Coordinating services and developing partnerships with other agencies

School leaders should conduct community needs assessments to determine problems and which community resources can help them develop collaborative partnerships. They should develop and apply planning tools to guide their needs identification and monitoring how they address them through partnership development. They can then contact agencies, foundations, and other resource organizations and request products, services, information, funding, and support to facilitate building collaborative relationships. Leaders should also consult the most current, important research and published planning guides to establish and reinforce parental and community agency partnerships. They can study existing successful collaborations as models for developing their own, and communicate with agencies providing students services. They should establish information-sharing mechanisms, encouraging agencies to share information with their schools. Leaders should encourage school staff to work with community agencies and parents on developing student services and programs. They should locate services most accessible for students. Leaders can establish coordination committees to interact with external agencies for reinforcing

Copyright © Mometrix Media. You have been licensed one copy of this document for personal use only. Any other reproduction or redistribution is strictly prohibited. All rights reserved.

connections. Referring to their own school vision or mission statement, they can work to develop a collective interagency vision.

Sharing recreational resources to enable more physical activity opportunities

Opportunities for regular physical activity decrease risks of obesity, and afford many additional health benefits. To help children and adults to be more active, a critical strategy is to furnish them with access to convenient, affordable, safe recreational facilities. This is particularly important in communities with lower incomes and racial minorities, which frequently do not include these facilities. The Centers for Disease Control and Prevention, the American Academy of Pediatrics, the U.S. Department of Health and Human Services, and other foremost public health authorities recommend that schools and communities share recreational facilities to increase physical activity opportunities. The objectives of the Healthy People 2020 initiative recommend opening recreational facilities to the public before, after, and during school hours; and during weekends, holidays, and summers. Because schools frequently have central locations in communities, if their playgrounds, gymnasiums, playing fields, tracks, and courts are available beyond school hours, they afford community residents opportunities to be active. When schools offer free joint or shared use of their facilities to community members, this cost-effectively promotes physical activity. Reciprocally, schools could use local park facilities through joint-use agreements.

Providing youth with access to recreational facilities outside of school hours

Multiple studies find children more active physically with access to renovated and existing school recreation facilities outside regular school hours. A survey in Boston, Cincinnati, and San Francisco found with after-school access to play areas and playing fields, adolescents were far more likely to be physically active. Another study in two lower-income New Orleans communities revealed children who were very active and/or walking in schoolyards or neighborhoods numbered 84 percent more in a community with a schoolyard open to public play than with closed schoolyards. More active children also spent fewer weekday hours watching TV and movies and playing video games. Another study, comparing three control schools to six public schools with renovated schoolyards in lower-income, inner-city Denver neighborhoods, discovered children's physical activity increased significantly outside school hours in the renovated schoolyards, and their overall activity also increased significantly. A shared-use program between a large local Honolulu high school and the parks and recreation department was found in an evaluation to attract over 1,000 participants including students, teachers, school staff, and community members, offering new opportunities like adult and senior fitness classes, recreation programs, and teen strength training.

Surveys and other studies that multiple researchers have conducted with school leaders in low-income and minority communities who do not allow community access to school recreational facilities outside of school hours reveal that they identify a number of reasons as most important for restricting access, including liability for injuries and insurance concerns, the expense of running programs and activities, security and maintenance staffing issues, concerns about safety, and the expenses and responsibilities for maintenance. Lack of funding and the risks of vandalism were also reported by school leaders in these studies as reasons for not opening schools to the public outside of school hours, as were the need for supervision and concern about overuse of the facilities. These concerns were expressed by school leaders regarding both indoor and outdoor school recreational facilities. These

Copyright © Mometrix Media. You have been licensed one copy of this document for personal use only. Any other reproduction or redistribution is strictly prohibited. All rights reserved.

results were reflected by studies conducted in specific U.S. states; national surveys; those surveying low-income and racial minority communities; and those surveying several U.S. communities whose educational, racial, and socioeconomic demographics varied.

Applying community resources to support student learning

When school leaders collaborate with communities to provide resources for students, they should not only consider school mission and goals, community alignment with goals, and how they engaged families and community in establishing and meeting these, but moreover how they will measure the results they have attained. They must also consider methods they will use to report these results to families and community. School leaders and staff need to evaluate the effects of their endeavors to engage the public, just as they need to evaluate student progress annually, and use the findings of their evaluations to make corresponding adjustments in what they are doing. In addition to their actions, they must evaluate their communications. School leaders can ask students' parents and other community members about their ideas for ways to improve how they communicate with them. When they have these conversations, they should respond to the feedback parents and community members give them by discussing how they plan to include all or some of this advice in their community engagement plans. They should also share the feedback and resulting plans with school staff.

Involving and utilizing family and community members as resources

To evaluate how well they have engaged and utilized family and community members as school resources, school leaders should consider whether they are fulfilling their goals and objectives for family and community involvement. They should determine what contributions parents and other community members are making to their decisions regarding student learning. School leaders can examine whether school training sessions, workshops, and events are receiving good attendance by families and school staff and think about why they are or are not. They can ask themselves what methods and strategies they have used to integrate the cultures and languages of their community into the curriculum and events in their school. They should consider whether they have had interpreters easily available for family and community members who need them to communicate with school personnel. School leaders should review whether they have a parent or community liaison(s) with solid community connections for the school. They should evaluate whether their school includes a family center, and whether the atmosphere at their school is inviting, welcoming, and warm.

Utilizing community resources to support student learning

To improve their schools through engaging community resources, school leaders must not only make sure the resources available and what they can offer are aligned with the school's vision, they must moreover ensure these resources and the activities they enable are sustainable over the long term—and even whether resources and activities will remain after they are no longer there as school leaders. Every time school leaders discover a resource, or are offered an opportunity or proposal for a resource, they should ask themselves specifically how it fits together with the school's vision, mission, and what they are trying to accomplish. They should consider whether the resource will further or impede their goals. Without considering such pointed questions, leaders will find their interactions with community resources undefined and nebulous, accomplishing little. They may want to

Copyright © Mometrix Media. You have been licensed one copy of this document for personal use only. Any other reproduction or redistribution is strictly prohibited. All rights reserved.

assign an administrative team as a clearinghouse for all proposed ideas from prospective community partners. They could also hold an election of an advisory board composed of students, teachers, and family members to ensure the school vision is furthered by all resources and activities it employs.

Communicating with community businesses that may provide resources to the school

Among the many community organizations that can support school visions and missions for improvement to help students learn, businesses can offer valuable resources that school leaders may want to access. When they communicate with prospective partners or resource providers from the business world, they must remember that the customs and language they use can be very different from those used in the education world. Effective school leaders advise it is important to learn and speak the language of business people when interacting with them. Business executives tend to use language that is more proactive than reactive, for example. Community-based organizations, like businesses, can also use different language for discussing problems and solutions. Another consideration for school leaders is to identify business and organizational missions that overlap or match with school missions and visions. They must not only exchange their visions and missions with these stakeholders, they must moreover identify where these overlap. Then they need to help prospective resource partners realize how the partnership will benefit them. As great as the variety of organizations interested in collaborating with schools is, their motivations are equally varied. School leaders must clarify what they need, what stakeholders want, and how these can coincide.

Sharing information with prospective community resource partners

Any community stakeholders who might partner with schools to provide resources they need must be given a clear comprehension of the school's assets and what things it needs most. Clarifying these things helps both the school leader and the community partner to define their expectations. School leaders can often communicate what their schools need by simply approaching prospective partners and asking them to listen to what they have to say. School leaders may find it intimidating to ask for help from strangers or people they do not know well. However, some leaders have discovered through experience that all they needed to do was to share their school's story with community leaders, and this would communicate to them what the school needed. Another thing that school leaders can do is to ask prospective community resource partners about their own past experiences with education, and ask them how these experiences influenced the people they are today. When community leaders make connections between their personal educational experiences and a prospective school partnership, they find these intellectually and emotionally meaningful, motivating them to engage and act to help.

Accessing community resources to support schools in advancing student learning

The National Association of Elementary School Principals (NAESP) suggests that school leaders use the following four general strategies: (1) create more ownership of the school's work by engaging the community. (2) Share decision-making and leadership. (3) Invite parents to get involved meaningfully with their children's learning and with their schools. (4) Make sure that families and students have the social, health and human services they require to maintain their focus on education. The National Parent and Teachers Association (PTA) also has six national Standards for Parent and Family Involvement Programs. (1)

Copyright © Mometrix Media. You have been licensed one copy of this document for personal use only. Any other reproduction or redistribution is strictly prohibited. All rights reserved.

Communicating: there must be reciprocal, meaningful, regular communication between schools and homes. (2) Parenting: schools must support and promote parenting skills. (3) Student Learning: parents perform an essential part in assisting students in learning. (4) Volunteering: schools make parents welcome, and they seek the help and support of parents. (5) School Decision Making and Advocacy: in all school decisions that have effects on students and their families, the students' parents are full partners. (6) Collaborating with Community: schools utilize community resources to make schools, student learning, and families stronger.

Overcoming differences between schools and major corporate resources

When school leaders want to form partnerships with major corporations to access their resources, they may think the obvious disparity between their financial resources makes for a very unequal relationship and feel discouraged before they begin. However, they need to view such relationships in terms of the different assets each partner can offer. For example, partnering with schools can give corporations ways to build greater goodwill toward their company. It can also offer them many new insights whereby they can understand their community in new and different ways. In addition, corporate employees will discover opportunities for personal growth when they engage in activities through the partnerships their companies form with schools. They reap these benefits in exchange for the resources of power, money, and personnel that the corporations can provide to the schools. When school leaders help to clarify the kinds of resources that each partner is exchanging in *quid pro quo* terms, they can help to achieve more equitable, and hence workable, relationships and partnerships.

Findings about elements present and absent in school-community partnerships

According to some research, many school-community partnerships seem to focus on vocational education programs, community businesses and agencies giving vocational education students internship opportunities, and school-to-work programs. However, this study finds much less evidence of partnerships between mental health, social services, and similar community service providers and schools. This indicates a need for school leaders to further student and school success by doing more to reach out to community agencies for opportunities. According to the Institute for Educational Leadership (IEL), school and community leaders should utilize some fundamental "rules of engagement" for developing and maintaining partnerships: (1) find out about one another's needs and interests. (2) Reach out to prospective partners by offering specific help in their own territories. (3) Spell out the terms and purposes of partnerships, including what each person will do, and by what time. (4) Work out problems as they occur and modify approaches as needed. (5) Build out from successful endeavors by sharing good results and promoting increased endeavors. ("Education and Community Building: Connecting Two Worlds")

Recommendations arrived at through experiences in creating successful community schools

To create successful community schools, school leaders recommend the following: (1) prepare the way for succeeding by believing in the idea of collaborative leadership. In addition to letting agencies work in their schools, leaders must also show through their leadership and actions that community resources and involvement are critical elements of student success. (2) Develop solid relationships by convincing partners they want and need

Copyright © Mometrix Media. You have been licensed one copy of this document for personal use only. Any other reproduction or redistribution is strictly prohibited. All rights reserved.

their interaction: the school's story and success are the partner's story and success. (3) Stop, suspend judgment, and listen to partners before assuming they are the only ones who know the solution to a problem. (4) Develop criteria determining what results they want community school endeavors to accomplish and which actions will support them, discarding less relevant ideas. (5) "Lead from behind," being engaged but delegating everyday program operation responsibilities to coordinators or assistants. Exert school leader influence to find funding and partners for on-site, full-time support. (6) Use collaborative planning and trainings to involve and give school staff opportunities to enrich classroom teaching through extended-day activities. (7) Get head starts through networks for technical assistance, materials, training, and support from community school colleagues.

Copyright © Mometrix Media. You have been licensed one copy of this document for personal use only. Any other reproduction or redistribution is strictly prohibited. All rights reserved.

Ethics and Integrity

NASSP behavioral standards

The National Association of Secondary School Principals (NASSP) states that school leaders must be examples of professional behavior because they are leadership models for students, teachers, and their communities. NASSP upholds the Council of Chief State School Officers' (CCSSO) 2008 Educational Leadership Standards calling for educational leaders to further all students' success by behaving ethically, fairly, and with integrity. It also gives recommendations in its position statement on wireless and Internet safety for school leaders to protect student First Amendment rights, encourage educational Internet use, and also protect students from predators online. NASSP recommendations for ethical school leader behaviors include: meeting professional duties honestly and with integrity; obeying federal, state, and local laws; basing all decisions and actions on the value of student success and well-being; implementing the administrative regulations, rules, and policies of their local board of education; and taking suitable actions for modifying any policies, regulations, and laws that they find are not compatible with valid goals for education.

The National Association of Secondary School Principals (NASSP) has issued ten recommendations to guide school leaders for engaging in fair, honest, and ethical behaviors and using integrity in all of the actions they take as role models who set examples of ethical behavior not only for students and teachers in their schools, but for members of their communities as well. Among the NASSP's recommendations for school leaders, included are: avoiding using the power of their job positions for attaining any personal gains by exerting any social, economic, religious, political, or other kind of influence; only accepting professional certifications, academic degrees, or other credentials from institutions that are duly accredited; honoring all contracts into which they enter until they are released, dissolved, or they have fulfilled their terms, with the reciprocal agreement of all parties involved in the contracts; and upholding the standards of their profession, and endeavoring to improve the efficacy of their profession by pursuing ongoing professional development and conducting research.

Ethical standards issued by the AASA

The American Association of School Administrators' (AASA) Code of Ethics states that educational leaders base decision-making on student education and well-being; behave in responsible, trustworthy ways and discharge professional duties honestly and with integrity; uphold due process principles and protect all individual human and civil rights; implement national, state, and local laws; advise school boards and implement their administrative regulations, rules, and policies; take applicable actions to change policies and regulations not in students' best interests or inconsistent with valid educational goals; do not use their positions to wield any economic, social, political, religious, or other influence for the purpose of obtaining any personal advantages; accept professional certification, academic degrees, or other credentials only from institutes with accreditation; fulfilling the standards of their profession, and working to enhance their profession's effectiveness, by doing research and participating in continual professional development; honoring contracts until all parties agree to their dissolution, fulfillment, or release;

- 84 -

Copyright © Mometrix Media. You have been licensed one copy of this document for personal use only. Any other reproduction or redistribution is strictly prohibited. All rights reserved.

assuming accountability and responsibility for their own behaviors and actions; and committing to serving others over themselves.

Actions that would constitute ethical breaches on the part of an educator

According to the National Education Association (NEA) Code of Ethics, under the principle of Commitment to the Student, educators must not restrain any student unreasonably from taking independent actions to pursue learning. They must not deny student access to various perspectives in an unreasonable manner. They are prohibited by this principle from purposely distorting or suppressing any information that is pertinent to student progress. They are enjoined to make reasonable efforts to safeguard students from any conditions that could harm their health, safety, or learning. Educators are also expected not to subject students intentionally to disparagement or embarrassment. Educators are also prohibited by this principle from discriminating against students based on race, color, gender, sexual orientation, national origin, creed, religious beliefs, political beliefs, marital status, family background, cultural background, or social background. This includes denying any students any benefits, granting any students any advantages, and excluding any students from participating in any programs. Educators must not exploit professional relationships with students for private gains. They must also not disclose student information, except if legally or professionally required.

NEA Code of Ethics principle

The National Education Association (NEA) professional commitment principle prohibits educators from purposely falsifying, or failing to disclose, material facts about qualifications and competency in applications for professional positions; and from misrepresenting their professional qualifications. The NEA's Code of Ethics also prohibits educators from helping any person(s) unqualified by education, character, or other pertinent characteristics to enter the profession. Educators are enjoined not to make any false declarations knowingly about the qualifications of any candidate applying in a professional capacity. This NEA principle also states that educators must not help non-educators to practice teaching without authorization. Under this principle, the NEA additionally stipulates that educators must not disclose any information about their colleagues which they have acquired through their professional service, with the exceptions of doing so for "compelling" professional reasons or as legally required. Educators must not consciously make malicious or inaccurate statements about colleagues. This principle also prohibits educators from accepting favors, gifts, or gratuities that would impede or apparently influence their professional actions or decisions.

Legal proceeding wherein a parent accused a school administrator of violating ethics

In a 2002 case brought before a School Ethics Commission, a parent filed a U.S. Department of Education (ED) civil rights complaint that a middle school leader, superintendent, and Board of Education violated the School Ethics Act by giving the School Board attorney and representatives of the ED access to his child's student record without parental consent, and misrepresenting the records' contents. The respondents filed answers that the Commission had no jurisdiction over an issue regarding student records, and that their actions related to the complaint were appropriate and did not violate the School Ethics Act. The complainant alleged the school leader edited documentation of harassment incidents out of the student's record, shared these edited records without his consent outside school, and used his

- 85 -

Copyright © Mometrix Media. You have been licensed one copy of this document for personal use only. Any other reproduction or redistribution is strictly prohibited. All rights reserved.

position to gain himself or others unjustified advantage. The Commission found the school leader had complied with an ED notice requiring information access for determining compliance with Title VI of the 1964 Civil Rights Act, and had no financial or personal involvement with the records wherefrom he could obtain any benefit. Therefore, it found no probable cause to credit the complainant's allegations.

Accountability for ethical behavior

School leaders are responsible not only for their own actions and the results of those actions, but also for what others do and what events occur under their leadership. In the same way school leaders hold their school staff members accountable for performing their job duties and for any judgment errors they make, school leaders must equally hold themselves accountable and also permit others to hold them accountable. To lead ethically, school leaders should build formal and/or informal accountability into their job positions. They should furthermore be prepared to deal directly with the consequences of the decisions they make and actions they take. The school leader's job includes assuming responsibility for working to improve unacceptable employee performance and correct others' mistakes. It also includes ensuring that all school organization interactions with others are ethical. Overall leader responsibility for mitigating the errors of others or their failure to perform their jobs in certain situations is not eliminated by blaming others, even those who did those things. Blaming others only gives leaders a cowardly appearance.

One way in which school leaders can hold themselves and others accountable for ethical behavior is to institutionalize means whereby other people are able to question the leaders' authority. Experts make the point that, except possibly when organizational goals are for conquering the world, starting a war, or purely for profit (and maybe not even then), leadership by autocracy is detrimental. For one thing, school leaders cannot advance their efficacy and make better decisions without information and feedback from others, and they will not receive these if they lead autocratically. For another thing, autocratic leadership is likely to incur resentment and dissatisfaction in those being led. This can result in their consciously or unconsciously becoming less effective in performing their duties. Also, staff creativity and input beyond that of the leader are sacrificed, meaning that staff will not take ownership of the school philosophy and decisions. This can cause more staff turnover. Hence, leading autocratically is bad for the leader, the employees, and the organization. School leaders should ensure that all employees and other stakeholders share in making decisions that directly affect them, and enables good job performance without interference.

Determining that one's decisions and actions are ethical in nature

Some experts (Pinnell and Eagan, West Virginia University Extension), in a course designed for volunteer leaders, advise that to get an idea whether any decision or action that one makes or takes is ethical in its nature, a leader should ask himself or herself four questions: (1) "Kid on Your Shoulder" – ask yourself whether you would do what you are considering or planning if your own kids were observing it. (2) "Front Page of the Newspaper" – ask yourself whether what you are considering or planning to do is something that you would want to see published on the front page of your local newspaper. (3) "Golden Rule" – as this rule says to treat others the way you would like them to treat you, ask yourself if you would like being the recipient of the decision or action that you are considering making or planning to take. (4) "Rule of Universality" – ask yourself whether what you are considering or planning to do would be acceptable for everybody to do.

Copyright © Mometrix Media. You have been licensed one copy of this document for personal use only. Any other reproduction or redistribution is strictly prohibited. All rights reserved.

Ethical leadership

Ethical school leaders need to be able to defer their personal interests to the needs of the students, staff members, and community stakeholders they serve; to the needs of the school organizations they lead, and the causes they support; and the greater good of the community, state, nation, and/or world. They must be willing to encourage differing opinions; challenges to their ideas, proposals, and actions; and to take feedback seriously. They need to encourage leadership in other people. They should make it a part of the school culture to consider and discuss ethics and ethical questions regularly. To those trusting them to lead their schools, by methods with the most efficacy and highest quality, in the right directions, school leaders must sustain and extend their own competence, which they owe them. They must be accountable and accept responsibility for their viewpoints, proposals, decisions, and actions. School leaders demonstrate that they understand the power associated with leadership and know how to use it wisely when they share that power as much as they can; avoid ever abusing it; and only exercise it to the benefit of the people, organizations, and communities with whom they work.

School leaders need to ensure that every individual in the school or community has an opportunity to exercise leadership whenever it is appropriate. This can include initiating decisions and actions, questioning others' decisions and actions, promoting the school's integrity, or being a role model in certain circumstances. School leaders must realize, whether they choose to be or not, that they are role models. Because of their positions of authority, people will take cues from them about the school culture, characteristics the school should have, and what ethical behaviors are. This means school leaders must attend not only to what they do and say, but also to how their actions and statements appear or could be interpreted. They must avoid doing anything that could be interpreted as unethical, even if it is not unethical in reality. School leaders should also fulfill their roles as ethical leaders by encouraging and mentoring leadership in others. This cultivates ethical leadership development in the school and community, enhancing functioning and providing more resources in the event of crises or problems. It moreover trains new leaders to assume more responsibilities over time, relieving school leaders of pressure and enabling others to take over when they leave.

Placing the importance of the good of the school ahead of one's own ego and interests

Experts say one genuine test of ethical leadership is whether a school leader makes a decision that is best for the school, even when this is not in the leader's self-interest. For example, during recessions or budget shortfalls, leaders might take a salary cut to facilitate programs and services, or sacrifice some of their own decision-making powers to extend those of others. School leaders need to be able to differentiate between their own good and the good of the school, which is not always obvious. For example, it may seem significant for the school when the leader assumes a new project. However, if that project spreads the leader's energy and attention too thinly, causes burnout, or takes away time to complete other necessary duties, it could be counterproductive. Leaders of small schools with fewer resources must take particular care in not sacrificing themselves to the point that they are no longer useful. However, they do need to be willing to put aside their own egos and self-interest to do what is best for the school and members of the learning community.

Copyright © Mometrix Media. You have been licensed one copy of this document for personal use only. Any other reproduction or redistribution is strictly prohibited. All rights reserved.

Ethical school leadership should be open and involve collaborative decision-making

The school leader's ethical principles should be congruent with those of the school vision and mission. An ethical school leader would not do anything that would compromise the school philosophy and/or vision—for example, accepting funds whose donor stipulated that the school utilize methods that the school leader and staff believe are harmful or ineffectual. To support an open, ethical decision-making process, school leaders should regularly engage staff and stakeholders in conversations about ethical questions and all participants' ethical assumptions (including those of the leader), which will facilitate self-examination of assumptions and development of ethical understanding. Because frameworks of ethical principles develop out of everything one experiences and learns, it follows logically that one's ethical framework continues to grow throughout life. School leaders should have the ability and willingness to explain and defend their ethical principles and decisions to others and stand up for their beliefs through their actions, not just their speech. They will also promote open, ethical decision-making when they accustom everyone in the school community to analyzing any decision's or action's ethical implications and how those should influence their approaches, which makes ethical discussion an integral part of the school culture.

School leaders should make every effort to be inclusive by creative use of diversity in being open to discussing diversity in the event of disagreement or conflict; encouraging others to learn about each other's perspectives and traditions and value these; and by being willing to hire and work with people from all races, ethnicities, cultures, social classes, sexual orientations, etc. They should also establish and sustain channels for communication with and among all staff and learning community members. Creating a reputation of transparency reduces suspicion, resentment, innuendo, and rumors among others and enhances their trust in the school leader. Maintaining sense of humor and perspective also keeps school leaders ethical, effective, and "human." Taking themselves too seriously tends to promote excessive protectiveness of leadership territories, which can undermine ethical reputations. Inviting appropriate collaboration not only admits more valuable input, but also shows that school leaders care more about providing the best services than protecting their authority.

Constraint to the sharing of data between schools and OST programs

Experts find sharing data between schools and out-of-school time (OST) programs is a process critical to supporting student development and learning, yet many factors make it difficult to navigate. Limited resources, lack of openness, and privacy issues are just a few among the barriers. However, some OST systems have found ways to work around these obstacles to form shared visions, mutual support, and solid partnerships with local school districts. One area of challenge is legal constraints on sharing data. One factor that should improve this area is that, in 2011, the U.S. Department of Education made some changes in the Family Educational Rights and Privacy Act (FERPA) regulations altering who can share data. Now, state and local education authorities can share data with other government agencies not under their direct control that are involved in federal- or state-supported education programs, which the previous interpretation restricted. Another approach is exemplified by the Providence After School Alliance (PASA) and Providence Public School District, which after building their relationship for seven years, signed a memorandum of understanding eliminating parental consent requirements by making PASA a "quasi-district" that provides services the district cannot.

Copyright © Mometrix Media. You have been licensed one copy of this document for personal use only. Any other reproduction or redistribution is strictly prohibited. All rights reserved.

ISLLC

The Interstate School Leaders Licensure Consortium (ISLLC) was formed by the Council of Chief State School Officers (CCSSO) with representatives from 37 U.S. states to develop a new set of standards for school leaders for guiding school leader preparation, state school leader standards development, evaluation, and licensure with success for all students in mind. Of six standards the ISLLC developed, Standard 5 is: "A school administrator is an educational leader who promotes the success of all students by acting with integrity, fairness, and in an ethical manner." Under Dispositions, school leaders are directed to value, believe in, and be committed to bringing ethical principles to decision-making processes. In doing so, they also model ethical decision-making for all participants. Under Performances, included are: "demonstrates values, beliefs, and attitudes that inspire others to higher levels of performance"; "serves as a role model"; "considers the impact of one's administrative practices on others"; "recognizes and respects the legitimate authority of others"; and "expects that others in the school community will demonstrate integrity and exercise ethical behavior." These all relate to holding others accountable for ethical behavior.

Types of power

According to Erich Fromm (*Escape from Freedom,* 1941, 1969), there are two types of power: "power over" and "power to." "Power over" controls other people for one's own purposes, while "power to" achieves one's purposes without requiring control over others. Rather than "power over," for ethical leadership, school leaders use "power to." They use it both in the form of personal, internal resources (e.g., knowledge, skills, etc.); and for accessing and utilizing external resources (e.g., funding, time, people, etc.) to accomplish school goals. By leading ethically, ethical school leaders serve as role models who set examples for others, including school staff, students, and community members. They encourage and mentor others in developing and exercising leadership. They share their power in appropriate ways, both to enhance the probability of succeeding and to accelerate new leadership development. They not only make decisions and act ethically, they also lead ethically, in their attitudes; in how they treat people during their everyday interpersonal interactions; in how they encourage others; and in which directions they steer their schools, committees, and initiatives.

Leading ethically and competently

To lead ethically, school leaders must continually work to enhance their own competence. Included in this effort is the self-knowledge to recognize and acknowledge what they are not good at doing. Other than improving their skills, they can often delegate these duties to others who are much better at them. For example, a school leader may be competent at supervising buildings and grounds managers, but not at the actual maintenance for which he or she has hired the managers who excel at it. Competent leaders also do not assume tasks or responsibilities they lack the resources or time to complete or manage. Community organizations including schools must develop, change, grow, and mature over time. Ethical and competent school leaders are able to identify when they have accomplished everything that they can, and/or when the school needs another leader to continue developing. Refusing to recognize this is called "founder's disease." Experts compare it to refusing to let go of children as they grow up and become independent. School leaders must not overstay

Copyright © Mometrix Media. You have been licensed one copy of this document for personal use only. Any other reproduction or redistribution is strictly prohibited. All rights reserved.

their utility and damage their schools; they must let go when schools need to grow beyond their influence.

FERPA and IDEA

States have freedom of information, or sunshine laws, which allow public records access including school district records, for inspection and monitoring purposes. Parents and guardians also have rights to their review, and interpretation and explanation to them, of their children's educational records. Family Education Rights and Privacy Act (FERPA) (as well as the Individuals with Disabilities Education Act [IDEA] for special education students) protects student rights to confidentiality of their records, and school leaders are responsible for enforcing these rights. However, there are also exceptions when student records must be shared with law enforcement officials and others. Therefore, school leaders must understand what the laws guarantee in records confidentiality and when they can and must disclose student records information. Under FERPA privacy protection, which limits third-party access and makes personally identifiable information confidential, school leaders must get written parent or guardian consent to disclose information to third parties. Parental rights transfer to students judged competent for informed consent when they reach age 18. School leaders are responsible to establish policies determining who else besides parents or eligible students may access records, what directory information will be available without parent consent, and when interests in records review are legitimate.

Both the FERPA and IDEA define educational records as special education and discipline records; official records about student school status; medical records; external agency (e.g., juvenile authorities, psychiatrists, and psychologists) evaluation reports, created and maintained by schools, school employees, or their agents; and any permanent information kept by school officials. FERPA determines educational records destruction via state laws. Records kept personally only by school leaders, teachers, nurses, or police liaisons are not included unless shared with anyone except substitute teachers. Directory information, which can be disclosed without consent, includes student attendance records, schools attended, academic status, degrees earned, awards received, school activities, place and date of birth, and address. IDEA amendments are informed by FERPA regarding records collection, maintenance, disclosure, destruction, and confidentiality protection and rights transfer. However, rights transfer is not automatic under the IDEA: it grants state legislatures the option to enact legal provision for transferring procedural rights to competent students with disabilities at age 18. The IDEA additionally requires designating special education records custodians to ensure all school leaders, teachers, special educators, and others collecting confidential information are instructed and trained; FERPA does not.

Parents and eligible adult students can protect the confidentiality of their educational records from some third parties by refusing to give signed, written consent. However, school leaders can still disclose student records without such consent to law enforcement officials, organizations or their employees considering financial aid for the students of record, and school officials and employees if they have a "legitimate need to know." Parents and eligible adult students have the right to request copies of all records disclosed without their consent to any third parties. Under the law, there is a provision for access to appropriate information by those with a legitimate educational interest about a student who has been disciplined for behavior threatening others' safety and well-being. For example, if a school leader has disciplined a student for conduct that presented a risk to the

Copyright © Mometrix Media. You have been licensed one copy of this document for personal use only. Any other reproduction or redistribution is strictly prohibited. All rights reserved.

well-being and safety of students or others in the school community, and that student then attends an event at another school and the school leader believes the student could represent a threat to others, then the school leader can share confidential disciplinary records with the other school's leader and officials.

Sharing school data and needs with staff and communities

Experienced school leaders advise those new to the position to seek allies among their faculties and communities. They should identify those who are not necessarily the most vociferous, but will support and help them in making needed changes to realize their vision. For example, school leaders can host a community forum the week before school starts. There they can share their vision, their action plan, and specific data showing the school's current status and expectations for its ideal status. They should also be sure to acknowledge their need for assistance from school staff, parents, and other community members. By being transparent with data and honest about school problems and needs, school leaders pave the way for community involvement in school success. School leaders using these practices report substantial gains in community school engagement, including local business partnerships; university deans, community members, and business owners' joining school management and planning teams; classes facilitated by community members; regular community forum scheduling; and community stakeholders' joining school administrative staff to canvass neighborhoods and give parents materials to help support their children's school success, school program offering overviews, and invitations to join the Parent-Teacher Association.

According to successful school leaders, when their staff sees them, they should also see their vision for the students and the school. When school leaders plan for their school's future success, they should imagine what the school should look like in six months, one year, and five years. They should also ask their school leadership team what they think the school would be like at each of these points in time. The school leader must spearhead an action strategy for the school that focuses on creating a core curriculum, building capacity, engaging students, and developing relationships. School leaders can divide their action items within each of these categories as quick, moderate, and difficult—i.e., what they can accomplish right away, what they can achieve by next year, and what they can complete within five years. Experienced leaders note the conflict inherent in advancing school progress: between having to evaluate and lead teachers, and also needing to give those teachers authentic assistance. They say the way to address this challenge is by treating it as an opportunity for listening to staff and student interests and concerns. Doing so is critical to creating collegial school culture and climate.

Gathering and applying informal data to develop school improvement plans

Some effective school leaders started during summer school by holding student focus groups and one-on-one interviews, asking students what was and was not working for them in school, and interviewing faculty and community stakeholders. They asked every staff member before the school year began not only the same questions they asked students, but additionally how their students learned; why they thought students were not achieving highly; and, if they were the school leader, what they would do first. They invited parents to informal school meetings and sent surveys to community stakeholders to involve them in school improvement conversations and acquire all different perspectives. They also conversed with summer school custodians and support staff. They used all the responses

Copyright © Mometrix Media. You have been licensed one copy of this document for personal use only. Any other reproduction or redistribution is strictly prohibited. All rights reserved.

they received to develop action theories and plans. They listed programs for promoting student achievement. They outlined intervention processes for unsuccessful students. They identified the data to use for reviewing and updating their school improvement plans. They asked their school leadership teams to establish priorities, goals, and benchmarks. They worked with them to align school improvement plans with state and district goals. They also developed a process to start continuing evaluation of school improvement plan initiatives.

Identifying school areas needing improvement

Experienced school leaders counter the familiar advice to new leaders not to change anything in their first school year with the observation that, if nothing changes for the better, there may be no second year. They advise new leaders and those at new schools to work for change while proceeding with caution, and get directions for change from data. They should review not only standardized test scores, but also grade reports, school history, attendance reports, discipline reports, incident reports, teacher observations, etc. They should evaluate what they have too little of and too much of—e.g., too few honor students, teachers achieving good outcomes; too little appreciation for staff and student contributions; too many absences, tardy arrivals, failing grades—and determine how to change them. They can look at teacher grades and make needs assessments for teacher professional development; call parents, introduce themselves, and discuss how tardiness and absences affect new school routines and success; and distribute student successes and expectations in parent bulletins. Some leaders coordinated district resources and support with teachers, students, and community volunteers in school renovation and beautification projects. The transformations pleased students and gave volunteers anticipation of other improvements to come.

Open sharing of data with students and staff

Co-school leaders at some schools, including elementary schools, have set goals that their school will prepare every student for college by making every student proficient or advanced in reading, language arts, and mathematics. They refer to their approach as "No Excuses," and work to achieve their goal through creating a school culture of universal achievement and developing exemplary systems for collecting, analyzing, applying, incorporating, and sharing data. They say they involve every student in the process, and every staff member participates in developing assessment plans. Every individual student's goals are based on his or her specific data measures. These leaders have accomplished students' close involvement with monitoring and knowing their own data, and the assurance by teachers that their classroom instruction is driven by the data they use. Administrators and teachers collect classroom data, analyze them, and incorporate the outcomes into teachers' action plans. All staff members are committed to discovering new means of identifying correlations between assessment scores and needed intervention types.

Two school leaders at one elementary school have instituted an approach whereby they, other administrators, and teachers all collect data from their classrooms, analyze them, and integrate what they find into teachers' plans. They have found that they are able to respond more quickly to all students' needs through using the data for developing instructional improvement frameworks. Moreover, they have engaged every student in knowing what their own data say and keeping track of it. These leaders' goal for their school is that no

Copyright © Mometrix Media. You have been licensed one copy of this document for personal use only. Any other reproduction or redistribution is strictly prohibited. All rights reserved.

student will fail; and that every single student, with no exceptions or excuses, will be proficient in math, reading, and language arts and ready for college. This Title I school includes students speaking 35 different languages. The leaders find that their approach of supporting universal achievement through analyzing, applying, and sharing data is achieving salutary results. They find every student subgroup is succeeding and thriving. Consequently, they have established 14 such schools nationwide. They say they want to create a "revolution" by showing educators that "there is a system for creating systems."

Respect for individual dignity and worth

School leaders should work to develop their own interpersonal and cultural sensitivity and competence. Leaders who treat all individuals and groups fairly, honestly, and respectfully will encourage mutual respect. Some U.S. states have passed legislation to ensure this. For example, New York State passed the Dignity Act (Dignity for All Students) as Article 2, an amendment to State Education Law, signed in 2010, effective in 2012, with amendments in 2013. This act aims to give elementary and secondary school students safe, supportive environments without discrimination, intimidation, harassment, taunting, and bullying in schools, on school buses, or at school events. It moreover amended Section 801 of N.Y. State Education Law, adding to citizenship, civility, and character education with awareness and sensitivity in human relations including various races, ethnicities, national origins, religions and religious practices, mental and physical abilities, sexes and sexual orientations and gender identities, and weights extending the concepts of dignity, tolerance, and respect for others. This law also requires Boards of Education to incorporate language in their conduct codes addressing the Dignity Act.

Under the Dignity Act, which amended New York State Education Law, schools are responsible not only to instruct students in awareness, sensitivity, tolerance, respect, and dignity for various groups of people, and include wording pertaining to the Dignity Act in their codes of conduct, they are also accountable for collecting and reporting data on material incidents of harassment, discrimination, and bullying—including cyberbullying. The state has established an online portal for submitting an annual reporting form. It also provides guides for local implementation, updating conduct codes, and resources and promising practices for school administrators and faculty. The Dignity Act requires, in the preparation programs of school professional leaders and teachers applying for new certification and licensure, at least six hours of coursework and training in patterns, prevention, and interventions regarding harassment, bullying, and discrimination. In the N.Y. State Code of Ethics for Educators, its first principle reflects the essence of the Dignity Act. Nationally, the Council of Chief State School Officers (CCSSO) has established six Educational Leadership Policy Standards emphasizing the responsibility of local school leaders to provide strong leadership, as the N.Y.S. Code of Ethics for Educators also does.

According to authors from the New York State Education Department (NYSED), the first principle of the state's Code of Ethics for Educators reflects the essence of NYSED's Dignity Act. It stipulates that educators cultivate every student's physical, intellectual, emotional, social, and civic potential. Educators are to advance all students' growth by integrating these learning domains. They respect the intrinsic worth and dignity of every person. They assist students in reflecting on what they learn and relating it to their own life experiences. Educators are also expected to get students engaged in activities that encourage them to adopt diverse solutions and approaches to the issues they encounter, as well as to offer their students a variety of means by which they are able to show their skills and what they

Copyright © Mometrix Media. You have been licensed one copy of this document for personal use only. Any other reproduction or redistribution is strictly prohibited. All rights reserved.

have learned. This principle also indicates that educators nurture the development of students such that students are able to analyze information, synthesize it, evaluate it, and communicate it, doing all of these with effectiveness.

School leaders must not only demonstrate their own responsibility and respect for all individuals and serve as role models who set examples for all members of their learning communities, but they must also be the ones who establish the general tone of respect and responsibility for all of the students, faculty, staff, parents, and other community members. The CCSSO's six Educational Leadership Policy Standards articulate how school leaders do this: (1) establishing widespread shared visions regarding learning; (2) developing instructional programs and school cultures that promote staff professional growth and student learning; (3) assuring that school operations, resources, and organization are managed efficiently to provide safe, effective, efficient learning environments; (4) responding to interests and needs of diverse community constituents, activating community resources, and collaborating with faculty and community; (5) behaving ethically, fairly, and with integrity; and (6) understanding the social, cultural, legal, and political contexts, responding to them, and influencing them.

Showing respect, understanding, and value for diversity

When they develop their school vision, school leaders should make sure that it includes high expectations for every student, irrespective of their socioeconomic status, race, ethnicity, language, national origin, or gender. In directing and managing their school operations, school leaders should offer the school and community multiple ways for celebrating diversity. They should make sure that all of their teachers create differentiated lesson plans and curriculum guides that contain learning units which are not only developmentally appropriate, but also incorporate cultural diversity and sensitivity. School leaders can also help to make sure that representatives from diverse community groups participate actively in school decision-making processes by recruiting the involvement of suitable stakeholders. By their own attitudes and behaviors showing respect for diversity in the school and the surrounding community, school leaders should model this respect for all others whom they influence. They should additionally ensure the presence of equity in all parts of their school programs for all students, and hold all school community members accountable for these values.

Inclusive school community

School leaders who are sensitive to the needs of all students contribute to inclusive school communities. School leaders should devise opportunities for students who come from diverse backgrounds to contribute their efforts to realizing the school vision. They should also make sure that all of these students are able to access these opportunities. As part of their jobs, school leaders must identify any obstacles to learning which show a lack of sensitivity to the needs of student populations with diverse characteristics. They then need to create and implement plans of action to eliminate or reduce these obstacles for students. School leaders should also help others identify the diverse elements within their community, and assist with the inclusion of representatives of these groups in the school's decision-making processes regarding its instructional programs. In addition, school leaders should make active efforts to assure the access of all individuals to equal learning and teaching opportunities.

Copyright © Mometrix Media. You have been licensed one copy of this document for personal use only. Any other reproduction or redistribution is strictly prohibited. All rights reserved.

Inclusive education of students with disabilities

Research has found that the leadership of the school leader is viewed as the central variable to determine successful school reform to implement inclusive education of students with disabilities in general education classrooms. Because their role is so important, school leaders need to display behaviors that promote accepting and integrating students with disabilities in general education classes, and advance these students' success there. Studies have established that school leaders' beliefs and values primarily determine decisions for inclusive education. Researchers identify the following ways in which school leaders demonstrate their beliefs, values, and priorities: the way they make commitments and honor them; in which things they show interest, and which questions they ask; what they say in informal and formal situations; their preferences in the people they interact with and the places they go; when they decide to take action, and how they make their actions known to others; and the ways in which they organize their physical settings and school staffs.

Research from the Council for Exceptional Children (Praisner, 2003) found from surveying elementary school leaders that, while the majority of them were uncertain about inclusion of students with disabilities, 20 percent of them had positive attitudes toward inclusion. Those with such positive attitudes had experienced more exposure to special education concepts and more positive experiences with students who had disabilities. School leaders who had such positive experiences and attitudes regarding students with disabilities were found more likely to place these students into settings that were less restrictive. School leaders were found to have different experiences and to make different placements of students with disabilities depending on various categories of the students' disabilities. According to the author, the findings of this research pointed to how important it is for school leaders to engage in inclusive practices, which afford more positive experiences for them with students who have all different kinds of disabilities. The researcher also found the results to indicate the importance of giving school leaders more specific training regarding disabilities and special education.

Some research conducted in 2000 (Praisner) found school leaders surveyed were most likely to choose least restrictive placements for students with speech and language disorders (93.7 percent). Second highest were students with physical disabilities (87.4 percent), then the category of Other Health Impairment (84.9 percent), then specific learning disabilities (81.9 percent), then deafness and hearing impairment (74.5 percent), and then blindness and visual impairments (71.9 percent). School leaders responding were far less likely to choose regular education classroom placements for students with autism (30.1 percent) and serious emotional disturbances (20.4 percent). Over half (63.6 percent) of school leaders surveyed selected the most segregated special educational service settings, outside of regular education schools and special classes, for students with serious emotional disturbances; almost half (49.8 percent) selected such settings for students with autism and/or pervasive developmental disorders. These restricted settings were chosen by 29.4 percent of school leaders for students with intellectual disabilities, 36.9 percent for students with neurological impairment, and 39.1 percent for students with multiple disabilities. School leaders responding mostly (62 percent) selected part-time special or regular education and resource rooms for students with specific learning disabilities and intellectual disabilities (59.7 percent). Serious emotional disturbance was the only category respondents largely associated with negative experiences.

Copyright © Mometrix Media. You have been licensed one copy of this document for personal use only. Any other reproduction or redistribution is strictly prohibited. All rights reserved.

In one Florida elementary school, the school leader places special-needs students in one class at each grade level, assigning one classroom teacher and one special education teacher to each. Classroom teachers give content lessons, and then special education teachers instruct assigned groups focused on their special learning needs and strengths. At a Louisiana elementary school, 20 percent of students are identified with special needs. Their school leader divides six special education teachers, assigning three to self-contained classrooms of students with mild, moderate, and severe intellectual disabilities who function two or more years below age and grade level; and the other three to inclusive classrooms—one each for grades 1-2, 3-4, and 5-6. This leader finds grouping the most efficient use of teachers, meaning some classrooms include more special-needs students than others. In grades with the most special-needs students, their special education teachers divide their time across two or three classrooms. A Washington junior high school leader includes most special-needs students in regular classrooms, reporting included students behave better whereas segregated groups display collective behavior problems. She assigns a special education teacher or paraprofessional whenever a regular class includes more than 12 special-needs students.

One middle school leader has established centrally located "learning centers" in the school's primary academic wings. A special education teacher or paraprofessional in each center helps special-needs students with projects they are assigned in regular classrooms. Students experiencing academic or behavioral difficulties can relocate to the learning centers for more individual attention and a quieter setting. This school leader also provides "resource room" classes for students with writing or math needs that cannot be met in regular classrooms. This leader finds that by making such resources available, as safety nets for special-needs students and as support for general classroom teachers, inclusion succeeds. Another middle school leader of a math and science magnet school, who has experience as a former special education teacher, finds staffing the key to inclusive education. She hires special educators who have training and commitment for inclusion, carefully matching them with classroom teachers for complementary pairings. The educators she selects work well as teams, and equally well with students and parents.

Establishing classrooms that include special education students

Many school leaders find the greatest challenges to establishing inclusive classrooms are logistical. For example, special education teachers are in short supply; their available numbers frequently determine school inclusion approaches. Also, special educators must work around established schedules, including lunchtimes, literacy blocks, etc. This can force schools to group special-needs students instead of distributing them evenly among classrooms. Because federal law mandates educating exceptional students in the least restrictive environment, some school leaders have a school administrator and secretary assigned specifically to them. Some school districts have these personnel for every school. Some bigger schools have their own exceptional student education (ESE) counselors. School leaders may have ESE teacher-consultants work with students, parents, teachers, and district offices. In some districts, all ESE teachers have laptops with software to expedite updating student IEPs. Some school leaders have mainstreamed even profoundly disabled students, with ESE teachers accompanying eight to 10 special education students to regular education classrooms, giving them added help, and team-teaching with classroom teachers. Special and regular education teachers collaborate to benefit all students.

Copyright © Mometrix Media. You have been licensed one copy of this document for personal use only. Any other reproduction or redistribution is strictly prohibited. All rights reserved.

Positive and negative aspects of school cultures

Experts observe that positive school cultures typically include a caring and nurturing atmosphere, positive attitudes, and an overall sense of responsibility for students' learning. They share values that support professional development for teachers. They have informal "grapevines" whereby staff members share information about things going on in the school, and informal "hero" and "heroine" networks. Leaders, other administrators, and staff in positive school cultures believe in their own ability to attain their visions. They emphasize collaboration and accomplishment, celebrate successes, and promote individual and collective commitment to student and staff learning. In contrast, negative school cultures have no faith that they will realize their visions, or that students can succeed. They demonstrate overall negative attitudes. Rather than encourage collaboration, they discourage it. Hostility and conflict among staff members is common, as they give no effort or support to working together cooperatively. Rather than celebrate accomplishment and success, they blame students when progress is lacking; they are not committed to students' or their own learning.

Experts (cf. Peterson, *Shaping School Culture: The Heart of Leadership*) say that school culture is composed mainly of underlying normative beliefs and values about teaching and learning held by administrators. In addition, rituals and traditions that schools use to reinforce those values and to build community contribute to school culture. Core belief sets based on fundamental assumptions regarding things like which teaching methods are effective, how important staff development is, how open the school's staff is to change, and what staff members will talk about at meetings are the underpinnings of overall school culture. School environments that are primarily negative include negative staff attitudes in general, staff members who do not believe in their students' ability to succeed, and frequent conflicts in the interactions among teachers. Negative or damaging school cultures include norms that support inertia, lack clear senses of purpose, discourage collaboration among members, blame students for their lack of progress, and often demonstrate active hostility in their staff relations.

When a school culture is primarily negative, leaders and staff must assess the school culture's fundamental values and norms first. Then they must work collaboratively to change these to make their school culture more supportive and positive. According to educational experts, school leaders need to "read" their schools. They should initiate conversations with long-term staff members able and willing to tell stories about the school's history. They should work with staff to review what they have learned about their school culture, asking each other which elements of the school culture are positive, for them to reinforce; and which elements of the school culture are negative, for them to change. School leaders and leaders among staff can cultivate positive school culture attributes by taking advantage of every opportunity to relate accounts of successful collaborations and accomplishments; formulating and utilizing clear, common vocabulary during professional development that promotes commitment to staff and student learning; and using all school ceremonies and staff meetings to celebrate successes.

Ensuring cultural equality and preventing or eliminating racism

Some appropriate actions that school leaders can take in the form of instituting and implementing equitable school policies include: incorporate cultural pluralism as goal of education in their school philosophy, vision and mission statements, and norms. Establish

Copyright © Mometrix Media. You have been licensed one copy of this document for personal use only. Any other reproduction or redistribution is strictly prohibited. All rights reserved.

official school policies not to tolerate racism, and clearly define the consequences for any members engaging in racism. Train students in mediation and conflict resolution skills for settling disputes. Acknowledge students from varied racial and cultural groups when giving honors and awards. Ensure the school board's cultural and racial composition reflects that of the student population. Evaluate whether school board policies are racially and culturally sensitive; if they are not, revise them to be. Consider whether the school judges or sorts students by standardized test scores; if so, change this. School tracking policies should also be avoided or replaced. Examine whether racial and cultural minority students are disproportionately represented in special education programs and classes. If so, administer more culturally fair tests, and use the results to revisit eligibility determinations.

School leaders should ensure that their curriculum materials selection committee chooses learning materials that are culturally and racially diverse. They should lead faculty in making curriculum decisions that take into account the needs of racial and cultural minority students. Leaders should counsel teachers who read to younger students and assign reading to older students to analyze whether the books they choose contain inherently prejudicial or discriminatory content. They should view their school's curriculum, and instruct teachers to view it, as constantly changing to meet perpetually changing student population needs, and pluralistic in nature. Leaders should assure their school offers materials teaching about different cultures and races, and opportunities for staff and students both to learn about other cultures and races. They should have their schools include a multicultural education among their curriculum goals. Multicultural education in their schools should constitute more than just festivals, food, and fun activities. Books, videos, films, recordings, photos, and other media should provide students with vicarious multicultural experiences. Curriculum should reflect the real lives of all students, including minorities. Teachers should connect minority students' knowledge and experiences to new curriculum content equally as others'.

School leaders can consider whether teachers and other staff understand the learning styles of all student cultural and racial groups in their classrooms. If not, they can implement trainings and staff peer mentoring in culturally diverse learning styles. Leaders should model for teachers to model for students the acceptance and appreciation of diverse language and learning styles, ideas, and opinions. Leaders should ensure that teachers generally understand their students' cultures and races; and that teachers endeavor to understand each individual student's cultural and racial characteristics. They should provide staff development programs that help employees better understand the styles and needs of minority students. School leaders should examine whether their faculties use any teaching practices that might conflict with any student cultural beliefs, values, or practices. If so, they should instruct teachers to modify or replace these. Leaders should assure that every teacher knows a few phrases or words in each student's native language to make their classrooms psychologically safe and welcoming learning environments for all students. They should make sure all staff members learn to pronounce student names correctly.

School leaders should consider whether their school has a committee for identifying and procuring racially and culturally diverse learning materials. Whether the school has a policy against racist language, slurs, and jokes is significant, as is whether it has anti-discrimination rules. School leaders and staff should teach appropriate ways of asking others about race and culture. They should regularly and consistently offer materials teaching about various races and cultures. They should examine whether they offer students opportunities to learn about their own race and culture. School activities

Copyright © Mometrix Media. You have been licensed one copy of this document for personal use only. Any other reproduction or redistribution is strictly prohibited. All rights reserved.

encouraging students to meet people of other races and cultures are important. Leaders should question whether their school teaches students that conflict is a part of everyday life. They should ask if they give students and adults alike chances for learning about other people's races and cultures, and if their school encourages teachers to apply cooperative learning methods as a means of helping diverse students to work and play with each other. They should ensure that community racial and cultural groups are represented in school advisory councils; they can ask whether these advisory groups resemble their student bodies.

School leaders should consider whether their school has rules that require students and staff to learn about different racial and cultural groups. Their policies should reflect that they value human differences. They should teach all learning community members how their own races or cultures affect the people surrounding them. They should make explicit that they hold educators accountable for having and communicating high expectations for students from racial and cultural minorities. They must educate students and staff about the rules that will ensure respect for racial and cultural differences. School leaders should examine whether all levels of their workforces are mixed racially and culturally or not. They should see that their schools encourage activities that value the common human qualities of all people. At the same time, their schools should also offer activities that recognize the differences among racial and cultural groups. Leaders should hire and promote educators whose racial and cultural memberships reflect the racial and cultural composition of their school's student body. School leaders and their staff members should teach students how to solve problems cooperatively.

School leaders should lead their faculty in teaching students how to engage in and sustain positive interactions among people from different racial and cultural backgrounds. Leaders and staff should encourage students to talk about race and culture differences without judging them. Schools should offer students activities acknowledging various needs and strengths of every racial and cultural group. School leaders should institute rules, and assure they and their staffs enforce them strongly, prohibiting racist language, slurs, and jokes. They should lead their schools in ensuring their community's racial and cultural groups are represented in all school decision-making groups. They can offer trainings to foster racial and cultural understanding among all school employees. School leaders must be sensitive, and teach staff members sensitivity, to detect very subtle racist behaviors and consistently correct these. They should see that their schools have effective conflict intervention strategies, teach that various races and cultures frequently communicate in different ways, encourage school staff to discuss racial and cultural differences, and have staff teach all students how to respect cultural and racial differences.

Common public views and perceptions related to professional development

According to research conducted by some state education departments, the public believes that a school leader's strategy of recruiting and keeping better teachers has more potential to improve schools than their strategies for decreasing class sizes, requiring standardized assessments as a promotion contingency, or convincing state education departments to allow more control at the local school level. These sources find that the majority of the public supports professional development opportunities financed by the schools as a way to find and retain teachers. Studies show that, among school investments, expanding teacher education increases student achievement more than raising teacher salaries, expanding teacher experience, or reducing class size. Research also finds that among the factors of

Copyright © Mometrix Media. You have been licensed one copy of this document for personal use only. Any other reproduction or redistribution is strictly prohibited. All rights reserved.

class size, family involvement and support, family socioeconomic status, and teacher qualifications, 44 percent of the impact on student learning is due to teacher qualifications. Surveys find the majority of the public believes professional development funding should be increased to keep teacher knowledge and skills current. A Gallup Poll in 2000 found that more than half of the public felt assuring every classroom had a competent, qualified teacher was the most promising strategy to improve student achievement.

State education department research finds only a small proportion (10 percent) of teachers think professional development (PD) programs in general are wastes of time. Among strategies for enhancing teacher quality, superintendents and school leaders surveyed found providing more PD opportunities for teachers to be more effective than raising teacher salaries, requiring high school teachers to major in the subjects they will teach, or decreasing class sizes. Teachers surveyed responded that improving student achievement was the leading reason for professional teacher growth, ahead of improving their teaching skills, advancing their professional careers, or networking with other professionals. In one survey, 82 percent of teachers responding believed that scheduling weekly collaborations with other teachers made their classroom instruction better. School leaders surveyed believed that creating a supportive environment for teaching and learning was their most important role, more than supporting parental involvement in student education, maintaining school safety and discipline, or managing school budget and securing more funds. School leaders believed that giving new teachers mentoring and ongoing support was a more effective strategy for attracting and retaining teachers than financial incentives, career growth opportunities, or involving them in policymaking.

Personal professional development activities

School leaders can attend professional conferences, workshops, and institutes. New school leaders can request coaching or mentoring from more experienced leaders. Those with some experience can mentor others, peer coach, and conduct peer observation and analysis. Collecting and analyzing student data is professional development (PD) for school leaders, as is conducting action research. Leaders can attend cross-grade-level meetings and grade-level meetings. Developing curriculum adds to PD. Lesson studies and independent studies are also avenues. Leaders can join professional organizations and networks, invite colleagues to observe them and then give debriefings, and view or listen to video and audio presentations. Keeping reflective journals contributes to PD. Leaders can present mini-workshops to their colleagues, and present at conferences. They may participate in research studies, book discussion groups, research studies, and online PD activities. They can serve on school improvement teams, and on school-level or district-level staff development committees. They may collaborate with teachers in lesson-planning. Reading professional books and journals, reviewing literature for best practices, shadowing, university courses, summer retreats, visiting schools with model programs, and writing professional articles are additional PD avenues.

Supporting ongoing professional development

Experienced, successful school leaders advise colleagues to create opportunities and for they and their teachers to participate in continuing professional development (PD). They say educational improvement and positive change are only maintained by building educator capacities via PD that is ongoing, focused, and high in quality. They can seek out schools that have implemented successful PD programs, and then they and their staff members can visit

Copyright © Mometrix Media. You have been licensed one copy of this document for personal use only. Any other reproduction or redistribution is strictly prohibited. All rights reserved.

these schools to observe, learn from, and share what they learn with other faculty members. School leaders and teachers can volunteer to visit schools as members of accreditation teams. They can write grant proposals to offer funding for PD programs. They could attend trainings, like the National Association of Secondary School Principals' (NASSP) *Breaking Ranks*, with administrator and leadership team members. They can send school administrators to state-run data workshops. To start and/or continue funding for school improvement, personalization, community forms, and leadership mentors, they can apply to obtain Smaller Learning Communities (SLC) grants. School leaders should assure that their school's PD is worth their effort and time, focuses on staff and school needs, engages teachers in their own training, and enables feedback opportunities.

Primary role of the school leader in professional development

School leaders should function mainly as nurturers, facilitators, and Socratic leaders of the PD process. They can do this by cultivating and maintaining staff professional growth and instructional programs that promote student learning; facilitating, developing, articulating, and implementing a shared school vision; managing the school organization to support an effective learning environment; practicing fairness and integrity with every member of school staff; collaborating with staff members to activate PD resources needed; participating actively in PD activities for school staff; helping the participants in PD activities focus on one major concept or "big idea" at a time; functioning as primary mentor for teachers; regularly visiting classrooms; and serving as facilitators to support teachers. For example, school leaders should lead school planning committees by facilitating their decisions about which PD activities to offer, while teacher leaders should facilitate the actual activities. Nonetheless, school leaders must participate actively and be role models in PD: research finds school leader PD participation determines effective school PD participation and its ensuing classroom impact.

Choosing a professional development model to implement

In considering the following PD models, school leaders and PD planning teams must consider the following aspects of each mode: in the training model, they must consider logistics, for example, whether to conduct workshops, large-group classes; whether to include role-play; whether to build follow-up sessions into the training, etc. In the observation and assessment model, they will need to decide who will do it, how, and when. In the process development and improvement model, they will need to consider such components as collaborative work, information review, curriculum review, and the individual and collective acquisition of knowledge. For the study group model, they will want to discuss group sizes, group focus, and which procedures to use for sharing. For the inquiry and action model, they should apply the philosophy of teacher as researcher. For the individually guided activities model, they will need to plan procedures for making personal PD plans. For the mentoring or coaching model, they will need to decide who will provide coaching and/or mentoring, when, in which skills and activities, and the provisions for collaboration.

Complying legally with federal regulations

In 2014, he U.S. Departments of Education and Justice released a school discipline guidance package with the stated purpose of helping states, districts, and schools create and apply school policies, practices, and strategies that will not only be federally legal, but also

Copyright © Mometrix Media. You have been licensed one copy of this document for personal use only. Any other reproduction or redistribution is strictly prohibited. All rights reserved.

improve school climates. These departments observe that although school violence incidents overall are fewer, many schools still encounter difficulty in establishing safe, positive learning environments. They believe non-discriminatory, fair, and effective responses to behavior issues, as well as welcoming atmospheres, can enhance school safety. They also seek to reduce the significant annual numbers of student expulsions, suspensions and their disproportionate representation of students with disabilities and from minorities. Their guidance package offers resources for establishing positive, safe school climates as necessities for closing achievement gaps and enhancing student academic performance. The U.S. Secretary of Education, Arne Duncan, stated that to keep students in classrooms where they can learn, these resources can help schools create and administer positive disciplinary policies rather than unfair discipline practices.

Federal government recommendation for school disciplinary policies

U.S. Attorney General Eric Holder has stated, "A routine school disciplinary infraction should land a student in the principal's office, not in a police precinct." The Supportive School Discipline Initiative (SSDI) addresses the "school-to-prison pipeline" and discipline policies and practices too often forcing students out of schools and into the justice and correctional systems. Its goals are to replace these with discipline practices keeping students in school while supporting safe, positive, inclusive learning environments. Through the SSDI, the U.S. Departments of Education and Justice (ED and DOJ, respectively) jointly produced a guidance package to support positive school discipline. Holder said, "This... will promote fair and effective disciplinary practices that will make schools safe, supportive and inclusive for all students. By ensuring federal civil rights protections, offering alternatives to exclusionary discipline and providing useful information to school resource officers, we can keep America's young people safe and on the right path" (2014). DOJ collaborated with ED not only because exclusionary school discipline leads to students' justice involvement, but moreover because DOJ enforces Titles IV and VI of the 1964 Civil Rights Act prohibiting discrimination based on race, national origin, or color by schools, law enforcement, and other federally funded agencies.

Presidential proposal to control gun violence

Motivated by recent incidents of gun and weapons violence, many occurring in school settings, and based on policy proposals made by Vice President Joe Biden, President Barack Obama issued a proposal in 2013, saying "now is the time to decrease gun violence," also known as Now is the Time. This proposal asked the U.S. Department of Education (ED) to collect and distribute best practices related to school disciplinary policies. It also charged ED with assisting U.S. school districts in the development and equitable implementation of school discipline policies in accordance with Now is the Time. Through the Supportive School Discipline Initiative (SSDI), ED and the U.S. Department of Justice (DOJ) collaborated to produce a guidance resource package to help schools develop and administer such policies. These departments solicited added input from civil rights advocates, philanthropic partners, and major educational organizations to ensure this resource would support Now is the Time. The guidance package includes a letter on civil rights and discipline explaining non-discriminatory school discipline compliant with federal law, guiding principles for research-based best practices to improve school climate and discipline, a Directory of Federal School Climate and Discipline Resources, and a Compendium of School Discipline Laws and Regulations.

Copyright © Mometrix Media. You have been licensed one copy of this document for personal use only. Any other reproduction or redistribution is strictly prohibited. All rights reserved.

Refocusing to effect school improvement

Consider a school which has been consistently failing to meet state standards over the past several years, while neighboring schools have been steadily evidencing academic advances. Not only is the school leader frustrated, but so are his teachers and support staff. They all believe in their students' ability to succeed academically, and all have been trying new initiatives and programs, as well as working hard, to this end, yet their standardized test results are not reflecting their endeavors. Consider another school which has met all benchmarks for Adequate Yearly Progress (AYP), whose students regularly outperform other students at nearby schools. Yet student achievement levels have not risen in the past few years. Even with their successes, the school leader, faculty and staff are perplexed how to enable further student performance increases. In both examples, comprehensive needs assessment can inform school improvement efforts, enabling personnel to refocus and gain new insights.

Comprehensive needs assessment to refocus on school vision and mission

There are three main steps in comprehensive needs assessment: (1) development of a clear, shared school program vision and mission addressing unique student and community needs; (2) collection and analysis of pertinent data; and (3) interpretation by administrators, teachers, staff, families, and community members of the data for developing data-based school improvement goals that all stakeholders support. A school vision statement is a clear, concise declaration of the school community's shared values. All stakeholders should define what is important to them and where they want the school to be five years hence. A school mission statement is based on the vision, but includes a longer, more detailed description of the vision and how to achieve it. Vision and mission statements provide structures for prioritizing improvements and designing goals and objectives. There are three categories of data to collect: (1) student demographics and achievement, including school-based and/or district-based formative assessments and annual standardized test scores. Student demographics can be derived by disaggregating achievement data by subgroups. (2) Program data cover instruction, intervention programs, professional development, school climate, parent involvement, etc. (3) Perception data are collected by surveying parents, students, and teachers about their views of the school program.

In conducting comprehensive needs assessment, there are several quality indicators that schools may use as categories for data collection, and respective examples of data to collect. (1) Aligned and rigorous curriculum: state standards, grade-level and subject-area curriculum guides, pacing guides, curriculum maps and other planning documents. (2) Effective instruction: teacher certification records, central office hiring procedures, teacher evaluation schedules, student achievement data and student subgroup achievement data, professional development calendars, professional development evaluations, teacher observations, lesson plans, pacing guides, school schedules, classroom activities, after-school programs, extended learning opportunities, pull-out programs, co-teaching, tutoring, and classroom instructional assistants. (3) Use of data from formative student assessments: formative or benchmark assessments, teacher grading records, report card schedules, lesson plans, and long-term instructional plans. (4) A positive school climate that focuses on achievement: orientation programs; counseling department records; transition plans; student, staff, and parent handbooks; written code of conduct; disciplinary referral, suspension, and expulsion logs; activities calendars; awards assemblies, and other non-instructional activities. (5) Effective school leadership: teacher leadership records and

Copyright © Mometrix Media. You have been licensed one copy of this document for personal use only. Any other reproduction or redistribution is strictly prohibited. All rights reserved.

evidence; agenda, committee rosters; surveys; meeting schedules; information-sharing via PTA, newsletters, brochures, emails, phone systems, homework lines, and websites. (6) Family and community engagement: parent meeting and program participation records, sign-in sheets, evaluations; information system; parent communication and guidance counseling office records.

Copyright © Mometrix Media. You have been licensed one copy of this document for personal use only. Any other reproduction or redistribution is strictly prohibited. All rights reserved.

The Education System

Explaining policies to school community members

School leaders need to have enough knowledge and understanding of school and government policies and regulations to administer and/or comply with them. In addition, they need to have the communication skills necessary to explain these policies and regulations to all members of the school community so that they also know about, understand, and can comply with them. For example, experts from the National Association of School Psychologists (NASP) suggest that to strengthen safety in schools, among other actions school leaders should write letters to their students' parents that explain the school's crisis prevention initiatives and safety policies. They additionally suggest that school leaders may want to make statements to other members of the community about these policies and procedures. NASP also recommends that school leaders formally review all of the school's safety policies and procedures, including emergency response procedures and crisis plans, so they can make sure these sufficiently address any issues of school safety that may develop.

Among policies for students, schools typically have policies concerning student behavior, including disruptive behavior, noncompliance with teacher and staff directions, behavior destructive or damaging to school property, assault on other persons, harassment, and bullying. In addition to published information in student handbooks, school leaders must also explain to students, parents, and other community members the behaviors prohibited, and the disciplinary actions included for violation of these prohibitions. Today, schools have also had to adopt policies concerning having guns or weapons on school grounds and resulting disciplinary action, as well as for threatening or inciting others to threaten personal injury or property damage; and for substance use, abuse, possession, sale, purchase, or storage, including tobacco possession or use on school grounds. Schools commonly have policies for student dress; even schools without formal dress codes may stipulate appropriate shoes for safety and health reasons. School policies regarding school visitors and standard building procedures are also common. School leaders are responsible for explaining these to school communities.

School policies are typically published in student handbooks, parent handbooks, etc. However, school leaders must also explain these policies and rules orally to school faculty and staff, students, parents, and other learning community members. Not everybody will read the handbooks, and even among those who do, some may not fully understand all of them or have differing interpretations and/or questions about some. Subjects with school policies that school leaders must explain include possession and use of cell phones and other telecommunications and electronic devices. Their explanations should include definitions of unauthorized use, whether confiscation and/or disciplinary action are responses, and administrative right to search video and audio recording device contents suspected of violating school regulations. They may also explain administrative disclaimers of responsibility for device repair or replacement. Leaders must also explain student records transfer policy, student organizations and clubs, and school homework policy. Student rights and responsibilities, special education procedures, and law enforcement involvement are also often considered policy areas which school leaders must explain, among many others.

Copyright © Mometrix Media. You have been licensed one copy of this document for personal use only. Any other reproduction or redistribution is strictly prohibited. All rights reserved.

Interacting with parents who are upset or angry

When they are confronted by a parent who is upset and/or angry over some issue, some effective school leaders begin by smiling and extending a hand. They report that this conveys a sense to parents that they respect them, and are willing to listen to them and look for a solution to whatever issue they perceive. To help themselves remain calm, school leaders also say that as they are welcoming an upset parent, they remind themselves the parent is not angry or upset with them personally, but with some event, or something in his or her own life. School leaders find that listening attentively accomplishes much toward resolving the majority of problems. Other school leaders observe that parents yelling in the school halls have an extremely negative effect, so they immediately invite them to converse privately in their offices. They find that knowing school leaders empathize and are willing to help nearly always enables angry parents to calm down.

Some school leaders find showing genuine concern for parent feelings to be the most important thing they can do. They report they always ensure the parent hears them say aloud that they understand, and that they will do whatever they can to right the wrongs parents perceive. Other school leaders agree that offering compassion to upset parents is critical. They realize that parents need to vent their emotions and will feel better when allowed to do so. These leaders find it counterproductive to react with defensiveness or anger, as this only turns the interaction into a power struggle wherein parents feel helpless and consequently lash out at them. Leaders point out that even if the parental complaint is something outside of their control, communicating to them that they understand how the parent feels is always a better response. Some leaders find many parents simply want them to listen to everything they need to say. Leader interruption implies disinterest in getting to the bottom of the issue, and/or placing priority on defending themselves, the school, or a teacher.

When parents approach school leaders in irate or agitated states, some school leaders not only listen, but also take notes. They tell parents note-taking records parents' exact concerns. This makes parents realize they are listening, and helps leaders understand issues better. Some leaders even offer parents to read their notes and add anything they find omitted. Other school leaders report eye contact and smiling help when greeting concerned parents. They make clear not only that they will hear parents out, but also that their office rules include adult behavior by adults, and behaving otherwise will instantly end their meeting. These leaders use active listening, restating parent utterances. They treat parents as they would want to be treated. Successful leaders note they ask parents to be advocates for children, but rarely teach them how, so they are advocating however they can. They remember parents often have heard children's incomplete or inaccurate accounts, and seek all information possible before reacting or deciding. Focusing on the student and not the parent, remembering parents react out of concern and love, putting themselves in the parents' shoes, communicating that the child is equally important to them, and never personalizing parental upset all help leaders stay calm.

Adopt-a-school and similar programs

School leaders can reach out on behalf of their schools to community businesses and government officials by inviting them into a formal partnership by adopting their school and becoming partners in school activities. These programs give stakeholders more direct

Copyright © Mometrix Media. You have been licensed one copy of this document for personal use only. Any other reproduction or redistribution is strictly prohibited. All rights reserved.

experiences with schools and greater awareness of their specific needs. Students also benefit from these programs when adults work directly with them, which can enhance their motivation and make their learning more relevant. Numerous advantages can be available to schools through such programs, such as gaining more volunteers; accessing professional speakers about careers; and receiving contributions of equipment and other resources, not to mention gifts of monetary funds. Reciprocally, when school leaders express their appreciation to these community partners, including recognizing the good in all people and things involved and celebrating all of the individual persons involved, the community partners will respond more positively toward the school leaders and their schools.

Inviting community member businesses and individuals to partner with schools

When school leaders invite businesses, individuals, and other community members to partner with their schools, their community partners become more informed about school functions and needs through their direct involvement and participation. They develop a sense of ownership in the school. They also derive satisfaction and pride from personally helping students learn. When school leaders then thank community partners for their efforts and participation, and acknowledge and celebrate everything they have done, these partners will not only appreciate, but may also remember what the school leaders did by reaching out to invite them and how they acknowledged them. Community partners will also remember and value things they have learned from the school and how they helped it through their participation. School leaders must also remember that their school belongs to their community: they should provide community access to school facilities by inviting or organizing special events, town hall meetings, legislative breakfasts, receptions, banquets, etc. This not only benefits the community, it also affords community members better understandings of the school and of what it is doing to make positive differences in students' lives.

Developing stakeholder relationships

One avenue for school leaders to build community relationships can be through conferences with parents, students, and teachers. However, such conferences are often scheduled due to the development of some problem, and the parent, teacher, or student involved is upset. These kinds of meetings often result in negative stakeholder impressions of the school. School administrators, teachers, and counselors can conduct these more efficiently, and resolve them more positively, when they understand what steps to follow. Experts (cf. Elmore, "Effective Parent Conferences", in *Principal Leadership,* February 2008) define the stages of productive conferences. Another avenue for community relationship-building has increasingly involved partnerships with local businesses and citizens, affording expertise, volunteers, and funding for student benefit. This also enables development of a sense of ownership in schools for community members. School leaders need to identify possible obstacles in the forms of attitudes, resources, time, and communication that could prevent community members from engaging, and apply various strategies to address these (cf. Hindman, Brown, and Rogers, "Beyond the School: Getting Community Members Involved," in *Principal Leadership,* April 2005).

In two counties of one state, 13 school districts were involved in a school violence and safety collaborative partnership project. School stakeholders responded with reports about the schools to focus groups, which collected the information. This project resulted in recommendations for more effective communication channels throughout the whole school

Copyright © Mometrix Media. You have been licensed one copy of this document for personal use only. Any other reproduction or redistribution is strictly prohibited. All rights reserved.

community, and strategies for recruiting community support in implementing effective programs for violence prevention and intervention. In another state's rural community, through a partnership formed by a city high school, city chamber of commerce, and county community college, the school career center started a work ethic certification program to help students learn effective communication, dependability, friendliness, and other "soft" skills needed for workplace success. Students earned tuition scholarships at the county community college, one semester for every year they met program requirements, including GPAs of 2.5 or more, community service participation, monthly skill-building lunchtime brown-bag workshop attendance, being on time to classes, and making portfolios of their experiences. Students completing the program for all four high school years earned free tuition for college degree programs.

Replacing a single individual with a team approach for implementing partnerships

Traditionally, school-wide partnership programs have been managed by one individual. However, programs like the National Network of Partnership Schools take a community collaborative approach. This program requires all participating schools to identify or form an action team. These teams include a school administrator; teacher, parent, and community representatives; and other interested stakeholders. They plan and implement school, family, and community partnership activities with the shared purpose of accomplishing significant school goals, realizing multiple advantages over individual management. In another example of school success through collaboration achieved by a school leader, one high school held the bottom-most rank in its city, with the state preparing to take over. Students recalled a chaotic setting rife with fighting; staff members reported feeling demoralized and overwhelmed. A new, first-time school leader implemented shared, collaborative leadership. She led staff in modeling behaviors, working cooperatively, and demonstrating student expectations collectively, "with one voice." Within three to four years, the school was transformed. Now, between classes, faculty and staff converse with students in hallways, students are fully engaged in classes and proud of themselves and the school, parents participate in school activities, and community members partner with the school regularly.

Educational equity

Among research conducted between 2007 and 2011, a study found that schools serving a majority of black students were twice as likely to employ teachers having only one or two years of experience, whereas schools in the same district serving a majority of white students employed half as many teachers with lesser experience and many more experienced teachers. Other research concludes that school leaders must have the capacity and willingness to take action to resolve achievement gaps and practice gaps that have persisted, which marginalize students in underrepresented minority groups. Other investigators have concluded that school leaders indirectly influence educational equity by changing staff members' beliefs about equity, getting training for staff to increase their technical skills, and building and strengthening their schools' partnerships with parents and community members. Another researcher observed that replacing educational models featuring segregation and tracking represented not only a shift in pedagogy and learning, but moreover "a moral act." Another investigator has found that many school leaders apply their leadership values based on a philosophy of "whatever it takes," seeking creative means of building trust, validating, and understanding their increasing numbers of diverse students.

Copyright © Mometrix Media. You have been licensed one copy of this document for personal use only. Any other reproduction or redistribution is strictly prohibited. All rights reserved.

According to researchers, school leaders can influence equitable school practices in the domain of community involvement by (1) recognizing parents' and other community member's expertise. By encouraging teacher acquaintanceship with student home cultures and religions, and assisting teachers with ways to scaffold instruction using cultural knowledge, school leaders can access the valuable social capital of family and community experience. (2) Establishing partnerships with parents in support of learning. School leaders should actively engage parents in home activities that support their children's learning. Additionally, they should explore service learning opportunities in the wider community, and partnering with social service agencies. In the domain of curriculum interpretation, school leaders can improve equity by (1) encouraging staff comfort to discuss diversity issues, social justice, and values; (2) confronting stereotypes and discriminatory language and modeling equity beliefs for staff through daily interactions; (3) clarifying misconceptions regarding equity (e.g., "deficit" theories); and (4) creating school environments that are safe and make all students feel welcome and valued, including establishing support networks for students subjected to harassment for their sexual, gender, or cultural identities.

In the domain of instructional practices, experts recommend that school leaders take steps to influence school equity by (1) enabling faculty to give students necessary support by helping teachers develop culturally relevant lessons; cultivating partnerships among classroom teachers and other staff, giving students needed additional scaffolding; and providing resources like visits to other schools, release time, etc. (2) Giving full curriculum access to all students, e.g., using school resources to compensate for limited home access to technology and cultural activities; (3) acknowledging potential racial or cultural bias in special education identification; and (4) supporting research-based instructional practices addressing achievement gaps. In the assessment and evaluation domain, school leaders should (1) use student data to monitor progress toward reducing achievement gaps. (2) Match testing accommodations to student needs, enhancing fairness and validity. (3) Discourage manipulation of assessment to omit reporting certain student results and artificially inflate scores to fool the accountability system, which impedes resolving achievement gaps. (4) Recognize and celebrate all students' performance gains, including those not meeting state standards. (5) Increase assessment reliability so score changes reflect performance, not test or tester changes. (6) Examine tests with staff for cultural, linguistic, and gender bias; discuss potential impacts on diverse students; and seek alternatives.

Furthering social justice and excellence in education

Some investigators who have empirically studied school leaders (cf. Theoharis, 2007) have found that those who entered the profession through a calling to advocate for equity and excellence in education were able to improve school organization, staff capacities, school culture, school community, and student achievement. Some of their practices accomplishing this included replacing special education and ESL pull-out programs they found discriminatory with heterogeneous group instruction, increasing both access to educational opportunities and their rigor, and insisting on all staff members' greater accountability for all students' achievement. The researcher cited above observed that, when these leaders replaced segregation or tracking models, this constituted not only a shift in teaching and learning, but moreover a moral imperative. These leaders refused to subscribe to a belief that failure by traditionally marginalized students reflected student deficits; they instead

Copyright © Mometrix Media. You have been licensed one copy of this document for personal use only. Any other reproduction or redistribution is strictly prohibited. All rights reserved.

attributed it to basic systemic injustice. They improved staff skills by hiring equitably; empowering staff with more professional freedom; providing continuing, equity-based training; and found non-traditional, multilingual and culturally relevant methods to engage diverse families. They met district, family, community, and staff resistance with proactive strategies including continued commitment, prioritization, more intentional communication, and establishing supportive administrative networks.

As researchers have discovered (cf. Larson, 2008), many education leaders commonly recommend certain practices to develop equity and excellence in schools: school leaders should build shared understandings of reasons for leading. They should be brave in confronting genuine challenges to developing leadership. They should design and maintain "nested" professional development opportunities. School leaders who effectively advocate for equitable, excellent education also advise others to establish collaborative approaches across systems to explore leadership practices from various viewpoints. They recommend furnishing opportunities for colleagues, staff, and other learning community members to develop addressed equity skills. School leaders should model the kind of dialogue that demonstrates courage for comprehending and confronting the power interactions inherent in racist and classist attitudes and practices. These professionals say school leaders must distinguish between their intentions and their actions. They advise studying systemic inequities, i.e., how they are part of the problem; and characteristics of equitable leadership, i.e., the solution to the problem. They recommend that school leaders be open to learning new things about equitable practice, and take risks they have not previously taken.

Lobbying and political activism to effect legislation to benefit education

According to journalistic reporting, legislators rely more and more on lobbyists and the groups they represent to help them determine how to vote on various issues. Legislators typically partner with corporations or organizations that sponsor them for most of the bills they propose. They gain the support they need to push laws through the legislative process from these partnerships. School leaders can contact government officials and lobbyists directly on the behalf of their students, their schools, and education in general. They can also engage in political activism through their memberships in professional organizations. The more school leaders who become members, the more influential these professional organizations can become. The largest organizations of educational administrators have their own registered lobbying staffs. These lobbyists liaison closely with state boards and agencies, meet often with legislators and their staffs, and manage all financial and policy issues that affect education in their states. School leaders can enlist their professional organizations to work within the legislative process to promote their local educational issues.

School leaders can send letters, emails, and faxes, and make phone calls to legislators to communicate with them about educational issues. They should first ensure they know the specific issues or agendas of the legislator they contact. They should then inform the legislator of their reasons for supporting or opposing a bill that legislator is proposing. They should include community lawmakers and leaders on the school mailing lists they use for communicating regularly with parents, parent-teacher associations, etc. They should also send their school newspapers, newsletters, and brochures to legislators. Experts warn school leaders not to complain when they communicate, as it never helps any situation and nobody likes listening to complainers. Instead, they should communicate professionally and clearly. When visiting local legislators, government leaders, and businesses, team

Copyright © Mometrix Media. You have been licensed one copy of this document for personal use only. Any other reproduction or redistribution is strictly prohibited. All rights reserved.

approaches help: school leaders should include administrative colleagues and/or school staff members, but in small groups (two to four people) to avoid overfilling small offices and overwhelming officials. Follow-up thank-you letters, including any promised information, are important after meetings.

Legislators rely on school leaders to be informed about educational issues

In view of term limits, legislators count on their lobbyists and staff members to furnish them with the information they need about legislative bills and current issues. The professions directly involved with school districts and individual schools are those that are most knowledgeable about educational issues. Therefore, politicians who get laws passed need to hear from school leaders about all issues that relate to education. It is not necessary for educators, including school leaders, to be professional lobbyists in order to influence their political leaders. They can advocate and lobby for their schools as individuals; through their professional organizations; and through a range of community contacts like local politicians, community leaders, and local businesses, all of whom can be equally important as the legislators. School leaders first must identify the names of individuals and groups they want to approach via community directories, the Internet, professional organizations, and district offices. These sources can provide information on local civic and district representatives, and community companies and individuals to contact. Then they can participate in grassroots initiatives sponsored by chambers of commerce, legislative action days sponsored by professional organizations, and other opportunities to lobby at federal and state levels.

Partnering with community stakeholders to inform and influence public laws and policies

School leaders have a range of methods for reaching out to their local communities. For example, they can be active members in their local chambers of commerce, community service organizations and clubs, and foundations. They can speak as frequently as possible before each of these groups about their schools and the educational issues that concern them. When special events are held in the community, school leaders can take advantage of these as opportunities to volunteer their student orchestras, bands, choral groups, and student clubs to entertain. Students can often accomplish more to keep their schools publicly visible and garner support for them than other community relations efforts can. School leaders should remember to view common student events like athletic events, plays, musicals, commencement ceremonies, and service projects as additional opportunities to advocate for their schools. Government officials, business people, and other community stakeholders can understand schools better through "adopt-a-school" programs.

Copyright © Mometrix Media. You have been licensed one copy of this document for personal use only. Any other reproduction or redistribution is strictly prohibited. All rights reserved.

Practice Text

Practice Questions

Answer Questions 1 through 3 based on the following description:

A school leader has been hired as the new principal of a public elementary school. State standardized test scores in English Language Arts (ELA) across all fourth-grade classes in this school have steadily declined over the past several years. Scores in reading, listening, and speaking have all declined, and scores in writing started out the lowest and have dropped the most since. The new principal and all fourth-grade teachers are meeting to study samples of student compositions and discuss how to improve writing achievement.

1. The teachers have each brought writing samples from their students to the meeting. The principal should advise them to take which of these steps first toward instructional improvements?
    a. Use the samples to identify students needing remedial instruction.
    b. Perform an analysis of all writing samples, and give scores to each.
    c. Review all of the writing samples and identify and group student needs.
    d. Identify samples for use as benchmark examples next school year.

2. Following the initial meeting, the new principal conducts observations of each fourth-grade teacher's classroom instruction. What should the principal mainly focus on in terms of improving students' state standardized ELA test scores?
    a. Whether teachers are aligning lesson objectives with state grade-level ELA standards
    b. Whether teachers are incorporating instructional strategies for diverse student needs
    c. Whether teachers are implementing their lesson plans as written in classroom activities
    d. Whether teachers are aligning lesson objectives with materials and teaching strategies

3. The principal wants to assist the teachers in identifying the best instructional strategies to augment their students' ELA achievement. Which of the following pairs of data sets would most inform this assistance?
    a. Fourth-grade students' reading levels; fourth-grade ELA instructional schedules
    b. Demographic information on the students; the vision statement for the school
    c. Fourth-grade teachers' years of experience; fourth-grade teachers' educations
    d. Student standardized test data, disaggregated; state grade-level ELA standards

Copyright © Mometrix Media. You have been licensed one copy of this document for personal use only. Any other reproduction or redistribution is strictly prohibited. All rights reserved.

4. A principal wants to develop a new school vision and goals associated with that vision. What applies most about implementing these?

    a. The principal must ensure that the vision and associated goals are all measurable for every student.

    b. The principal must differentiate measurable versus nonmeasurable vision and goals for every student.

    c. The principal must ensure vision and goals, rather than expectations are measurable, for all students.

    d. The principal must develop vision and goals, and school staff must develop an implementation plan.

5. Regarding a school's vision, mission, and related goals, the school leader's responsibility is to ensure these are congruent with which level(s) of education policy?

    a. With only the school and district policies

    b. With the school, district, and state policies

    c. With only federal and state-level policies

    d. With school, local, state, and federal policies

6. A school leader surveys key stakeholders regarding the school vision and goals to learn what they believe about the purposes of education. Which set of stakeholder groups is the leader LEAST likely to survey about this particular topic?

    a. Superintendent, central office administrators

    b. Members of school board, parents of students

    c. Community business owners, business workers

    d. Students, teachers, paraprofessionals at school

7. To gather feedback from key stakeholders about the relationship between their opinions about the significance of education and the school's vision and goals, which of these should a school leader do?

    a. Develop a series of critical questions appropriate to this topic.

    b. Develop a few open-ended questions to stimulate discussions.

    c. Develop a school task force to interview all of the stakeholders.

    d. Develop a series of meetings wherein stakeholders discuss this.

8. To implement the school vision and pursue the school goals, how should a school leader best invite others to share these commitments?

    a. Identify only members of the school staff with common perspectives to ensure cooperation.

    b. Identify members of school and community with common perspectives to attain consensus.

    c. Identify school and community members with diverse perspectives to assure representation.

    d. Identify only members of the school staff with diverse perspectives to implement equitably.

Copyright © Mometrix Media. You have been licensed one copy of this document for personal use only. Any other reproduction or redistribution is strictly prohibited. All rights reserved.

9. What does research show about school leaders distributing leadership responsibilities for implementing a school vision and goals?
   a. The most effective leaders are found to influence student achievement and school efficacy directly.
   b. Today's schools cannot be led by one principal without significant participation by other educators.
   c. The traditional model of single, formal leadership exists because teachers lack a principal's expertise.
   d. Educational programs developed by one principal are easier for principals who follow to maintain.

10. As part of an overall school reform initiative, a principal makes a plan to distribute leadership among educators and other stakeholders for implementing school goals. Which research findings exist to inform this decision?
   a. Distributing leadership improves professional development but nothing else.
   b. Educational reform changes demand efforts requiring a few superior leaders.
   c. The capacity building needed for school improvement limits leader numbers.
   d. School reform initiatives all share implicit distributed leadership in common.

11. Which statement is MOST accurate and complete regarding school leader skills for promoting staff communication and collaboration in problem solving toward school improvement and reform to realize school vision and goals?
   a. School leaders communicate school vision and goals to stakeholders, which suffices.
   b. School leaders evaluate staff leadership abilities and select those with the best skills.
   c. School leaders use consensus building and group-process skills in facilitating reform.
   d. School leaders evaluate staff collaborative skills and select those with the best skills.

12. To assess and monitor progress toward school goals, which type(s) of assessment would be MOST indicated for measuring student analytical and critical thinking and communication skills?
   a. Performance assessments, journals
   b. Standardized tests of achievement
   c. Extended student group projects
   d. Teacher's observations of students

13. Which of the following is the MOST effective strategy for a principal to communicate the school vision to school personnel?
   a. Morning announcements
   b. Sending a daily e-mail to staff
   c. Attending community events
   d. Meetings in one-way format

Copyright © Mometrix Media. You have been licensed one copy of this document for personal use only. Any other reproduction or redistribution is strictly prohibited. All rights reserved.

14. For a school principal to assess the effectiveness of his or her strategies to communicate the school vision, which method would be MOST informative?

a. Separately ask a group of students and a group of parents what the vision is; see if answers align.

b. Separately ask the teachers and a group of parents to state the vision, and compare their answers.

c. Separately ask different members of the school staff to articulate the vision, comparing responses.

d. Separately ask an educational leader, student, teacher, and parent the vision; see if answers align.

15. A principal forms and helps train a school vision oversight team before involving the whole faculty in developing a school vision statement. What best describes the primary purpose of this team?

a. To draft the vision because most school faculties are too big to be productively involved

b. To introduce the concept, engage faculty in writing a vision, and synthesize all their input

c. To represent the school leadership team on a smaller level by delegating some members

d. To represent all school department staff, including those who are not already educational leaders

16. School leadership experts have observed that many available forms of school data can be more significant for informing and guiding the school vision than the kinds of data educators tend to think of automatically. Which choice represents this default assumption that can exclude other valuable data?

a. Standardized achievement, state, local common, AP, and IB test results

b. Data that measure rates of student attendance, absence, and tardiness

c. Rates of attendance, absence, and turnover of grade or department staffs

d. Student extracurricular enrollments and incidents and dispositions in discipline

17. To address inherent barriers like staff fear of the unknown and resistance to change, school principals benefit from knowing common kinds of inner dialogues employees experience around school vision development for listening to and validating their thoughts. What do school personnel typically ask themselves about this change process?

a. Not what is needed for the vision but if they will be able to live with and support it

b. If they believe they and the school can realize the vision rather than if they believe in it

c. Whether they will be able to continue their instructional practices along with why or why not

d. What the vision will expect and how their lives will change more than practice continuity

Copyright © Mometrix Media. You have been licensed one copy of this document for personal use only. Any other reproduction or redistribution is strictly prohibited. All rights reserved.

18. A principal has assembled a school vision oversight team and provided them with a variety of school data for background knowledge. The team is ready to engage school staff in developing a new school vision. Faculty members review the current vision statement, examples of others' vision statements, and school data. The team divides staff into groups with discussion questions; for example, "What kind of school do we aspire to be?" What other question would apply?

    a. "How is our school just the same as any other school?"
    b. "What do we think our vision statement should reflect?"
    c. "What should we keep on doing to realize this vision?"
    d. "What is evidence we are meeting the current vision?"

19. Relative to developing and sustaining a clear school vision and learning goals, which choice correctly describes documented practices of effective school principals?

    a. They protect educators' instructional time via minimizing disruptions.
    b. They set aspirational goals that they do not expect everyone to meet.
    c. They have a clear vision for the school and always focus on one vision.
    d. They ensure continual progress monitoring regardless of school goals.

20. The research literature about school principals' roles in realizing the school vision and goals, and aligning instruction with the vision and goals, affords which of these conclusions?

    a. Principals with more effective schools focus on learning rather than on school improvement.
    b. Principals with high-achieving schools have more confidence in teachers than in themselves.
    c. Principals with effective schools delegate the roles of assuring instructional quality to others.
    d. Principals with high-achieving schools communicate to all stakeholders that learning comes first.

21. To create a culture of high expectations for students, some school leaders and teachers have instituted "no zeroes" grading policies wherein students received progressive interventions and new due dates to achieve at least 70% on assignments instead of 0% the first time. What best reflects student outcomes?

    a. Far fewer students received F grades.
    b. Missed assignments remained equal.
    c. More students received a D grade.
    d. More students received extra help.

22. Research into achievement gaps in suburban schools known for excellence found which of the following about students from racial and ethnic minority groups?

    a. Black and Latino students spent less time on homework and completed homework less.
    b. Researchers attributed differences in grades and homework to motivation and effort.
    c. Asian students had higher grades and finished more homework by spending equal time.
    d. Researchers attributed grade and homework differences to skill and home support gaps.

Copyright © Mometrix Media. You have been licensed one copy of this document for personal use only. Any other reproduction or redistribution is strictly prohibited. All rights reserved.

23. The Tripod Project and other research-based initiatives to close achievement gaps have identified aspects of student engagement. For example, when teachers help them consolidate new learning, students are prepared for the future. Among other aspects, each described here as opposing pairs leading to success or failure, which is incorrect?
    a. Trust and interest versus mistrust and disinterest
    b. Autonomy of students versus control by teachers
    c. Ambition in learning versus. ambivalence toward it
    d. Industry versus disengagement or discouragement

24. Among guidelines for school leaders to embed standards-based professional development (PD) into teachers' jobs, which pair is described accurately?
    a. Effective PD is student centered; teachers are actively involved in learning processes.
    b. Job-embedded and school-based PD is on-site; teachers independently problem solve.
    c. PD is supported and ongoing; teachers must know practical applications, not theories.
    d. PD is part of district-supported systematic reform; it must cover new, unstudied trends.

25. In steps for school leaders to take to develop professional learning communities for identifying instructional practices to augment student learning, the first is that school leaders and faculty endorse the school purpose of high-level learning for every student. Which of the other steps is represented correctly here?
    a. School leaders form staff teams whose members collaborate in accomplishing diverse goals.
    b. School leaders assign teams to develop, not administer, assessments nor design curriculum.
    c. School leaders and staff teams identify both exemplary and struggling teachers and students.
    d. School leaders let staff teams develop coordinated intervention plans but do not participate.

26. The National PTA identifies factors promoting family school involvement as a critical form of stakeholder collaboration. Which factor(s) is/are more the responsibility of school leaders than the collective responsibility of school leaders, faculty, and staff?
    a. Supporting the parenting skills of the parents or guardians of the students
    b. Actively participating in student learning and supporting parents to do this
    c. Engaging students' parents to become partners for school decision making
    d. Community outreach, encouraging family volunteers, and serving on PTAs

27. How can attending district school board meetings most help a school leader who is new to a school and community in both informing the leader and promoting leader willingness to change positions or beliefs about educational issues?
    a. By discovering how diverse the new school district is
    b. By witnessing how school boards accentuate diversity
    c. By seeing how school differences correlate to distance
    d. By realizing how districts are managed just like schools

Copyright © Mometrix Media. You have been licensed one copy of this document for personal use only. Any other reproduction or redistribution is strictly prohibited. All rights reserved.

28. As school leader responsibilities have increased, distributing leadership has become more important. Distributive leadership can have additive or holistic forms. Which of the following is correct about these?

    a. In the additive form, collective work by all leaders adds up to more than the sum of its parts.

    b. In the holistic form, every organizational member is a leader, regardless of his or her interactions.

    c. In the additive form, all organizational leaders must "sink or swim" together, not separately.

    d. In the holistic form, interdependent leadership among organization members is emphasized.

29. Regarding how school leaders involve students appropriately in school improvement teams and processes, which of the following is true?

    a. Planning school-wide forums is always a school leader's job.

    b. Some students have conducted school-wide survey research.

    c. Students have never participated in hiring any school leader.

    d. Students testifying in the state legislatures is against the law.

30. Which of the following things can school leaders do to give teachers a safe environment for expressing their ideas?

    a. Giving critical feedback about unusual ideas they express

    b. Scheduling regular, brief meeting times for original ideas

    c. Taking care not to let teachers undermine their authority

    d. Asking them how "safe" differs for teachers versus students

31. What have researchers found about the roles of school leaders relative to teacher risk taking?

    a. Principals who follow traditional authoritarian approaches receive more respect from teachers.

    b. When principals allow more freedom in curriculum design, teachers miss their leaders' control.

    c. Teachers attribute their success to empowerment by principals who give freedom to take risks.

    d. Researchers find that to meet student needs, school leaders must minimize teacher risk taking.

32. Regarding strategies that principals can use to give teachers effective feedback, which is true?

    a. Principals will make feedback fresher for teachers by delivering it unexpectedly.

    b. Principals should give feedback unrelated to their expectations or teacher goals.

    c. Principals enable perspective by delaying feedback after classroom observation.

    d. Principals convey criticism best following strengths and by requesting solutions.

33. Educational research into collaborative data analysis has identified four areas. Which of these areas involves the process of exploring learning standards, goals, and definitions?

    a. Calibration

    b. Student data focus

    c. Educator engagement

    d. Supportive technology

Copyright © Mometrix Media. You have been licensed one copy of this document for personal use only. Any other reproduction or redistribution is strictly prohibited. All rights reserved.

34. Among standards informing effective professional development (PD) for teachers, which is/are most characteristic of strong school leaders?
    a. Valuing ongoing learning, promoting continuous improvement, and inquiry, collaboration, and problem-solving
    b. Realizing good PD's value, promoting teacher participation, and communicating PD benefits to stakeholders
    c. Human, financial, and temporal contributions; allocation coordination; and investment return assessments
    d. Rigorous analysis of varied, disaggregated student data for proficiency standards, learning gaps, and results

35. Which of these is NOT one of the purposes of rigorous and relevant curriculum design?
    a. To challenge educator views on how students learn
    b. To incorporate the instructional skills of the teacher
    c. To impose a structure on existing instructional goals
    d. To incorporate new and different instructional goals

36. Among tenets of the philosophy of differentiating instruction that are compatible with standards-based instruction, which is described correctly here?
    a. The Zone of Proximal Development enables optimal learning.
    b. Designed learning opportunities are superior to natural ones.
    c. Activating prior knowledge enhances relevance, not learning.
    d. Sense of community aids social, not academic, development.

37. A high school teacher's Algebra II class includes some students learning independently, some progressing as fast as she could teach them, and some lacking prerequisite skills for the course. The teacher's dual goal is to help every student acquire a solid grasp of mathematics and also pass the standards exam. Which of the following practices help her achieve this?
    a. Letting students discover curriculum skills to master instead of telling them
    b. Devoting most small-group instruction time to students needing more help
    c. Dividing classroom time among varied instructional groupings and activities
    d. Focusing on introducing new concepts rather than prior student knowledge

38. Regarding data collection, recording, and submission for monitoring student progress and relating it to state assessments, which school leader responsibility to help faculty is MOST accurately described?
    a. Deciding how often, and to whom, teachers submit data
    b. Ensuring teachers collect data periodically, for example, quarterly
    c. Having faculty aid one another with data-recording forms
    d. Applying state-assigned rubrics to assessment for faculty

39. How must school leaders help faculty and other staff with curriculum and instruction to identify and meet student needs?
    a. They oversee but do not participate in designing curriculum and instruction.
    b. They review programs regularly to determine correct implementation only.
    c. They help faculty and staff meet unmet needs rather than implement plans.
    d. They help faculty and staff identify content and practices to address needs.

Copyright © Mometrix Media. You have been licensed one copy of this document for personal use only. Any other reproduction or redistribution is strictly prohibited. All rights reserved.

40. When school principals collaborate with others in making curriculum decisions, who else should be involved?
    a. Curriculum specialists and professional personnel
    b. Curriculum specialists, professionals, and board members
    c. The students and the school's professional personnel
    d. School professionals and members of the board of education

41. What best describes knowledge of instructional practices that school leaders must have?
    a. Helping teachers learn new methods but not predicting how long it will take
    b. Knowing the time effective planning takes regardless of the number of students
    c. Implementing new approaches, more importantly than networking teachers
    d. Knowing the time effective planning takes according to the levels of content

42. Which of the following applies to both horizontal and vertical curriculum alignment?
    a. Teaching the same content across all classrooms on the same grade levels
    b. Teaching content aligned with state or district assessments and standards
    c. Teaching to minimize achievement gaps through standardizing education
    d. Teaching across successive grade levels including preparatory scaffolding

43. School leaders should regularly review and analyze teachers' learning objectives, assessments, progress, and achievement data collection and use their analyses to determine which of the following?
    a. How well these elements align with one another within and across grade levels and curriculum
    b. How well these elements align with state or national standards rather than with one another
    c. How well these elements align with one another within grade levels rather than across levels
    d. How well these elements align with one another across grade levels instead of the curriculum

44. To assist teachers with integrating technology into instruction, which should school leaders do?
    a. Lead teachers first to encourage student technology use for enhancing research skills
    b. Lead teachers to avoid legal and ethical issues with technology as outside their scope
    c. Lead teachers to encourage student concept comprehension before using technology
    d. Lead teachers to target technology skills and content quality without differentiation

45. School leaders can organize teachers into data inquiry teams to identify and address student academic needs. What accurately describes something school leaders should direct these teams to do?
    a. Develop action plans according to data analyses.
    b. Support the implementation of the action plans.
    c. Analyze data from summative assessments only.
    d. Analyze data by classes, not individual students.

Copyright © Mometrix Media. You have been licensed one copy of this document for personal use only. Any other reproduction or redistribution is strictly prohibited. All rights reserved.

46. What best reflects research findings about factors influencing school achievement gaps?
   a. School curriculum and resources correlate with student achievement more strongly than socioeconomic status (SES).
   b. SES correlates more strongly with achievement than school resources.
   c. Student SES correlates more strongly with student achievement than school curriculum does.
   d. Student achievement correlates more strongly with SES and school resources than curriculum.

47. Which of these is recommended for school leaders to plan classroom visits effectively for giving teachers useful observational feedback?
   a. Completing a checklist during every classroom visit
   b. Giving teachers individual, not collective, feedback
   c. Making walk-throughs to give summative feedback
   d. Using statistics to give individual teacher feedback

48. Experts advise school leaders to create a clear vision for the best use of school-wide student achievement data and to communicate this vision. What else do they recommend for using these data?
   a. School leaders should institute supports to develop a data-driven school culture.
   b. School leaders should instruct faculty, not students, to understand and use data.
   c. School leaders should develop and maintain data systems specific to the school.
   d. School leaders should separate data from the cycle of continuous improvement.

49. School leaders can institute consistent, routine, effective data-based decision making by establishing strong school cultures for data use through forming a school-wide data team. What should this team do?
   a. Hold the staff accountable for data use.
   b. Supervise a school staff's data activities.
   c. Lead school staff by modeling data use.
   d. Provide school staff with expert advice.

50. Among classroom assessment principles that school leaders must know for effective collaboration with teachers, which choice is MOST representative?
   a. A few specific assessment instruments are error free.
   b. Authors and users typically overestimate testing error.
   c. Assessment reliability applies to tests, not test scores.
   d. Good assessment is valid, reliable, ethical, and fair.

51. Among school leader responsibilities for managing daily school facility operations, which is MOST likely to involve district support for hiring expert consultants to address contemporary issues?
   a. Managing the food services in the school
   b. Managing school environmental quality
   c. Managing school transportation services
   d. Managing custodial services in a school

Copyright © Mometrix Media. You have been licensed one copy of this document for personal use only. Any other reproduction or redistribution is strictly prohibited. All rights reserved.

52. Regarding school buildings and grounds maintenance, for which of these are school leaders directly responsible?
    a. Inspection and maintenance procedure development
    b. Allocation of budget for inspection and maintenance
    c. Inspection and maintenance schedules development
    d. Preventive maintenance procedures implementation

53. Leadership is one of the factors identified by research as instrumental in implementing school-wide technology adoption. This includes multiple roles for school leaders. Which set of responsibilities is associated with the role of learning organization leader?
    a. Making change a priority, supporting and encouraging teacher endeavors
    b. Making sure that teachers have what they need to meet goals for change
    c. Setting high learning and collaborative standards as conditions for change
    d. Leading initiatives, resolving problems, and providing learning opportunities for faculty

54. In a school's Acceptable Use Policy (AUP) for classroom Internet technology, which section is MOST likely to cross-reference or even duplicate the general school disciplinary code?
    a. Violations and sanctions
    b. Acceptable uses
    c. Unacceptable uses
    d. Policy statement

55. What is MOST true about how school district personnel and school leaders plan school budgets?
    a. They can predict employee benefits expenses more easily than salaries.
    b. Estimating next year's budget expenses excludes any emergency funds.
    c. Districts issue school budgets for leaders without enrollment numbers.
    d. School budgets omit necessary and costly expenses for transportation.

56. Researchers have identified which essential findings about how school leaders recruit, assign, develop, and retain highly qualified teachers?
    a. Effective schools avoid hiring good teachers from other schools.
    b. Effective schools assign new teachers preferentially to students.
    c. Effective schools improve teachers more but at the same speed.
    d. Effective schools retain superior faculty more than other schools.

57. To develop staff leadership skills that advance the school vision, which activities that school leaders can ask staff members to participate in fall into the category of helping staff increase their skill and knowledge bases?
    a. Serve on school leadership teams, lead faculty study groups, help on school improvement projects, and lead curriculum planning committees.
    b. Help screen and interview job applicants, attend district meetings, work on less familiar projects, and help others work with challenging parents.
    c. Discuss reasons and ways that school leaders handled situations as opportunities to observe and reflect, and journal leader practice observations.
    d. Join and participate in professional organizations, mentor new employees, and present information to other members of the school staff.

Copyright © Mometrix Media. You have been licensed one copy of this document for personal use only. Any other reproduction or redistribution is strictly prohibited. All rights reserved.

58. Related to school safety plans, goals for school leaders include which of these?
    a. Leading school needs assessments, safety plan development, and implementation monitoring
    b. Developing a system to monitor school incidents and crime that others share with stakeholders
    c. Appointing personnel to design safe traffic patterns inside and outside the school environment
    d. Adopting emergency evacuation procedures and delegating crisis management procedure choices

59. Developing a school safety plan requires the participation of which of the following and for which reason?
    a. School leaders and staff, because only they know their school and students best
    b. School personnel only, because schools are for controlling as well as for learning
    c. The entire community, because school crime data reflect community crime data
    d. Law enforcement and mental health professionals, because they address crimes

60. Among challenges that school leaders face in their efforts to promote student mental health, which of the following descriptions most represents the category of limited resources?
    a. Accountability law has shifted school counselors' duties from mental health to academic achievement.
    b. Prevention and promotion can address most student issues, yet costly treatments are routinely prescribed.
    c. The mental health resources available to public schools are not provided proportionately or equitably.
    d. Owing to our society's cultural traditions, the priority of mental health issues in schools is marginalized.

61. Which category of mental health obstacles to student learning and achievement includes the LEAST proportion of factors that can arise in and be addressed in schools?
    a. External stressors
    b. Educational problems
    c. Psychosocial problems
    d. Psychological disorders

62. The National Association of Secondary School Principals (NASSP) recommends that school leaders furnish comprehensive staff development in supporting student mental health. Which area of recommended training is most related to the Response to Intervention (RtI) model?
    a. Early identification of students having or at risk of mental disorders
    b. The use of referral mechanisms for school and community services
    c. Strategies to apply in promoting school-wide positive environments
    d. Models for consultation, coordination, and collaboration in schools

Copyright © Mometrix Media. You have been licensed one copy of this document for personal use only. Any other reproduction or redistribution is strictly prohibited. All rights reserved.

63. Among responsibilities of the school leader related to the school emergency plan are to conduct emergency response drills, evaluate staff responses, and revise the plan based on the results. These activities apply to which phase of emergency management?
a. Preparedness
b. Prevention
c. Response
d. Recovery

64. The U.S. Department of Homeland Security has adopted the National Incident Management System (NIMS) for all federal, state, and local government agencies in emergency response. This system includes the Incident Command System (ICS). School district and building emergency response teams are organized based on ICS management functions. Which of these functions develops incident response objectives?
a. Planning
b. Logistics
c. Command
d. Operations

65. What is true about school leader responsibilities for documentation related to school safety?
a. They must communicate rather than document implementation monitoring feedback.
b. They must document their observations from monitoring safety plan implementation.
c. They must document school safety incidents but not related feedback to stakeholders.
d. They must not allow others to document the safety management procedures they adopt.

66. Regarding school collaboration with key stakeholders to eliminate barriers to learning, which of the following is a valid reason for such collaboration related to mental health services?
a. Most school-age children in the United States have several options for mental health services.
b. Services like clinical psychiatric care are unfeasible and inappropriate in the schools.
c. Students and parents are more comfortable with familiar school settings and staffs.
d. Research studies find students are less likely to seek counseling services in schools.

67. Which statement is true with respect to segregated educational services for individual student needs and integrated comprehensive educational services?
a. Students benefit more from specific educator expertise through segregated than integrated services.
b. A principle of service integration is student centeredness, that is, targeting the student as a failure source.
c. Educators should design their curriculum and instruction beginning with appropriate differentiation.
d. Educators should develop curriculum for average students and then adapt it for individual students.

Copyright © Mometrix Media. You have been licensed one copy of this document for personal use only. Any other reproduction or redistribution is strictly prohibited. All rights reserved.

68. Regarding family involvement in educational decision making for their children, which of these statements is LEAST accurate?

　　a. Families are important to collaboration as their children's primary advocates.

　　b. Families are inspired to participate by the minority of families who volunteer.

　　c. Families can advocate for other families as aspects of school-based dialogues.

　　d. Families can provide service and support in developing learning communities.

69. Some successful school leaders have obtained public and financial support for their schools by communicating with community members. Which example of this is most applicable?

　　a. Sharing real estate data with the business community is unrelated to school success.

　　b. Local families are drawn to schools more by physical changes than better test scores.

　　c. Significant improvements for minority students are best shared within the first year.

　　d. Leaders should share substantial, overall school academic gains with families yearly.

70. School leaders and schools realize benefits from engaging community partners. Which of the following such benefits contribute(s) MOST to successful student interactions in the wider world beyond their immediate community?

　　a. Greater social capital through relationships

　　b. Access to needed health and social services

　　c. Safe opportunities to experiment and lead

　　d. Adult guidance and positive role modeling

71. School leaders are finding that communicating with the media helps them engage the public in education. Researchers find this public engagement reinforces community pride. What else do they find it does?

　　a. It has no effects upon local safety or security.

　　b. It increases public criticism of school reforms.

　　c. It helps the schools rather than communities.

　　d. It increases service to the school and community.

Copyright © Mometrix Media. You have been licensed one copy of this document for personal use only. Any other reproduction or redistribution is strictly prohibited. All rights reserved.

72. A constructivist model for evaluating educational programs incorporates multiple stakeholder perspectives. Which of the following correctly sequences the steps for school leaders and others to follow in this approach?

    a. Discover stakeholder concerns, issues, and assertions; furnish a method and context for collecting and analyzing stakeholder feedback; identify stakeholders; establish a forum enabling negotiation; gather and disseminate information for negotiating; use an agenda for negotiations; reach consensus within and among stakeholder groups; review any unresolved matters; and make and deliver a report to stakeholders.

    b. Identify stakeholders; discover stakeholder concerns, issues, and assertions; furnish a method and context for collecting and analyzing stakeholder feedback; reach consensus within and among stakeholder groups; use an agenda for negotiations; gather and disseminate information for negotiating; establish a forum enabling negotiation; make and deliver a report to stakeholders; and review any unresolved matters.

    c. Establish a forum enabling negotiation; gather and disseminate information for negotiating; use an agenda for negotiations; reach consensus within and among stakeholder groups; discover stakeholder concerns, issues, and assertions; identify stakeholders; review any unresolved matters; make and deliver a report to stakeholders; and furnish a method and context for collecting and analyzing stakeholder feedback.

    d. Furnish a method and context for collecting and analyzing stakeholder feedback; identify stakeholders; establish a forum enabling negotiation; discover stakeholder concerns, issues, and assertions; gather and disseminate information for negotiating; reach consensus within and among stakeholder groups; review any unresolved matters; make and deliver a report to stakeholders; and use an agenda for negotiations.

73. Measures of the effects of school community engagement strategies include changes in the behaviors and attitudes of parents, families, community members, and students. What represents some of these impacts on students?

    a. Greater school achievement and fewer school behavior problems

    b. Greater school attendance in spite of the same school enrollment

    c. Greater school enrollment but not necessarily school achievement

    d. Greater school achievement, although not necessarily satisfaction

74. When school leaders have engaged communities and families in school reform initiatives, what have they found about the responses of parents, families, and community members?

    a. Parents attended more school events and meetings than school trainings.

    b. School-to-family outreach would not engender family-to-school outreach.

    c. More parents became advocates and organizers for school improvement.

    d. Community members served on school councils more than parents would.

75. School leaders need to access multiple information sources to understand and address diverse student and community dynamics. As one type of source, their state education departments can share leadership and accountability and support school leaders. Which example of this helps school leaders in their jobs by facilitating their analyses of school strengths, needs, progress, and trends?

    a. Establishing online networks and electronic LISTSERVs for them

    b. Strengthening resources and refining data collection methods

    c. Organizing conferences designed especially for school leaders

    d. Initiating mentoring and coaching programs for school leaders

Copyright © Mometrix Media. You have been licensed one copy of this document for personal use only. Any other reproduction or redistribution is strictly prohibited. All rights reserved.

76. To engage diverse family and community members, school leaders and staff must make efforts to bridge gaps in language, culture, literacy, education, and so on. Which strategy MOST addresses cultural differences?
    a. Having multilingual staff interpret at meetings, trainings, school events, and home visits
    b. Suggesting parents ask children about assignments rather than help with homework
    c. Assigning parent and community rooms for teacher and other parent meetings and information
    d. Hiring community liaisons to help staff understand parental beliefs about education

77. Which choice best describes one of the benefits of collaborations among schools, community agencies, resources, organizations, universities, and businesses?
    a. They can coordinate among discrete visions and missions.
    b. They can share some resources but cannot pool funding.
    c. They can offer multiple services within the school setting.
    d. They can share little information because of privacy laws.

78. In seeking community support and additional resources, how do effective school leaders communicate with prospective partners?
    a. Define how school leaders' needs and stakeholders' wants can coincide.
    b. Speak reactive language when communicating with business executives.
    c. Identify business or organization visions exactly matching school visions.
    d. To motivate them, explain to partner prospects how schools will benefit.

79. To communicate information to prospective community partners about resources they have and those they need, which approach that school leaders have found effective for motivating community leader engagement is MOST based on evoking intellectually and emotionally meaningful connections?
    a. Simply asking prospective partners to listen to what they say
    b. Asking how education experiences shaped who they are now
    c. Sharing the story of their school with the community leaders
    d. Clearly identifying their school's assets and its greatest needs

80. The Institute for Educational Leadership defines some fundamental "rules of engagement" for developing and maintaining school-community partnerships using this mnemonic: "Find out, Reach out, Spell out, Work out," and "Build out." For example, "Find out" refers to discovering each other's needs and interests. Which of the others refers to sharing success and supporting greater endeavors?
    a. "Build out"
    b. "Spell out"
    c. "Work out"
    d. "Reach out"

Copyright © Mometrix Media. You have been licensed one copy of this document for personal use only. Any other reproduction or redistribution is strictly prohibited. All rights reserved.

81. The National Association of Secondary School Principals (NASSP) recommendations for ethical behaviors by school leaders include the following:

    I.   Fulfilling their professional duties honestly and with integrity
    II.   Obeying all the federal, state, and local laws and regulations
    III.   Basing all decisions on the value of student success and well-being
    IV.   Acting to change laws, policies and regulations against education goals
    V.   Implementing the local board of education regulations and policies

Which combination of these could MOST present a conflict for a school leader in some instances?
    a. I and III
    b. II and IV
    c. II, IV, and V
    d. III, IV, and V

82. The American Association of School Administrators (AASA) Code of Ethics and the National Association of Secondary School Principals (NASSP) recommendations for a code of ethical conduct for school leaders share many items in common. Which of the following standards does the AASA include that the NASSP recommendations do not?
    a. Not using positions for personal gain through political, economic, social, religious, or other influences
    b. Only accepting academic degrees or professional certifications from institutions that are accredited
    c. Sustaining standards and improving the profession's efficacy with research and professional development
    d. Accepting responsibility and accountability for their actions and committing to serve others over self

83. Under the National Education Association (NEA) Code of Ethics, Principle I, Commitment to the Student, educators are enjoined against doing a number of things, including that they: "[s]hall not disclose information about students obtained in the course of professional service unless disclosure serves a compelling professional purpose or is required by law." This reflects which of the following federal laws?
    a. The Civil Rights Act of 1964
    b. The Family Educational Rights and Privacy Act (FERPA) and/or the Individuals with Disabilities Act (IDEA)
    c. Americans with Disabilities Act (ADA) Amendments Act Title II
    d. Rehabilitation Act Section 504

84. On which of the following do the Individuals with Disabilities Education Act and the Family Education Rights and Privacy Act differ with respect to student records?
    a. Requiring instruction and training of educators on records confidentiality
    b. Defining which student records are considered to be educational records
    c. Determining conditions for destroying educational records via state laws
    d. Regulating records collection, maintenance, confidentiality, or disclosure

Copyright © Mometrix Media. You have been licensed one copy of this document for personal use only. Any other reproduction or redistribution is strictly prohibited. All rights reserved.

85. What is the MOST accurate description among ways that effective school leaders openly share data with students and staff?
	a. Involving identified students for developing data systems
	b. Involving designated staff in developing assessment plans
	c. Involving students in knowing and tracking their own data
	d. Involving overall school data as the basis for student goals

86. How can school leaders best promote openness and collaborative decisions in ethical school leadership and make ethical conversation integral to their school culture?
	a. They can analyze the ethical implications of any decision for the school community.
	b. They can maintain constancy in their ethical frameworks throughout their careers.
	c. They can accept needed funding even if the donors require less effective methods.
	d. They can regularly initiate discussions for self-examination and ethics development.

87. The Council of Chief State School Officers (CCSSO) has set national Educational Leadership Policy Standards for school leaders to guide school communities in respecting individual worth and dignity. Which of the following is NOT specifically included among these standards?
	a. Promoting staff professional growth
	b. Students monitoring their own data
	c. Assuring efficient school operations
	d. Responding to community diversity

88. Research into school leader perceptions and attitudes regarding inclusive education of students with disabilities has found which of the following?
	a. The majority of school leaders who were surveyed had positive attitudes toward inclusion.
	b. School leaders who were exposed more to special education ideas had negative attitudes.
	c. School leaders having positive experiences with disabilities made less restrictive placements.
	d. Different categories of disability had no influence on school leaders' placement decisions.

89. Which of these can school leaders appropriately do to prevent or eliminate racism and ensure cultural equality in their schools?
	a. They can change school board policies and also the school board's member composition.
	b. They should train their faculty in mediation and conflict resolution skills to settle disputes.
	c. They cannot do anything about minority student overrepresentation in special education.
	d. They can make official policies not tolerating racism that suffice without consequences.

Copyright © Mometrix Media. You have been licensed one copy of this document for personal use only. Any other reproduction or redistribution is strictly prohibited. All rights reserved.

90. How can a school leader evaluate and improve the school curriculum for cultural and racial equity?
    a. Instruct teachers to view curriculum as pluralistic and unchanging.
    b. Include multicultural education within the school curriculum goals.
    c. Assure books include diversity but not look for prejudiced content.
    d. Focus multicultural education on foods, festivals, and fun activities.

91. Which statement is MOST accurate concerning how school leaders can ensure that faculty instructional practices treat minority students equitably?
    a. Leaders can best get teachers to model appreciation of diversity for students by talking about it.
    b. If teaching practices conflict with student cultures, leaders instruct teachers to be aware of this.
    c. Having all teachers know a few words or phrases in each student's L1 is simply token lip service.
    d. Leaders should make sure that all staff members learn to pronounce students' names correctly.

92. What has research by state education departments found about public perceptions of school leaders' roles?
    a. The public believes school leaders most improve schools by requiring standardized tests for promotion.
    b. The public believes school leaders most improve schools by recruiting and retaining superior teachers.
    c. The public believes school leaders most improve schools by applying strategies to decrease class sizes.
    d. The public believes school leaders most improve schools by getting more local control from the states.

93. Studies have found that student achievement is increased most by school investments in which of the following?
    a. Expanding teacher education
    b. Expanding teacher experience
    c. Increasing the teacher salaries
    d. Decreasing the sizes of classes

94. In isolating factors that affect student learning, researchers have found which of these has the most impact?
    a. Family involvement and support
    b. Family socioeconomic status
    c. Qualifications of teachers
    d. The sizes of classes

95. Researchers for state education departments report that school leaders they surveyed found which of the following to be their most important role?
    a. Creating a supportive environment for teaching and learning
    b. Supporting parent involvement in the education of students
    c. Managing the school budget and procuring additional funds
    d. Ensuring and maintaining safety and discipline in the school

Copyright © Mometrix Media. You have been licensed one copy of this document for personal use only. Any other reproduction or redistribution is strictly prohibited. All rights reserved.

96. What do experts recommend to school leaders for explaining policies to the school community?
- a. Knowing and understanding policies are more important than communication skills.
- b. Good communication skills take precedence over policy knowledge and understandings.
- c. Making speeches to explain policies to parents is better than writing letters to them.
- d. With safety policies and procedures, school leaders should conduct a formal review.

97. School leaders may be confronted by angry parents complaining about something that is outside of a leader's control. In the experiences of successful school leaders, which of the following is most effective?
- a. Communicating that this is outside of their control
- b. Listening and then communicating understanding
- c. Responding to each parental complaint as it occurs
- d. Referring the parent to somebody who has control

98. Which of the following MOST accurately represents expert recommendations for school leaders to promote educational equity by influencing curriculum interpretation?
- a. Allowing harassed students to establish support networks
- b. Communicating with staff periodically about equity beliefs
- c. Clarifying misconceptions about equity, like deficit theories
- d. Talking about diversity issues regardless of staff discomfort

99. Regarding school leader involvement in lobbying to influence legislation that affects education, which of these is true?
- a. School leaders must inform lawmakers regarding educational issues.
- b. School leaders cannot lobby for their schools on any individual basis.
- c. School leaders can only lobby through a professional organization.
- d. School leaders must be professional lobbyists to influence legislators.

100. Researchers have identified which of the following practices that successful education leaders recommend to advocate for educational excellence and equity?
- a. They develop equity skills that spread through the learning community.
- b. They study system inequities to discover solutions to the problems.
- c. They study equitable leadership to discover their parts in the problems.
- d. They advise others to develop collaborative approaches across systems.

Copyright © Mometrix Media. You have been licensed one copy of this document for personal use only. Any other reproduction or redistribution is strictly prohibited. All rights reserved.

Constructed Response

1. You are the principal of a school that historically was majority White, non-Hispanic/Latino, non-bilingual. Over the last ten years, the geographical area and your school in particular has experienced a profound change in its demographic makeup. This school year 75% of the student body is Hispanic/Latino, and 25% is White (non-Hispanic), with a large number of English Language Learners/Bilingual students. The staff of the school is predominately White, not bilingual, and has largely remained unchanged in ethnic makeup from previous year. A significant group of parents have become increasingly upset by what they perceive as a major communication barrier between parents, students, and school teachers/staff. The district Superintendent has asked you to develop a new cultural competency program aimed at solving this problem. In 300-600 words, outline the program you would come up with. Include how the program would be implemented and whom the program would include.

2. You are the principal of a large suburban high school with a diverse student and teacher population. One day you overhear a group of students discussing one of their classmates and her relationship with the chemistry teacher, Mr. Bolyn. The students are debating if their classmate and Mr. Bolyn have had sexual relations yet or not. In 150-300 words, explain how you would address this situation.

3. A group of parents have become increasingly disruptive at basketball games at the high school where you are the principal. There has been swearing, yelling, derogatory comments, etc., from the home bleachers. In 150-300 words, discuss how this situation could escalate, causing serious problems for the school, and outline the steps you would take to prevent this from happening.

4. You are starting your first year as principal at Mendoza High School, which has a diverse student population of about 1,500 students. Over the past several years the pass rate on the state mandated English exam has been declining and is now notably lower than the pass rate in other area high schools. Last school year (prior to your beginning at the school) the English department in conjunction with the faculty audited the school's curriculum and adjusted it to align with the state standards. This year, the superintendent has told you that you will have an additional $12,000 in discretionary funds to support the initiative to increase the pass rate of the English exam. In 300-600 words, outline two important issues you should consider when preparing recommendations for the discretionary budget, explain one strategy you can use to determine budget allocations to recommend that will promote improved student performance, and explain why the strategy you have described will likely be effective.

5. You are the principal of a 900-student middle school (6-8). The school recently formulated a school vision, which includes a critical goal of improving the academic and social-emotional preparedness of the school's eighth-graders for the transition to high school. Over the past several years, teachers and administrators in the local high school have become increasingly concerned about the level of preparedness of entering ninth-grade students. The ninth grades have been increasingly socially immature and lacking in vital academic and study skills. Various stakeholders (parents, students, teachers in both schools) attribute the problem to different reasons and would prescribe different remedies.

Copyright © Mometrix Media. You have been licensed one copy of this document for personal use only. Any other reproduction or redistribution is strictly prohibited. All rights reserved.

You form a committee to formulate a plan to improve the readiness of the eighth graders in your school for their transition to high school. Committee members include teachers, parents, student supports (social worker, school psychologist), a special education representative, and a curriculum coordinator.

Write a 150-300 word memo to the members of the committee about the plan to improve eighth grade readiness for high school. Before you write the memo, state what assumptions you make about the school/community (rural/urban, demographics, socioeconomics). In the memo convey why you believe it is important for the school to succeed in this endeavor (improving preparedness for high school), describe 2-3 significant aspects of the school's instructional program that the committee will address in developing its plan. For each of these specific aspects/factors describe a type of data or other information that the team should analyze and explain why this type of information may be useful in analyzing the specific area of concern.

6. You are the principal of an 1800-student urban high school with a primarily African-American and Hispanic/Latino student population. The school has an active student newspaper with a much-beloved journalism teacher. Over the past several months, the student-staff have published several items of dubious origin that have caused controversy in the larger community. These items have typically had topics dealing with race relations. You have spoken to the journalism teacher after each incident about not allowing students to publish this type of questionable content. The newest issue of the student newspaper contains another such item. In 150-300 words, describe what you would do to address the situation.

7. You are the new principal of a 700-student elementary (K-5) school. The previous principal left the school in the midst of some controversy and there has been a significant turnover in teaching staff. In your first couple of weeks on the job, you notice a considerable amount of negativity among staff, in large part fomented by teachers who have been at the school for several years and have had multiple principals. In 300-600 words describe the strategies that you would use to address this negativity and change the culture of the school to a more positive tone and improve teacher and staff morale.

Copyright © Mometrix Media. You have been licensed one copy of this document for personal use only. Any other reproduction or redistribution is strictly prohibited. All rights reserved.

Answers and Explanations

1. C: The principal should help teachers design and deliver instruction that addresses the standards on which the test is based. Identifying individual students with the greatest needs (a) would help them but not writing instruction overall across all fourth-grade classes. Choices (b) and (d) reflect steps in the process of improving instruction, but neither should be the first step. Grouping student needs is most related to declining group test scores, so identifying those needs (c) is the first step to improve instruction.

2. A: Although meeting diverse student needs (b), implementing lesson plans accurately (c), and coordinating learning objectives with instructional materials and strategies (d) are all research-based best practices, only aligning lesson objectives with state grade-level English language arts (ELA) standards (a) directly addresses improving students' scores on state standardized ELA tests, which are based on those standards.

3. D: For making appropriate instructional decisions, the principal must be able to identify data required to inform them. Disaggregated standardized test data will inform identifying areas of student mastery and need, and state standards will inform designing curriculum and identifying instructional content. Knowing these together will inform identifying the best instructional strategies to increase student ELA achievement.

4. B: Although it is better for goals to be measurable, not all of them may be measurable for every student (a); it is more important that the principal identify which are measurable and which are not for every individual student (b). In particular, expectations must be measurable for all students (c) and aligned with the vision and goals. Whether a principal develops a vision, goals, and implementation plan alone or with staff varies, but research finds principal-staff collaboration more effective (d).

5. D: It is the school leader's responsibility to ensure that the individual school's vision, mission, and related goals are compatible with all policies issued not only at the building and school district level (a) and also at the level of the state education department (b) but also at the level of the federal (U.S.) education department (c).

6. C: Community business owners and employees are included among stakeholders in education; however, the school leader is less likely to survey them than those more key to this particular topic, including the superintendent of schools, administrators in the central office (a), members of the local school board, parents of the students (b), the students themselves, the teachers, and the paraprofessionals working at the school (d).

7. A: To gather this kind of feedback, the school leader should develop specific questions that are critical in nature and appropriate to this topic. Open-ended questions will stimulate discussions of many other stakeholder issues and concerns (b). Interviewing them all (c) is impracticable or at best very time inefficient. Discussion meetings (d) are both less focused like (b) and less time effective, like (c).

8. C: The school leader should share the commitment to implementing the school vision and goals not only with school personnel (a), (d), but also with community members (b), (c);

Copyright © Mometrix Media. You have been licensed one copy of this document for personal use only. Any other reproduction or redistribution is strictly prohibited. All rights reserved.

these participants should not all share common perspectives (a), (b) but rather should represent the diversity of backgrounds and viewpoints in the school and community (c).

9. B: Researchers have found that the most effective school leaders have powerful influences over student achievement and school effectiveness; that these influences are indirect (a); that today's schools cannot be led by one principal without other educators' participating significantly (b); that the traditional model of single formal leadership neglects utilizing the valuable expertise of teachers (c); and that it is harder to sustain programs and improvements instituted under one principal after that principal leaves the school (d).

10. D: Researchers report a wide variety of school reform initiatives studied all commonly share one factor: leadership implicitly distributed among multiple individuals at schools. Studies also find that distributing leadership improves not only professional development of teachers (a) but also curriculum, assessment, and the development of professional communities in and among schools, led by teachers. Research finds the prodigious effort needed to make educational reform changes requires many good leaders, not just a few (b); broader-based capacity building requires distributing leadership more broadly, not limiting numbers of leaders (c).

11. C: Federal and state expectations of school principals typically include communicating not only the school vision and goals but also the school's continuing progress toward achieving the school goals to stakeholders (a); evaluating staff leadership abilities and developing and nurturing these (b); using consensus building and group process skills to support school reform efforts (c); and not only evaluating staff collaborative skills but also supporting staff needs in collaborative skills through professional development (d).

12. A: Progress toward different goals often is best assessed or monitored using different types of assessment instruments. For example, performance assessments or journals are more appropriate to assess analytical and critical thinking and communication skills than standardized achievement tests (b), which are more appropriate for monitoring progress in academic competence. Student progress in working more thoughtfully through cooperative learning skills would be more appropriately monitored through extended group projects (c) or teacher observations of students (d).

13. B: Successful school principals report that daily morning public announcements (a) are best for communicating school vision to students. For staff, a brief, succinct daily e-mail is best for combining and connecting administrative details and useful information with school vision (b), also showing that principals value staff time. Attending community events (c) is best for communicating school vision to stakeholders beyond campus. Effective meetings are two-way interactions (d), best for staff affirmation, collaborative opportunities, and internal highlight sharing. Most one-way communications can be handled through e-mails (b).

14. D: It would be most informative for the principal to ask a representative of the greatest variety of types of stakeholders to articulate the school vision to see if their responses are aligned or not. This will show how well he or she has communicated the vision to all involved rather than only comparing student and parent responses (a), only teacher and parent responses (b), or only different school staff members' responses (c).

Copyright © Mometrix Media. You have been licensed one copy of this document for personal use only. Any other reproduction or redistribution is strictly prohibited. All rights reserved.

15. B: Although most school faculties are too big to develop a vision statement as productively and/or effectively as smaller groups, the vision oversight team does not replace or represent faculty: It is imperative to have all faculty's full investment regardless (a). The team's primary purpose is to introduce the vision concept to faculty, engage them in writing a vision, facilitate the process, and synthesize their diverse input (b). The principal may select team members from the school leadership team (c) or other staff representing all school departments, offering leadership opportunities to those not formally educational leaders already (d).

16. A: Experts observe educators often assume "data" simply mean test results. They point out school vision oversight teams and faculty should also review other available data significant for informing school vision, including student attendance, absence, and tardiness data (b); rates of staff attendance, absence—including most frequent days—grade-level and department staff absenteeism, and turnover rates (c); student enrollments in extracurricular activities (clubs, sports, etc.); disciplinary incidents—including referral types, referring departments, teams, and teachers—and dispositions, including detention, in-school suspension, suspension, and expulsion (d).

17. C: Principals can help staff cope with changes by listening to and validating their thoughts through understanding common internal dialogues. These include wondering whether they will be able to live with and support the vision and also what is needed (a); whether they believe in their and the school's ability to realize it and also in the vision itself (b); whether they will be able to continue long-practiced traditions and why or why not (c); and what the vision will expect of them, how their life will change, and whether they will be able to maintain continuity in instructional practices (d).

18. B: To engage them in developing a vision statement, questions the vision oversight team can ask small groups of staff (eight or fewer) to discuss include the following: how their school differs from other schools (a); what they think their vision statement should reflect (b); what they need to do differently to realize the new vision (c); and what evidence they can identify that they are meeting the current vision (d). These topics elicit key values, beliefs, and ideas as the genesis of strong visions.

19. A: Researchers have documented practices of successful school principals relative to developing and sustaining clear school visions and learning goals, including protecting instructional time by scheduling building maintenance and limiting public announcements to minimize disruptions (a); expecting teachers and students to meet the goals they set (b); not only having a clear vision but, when needed, having two visions: one for their school and their own school role and another for their school's change process (c); and ensuring continual progress monitoring related directly to school goals (d).

20. D: Based on the research literature, experts draw these conclusions about school principals' roles in creating and realizing school visions and goals, including aligning instruction with them: Principals who focus on school improvement have more effective schools (a). Principals of high-achieving schools have equal confidence in themselves, their schools, and their teachers to meet school goals (b). To be effective, schools need principals who ensure instructional quality rather than delegating this role to others (c). Principals of high-achieving schools communicate to all stakeholders that the most important mission of the school is learning (d).

Copyright © Mometrix Media. You have been licensed one copy of this document for personal use only. Any other reproduction or redistribution is strictly prohibited. All rights reserved.

21. A: At one school that instituted a "no zeroes" grading policy, outcomes included that 72 percent fewer students received F grades; missed assignments decreased significantly (b); 57 percent fewer students received grades of D (c); and 68 percent fewer students received extra help (d) because they did not need it.

22. D: Research found black and Latino students completed less homework, even though they spent similar amounts of time (a) as white and Asian students. Researchers attributed differences in grades and homework not to student motivation or effort (b) but to gaps in student skills and differences in home supports (d). Asian students had higher grades and finished more homework by spending more time (c) on studying and homework.

23. B: Student trust in the teacher and interest in the class lead to success versus mistrust and disinterest (a). Ambition in learning leads to success versus ambivalence toward learning (c). Industry in pursuing learning goals promotes student success versus disengagement from boredom or discouragement from difficulty (d). However, success is more likely through a balance of student autonomy and teacher control versus too much of either one (b).

24. A: Effective professional development (PD) is student centered, not teacher centered, and requires active teacher involvement in the learning process. Job-embedded, school-based PD can be outside the school if it emerges from and contributes to classroom practices and teachers perceive it as part of their daily work; it requires teachers to collaboratively problem solve (b). PD must be supported and ongoing; teachers must know and understand both underlying theories and their practical applications (c). PD must be part of district-supported, systematic reform, but school leaders should not let it cover new trends or fads that are unstudied, hence unsupported (d).

25. C: For developing professional learning communities (PLCs) and identifying effective instructional practices, experts recommend school leaders form staff teams whose members collaborate in accomplishing commonly shared, not diverse, goals (a); assign teams to develop and administer formative assessments and design curriculum (b); work with teams to identify both exemplary and struggling teachers and students (c); and participate with teams to develop coordinated intervention plans for struggling students (d).

26. D: The National PTA identifies supporting parenting skills (a) as something school staff as well as school leaders should do; actively participating in student learning and supporting parents to do the same (b) as something school leaders, faculty, and staff should do; engaging parents as school decision-making partners (c) as something for school leaders, faculty, and staff to do; and active community resource outreach, encouraging families to volunteer, and serving on PTAs (d) as something officers and teacher representatives to do more than responsibilities of school leaders.

27. A: By attending district school board meetings, a school leader new to a school and community can get a good idea of how diverse the school district and county or city is; witness how school boards unite and organize diverse schools, giving them a common framework (b); see how schools can differ widely whether they are far apart or close together (c); and realize how managing an entire school district differs from managing a single school (d), promoting new insight and respect for school boards.

Copyright © Mometrix Media. You have been licensed one copy of this document for personal use only. Any other reproduction or redistribution is strictly prohibited. All rights reserved.

28. D: The collective work of all leaders adds up to more than the sum of its parts (a) in the holistic form of distributed leadership, which emphasizes interdependent leadership (d). One way of describing interdependence is that all members realize they must "sink or swim" together, not individually (c). The additive form of distributive leadership, everybody is a leader, regardless of whether or how the members interact.

29. B: Ways that school leaders have appropriately involved students in school improvement efforts include allowing students to plan school-wide forums (a), conduct school-wide surveys (b), participate in hiring school leaders (c), and testify before education committees in their state legislatures, which is not illegal (d).

30. B: To create environments wherein teachers feel safe to express their ideas, school leaders should not criticize even unusual ideas (a); schedule regular, brief times during meetings for teachers to express original ideas (b); abandon their fears that teachers will undermine their authority (c) because leadership experts find that the more a leader shares power, the more authority he or she gains; and ask teachers what elements of a safe environment are similar, not different, for teachers in the school as for students in their classrooms (d).

31. C: Educational researchers have found that principals taking traditional authoritarian roles are not respected by teachers (a); teachers resent authoritarian principals' control as manipulative, leading to teacher job dissatisfaction, but appreciate more freedom in curriculum design (b) and other work areas; and teachers attribute their classroom success to empowerment by principals who give them freedom to take appropriate risks (c), which school leaders must encourage to meet student needs (d).

32. D: Teachers are more receptive to principal feedback that is not unexpected (a): principals should tell teachers their expectations and encourage teachers to establish goals before offering feedback related to these (b). As behaviorism has shown, effective feedback is immediate, not delayed (c). Effective feedback strategies include identifying teacher strengths first and then communicating criticisms in the form of requesting solutions (d).

33. A: Calibration is the process of exploring and reaching consensus about learning standards, goals, and definitions at building, system-wide, and district-wide levels. Student data focus (b) yields in-depth information, for example, how well students are meeting specific, time-limited learning objectives. Student profiles assist cross-curricular teams. Summative assessment data aid capacity building, help identify pedagogical strengths and needs and specific remedial student groups, and politically support long-term strategic information plans. Educator engagement (c) alleviates faculty mistrust under external accountability pressures and facilitates systemic, sustainable change. Supportive technology (d) facilitates teacher access to data and shares reciprocal support with data team collaboration.

34. B: Valuing ongoing learning and promoting continuous improvement, inquiry, collaboration, and problem solving (a) are characteristics of vibrant learning communities as professional development (PD) contexts. Realizing the value of good PD, promoting teacher participation, and communicating PD benefits to key stakeholders (b) are characteristics of strong school leaders. Human, financial, and temporal contributions, and assessments of allocation coordination and investment returns (c), are characteristics of sufficient resources and their effective use. Analyzing student data to identify proficiency

Copyright © Mometrix Media. You have been licensed one copy of this document for personal use only. Any other reproduction or redistribution is strictly prohibited. All rights reserved.

standards, learning gaps, and assessment and behavioral results (d) is characteristic of rigorous data analysis by schools and districts.

35. D: Significant purposes of rigorous, relevant curriculum design include challenging educator thinking about ways students learn (a) and how they evaluate these; incorporating teachers' instructional skills (b); and applying a structure to organize existing instruction and assessment goals (c) but not introducing new and/or different instructional goals.

36. A: The philosophy of differentiating instruction is compatible with standards-based instruction required for accountability as long as educators apply principles of effective curriculum and instruction. For example, differentiation principles include these: leading students into Vygotsky's Zone of Proximal Development (where students can do more with assistance than they can alone) optimizes learning (a). So do natural learning opportunities (b). Activating prior student knowledge not only makes new learning relevant to students but also enables them to learn best (c). Sense of community, wherein students feel respected and important, makes learning more effective both socially and academically (d).

37. C: Effective teachers combine standards-based instruction, enabling students to pass accountability exams with differentiated instruction and addressing individual student differences in skills and learning levels, using teaching methods including these: starting every textbook chapter by defining specific skills and concepts for students to master in each curriculum segment (a); allotting comparable small-group times for advanced, struggling, and mixed-level students (b); dividing classroom time among whole-class, small-group, teacher-led, and independent activities (c); and guiding students to connect new material to their prior learning (d).

38. A: School leaders are responsible for deciding how often and to whom teachers submit data; for example, they might want teachers to submit data every 2 to 3 weeks to their team leaders to enable structured data discussions during team meetings. School leaders are responsible to ensure teachers collect data continuously: quarterly (b) is insufficient to adjust instruction, can impede viewing monitoring as essential, and fails to further faculty instruction and assessment goals. School leaders are also responsible for helping faculty choose and develop data-recording forms (c) and ensuring faculty application of state-assigned rubrics to predict student performance on state assessments (d).

39. D: School leaders must collaborate with faculty and other staff to design curriculum and instruction (a); review programs regularly not only to determine correct implementation (b) but also to identify students' unmet educational needs despite implementing programs accurately (c); and in the event of such unmet needs, help faculty and other staff identify content and practices that will address these (d).

40. B: The practice recommended by education authorities is for principals to collaborate with not only curriculum specialists and school professionals (a), for example, faculty, educational specialists, therapists, and so on; not only students and professionals (c); and not only professionals and board of education members (d) but curriculum specialists, professionals, and members of the board of education in making curriculum decisions.

41. D: School leaders must know how to help teachers learn new instructional methods, and how to predict how long it will take for them to learn these (a); how much time effective planning takes, which varies with the number of students to be taught (b); how to network

Copyright © Mometrix Media. You have been licensed one copy of this document for personal use only. Any other reproduction or redistribution is strictly prohibited. All rights reserved.

teachers learning new approaches as the school leaders implement these approaches (c); and how much time effective planning will take, which also varies with the levels at which teachers will instruct students in academic content (d).

42. C: Teaching the same content across all classrooms at the same grade levels (a), and teaching content aligned with state and/or district assessments and standards (b) are characteristics of horizontal curriculum alignment. Teaching content that progresses through grade levels, incorporating scaffolding to prepare students for the next grade (d), is characteristic of vertical alignment. Teaching to minimize achievement gaps through standardizing education (c) is accomplished through both horizontal and vertical curriculum alignment.

43. A: School leaders should use their analyses of these elements of teacher curriculum, instruction, and assessment implementation to determine how well they align with one another, within (c) and across (d) grade levels, across the curriculum (a), and with state and/or national standards (b) as well.

44. C: School leaders should lead teachers to encourage solid student comprehension of concepts first, and only encourage students to use technology for enhancing their research and problem-solving skills after, not before (a), they understand concepts. They should not only lead but require teachers to instruct students in legal and ethical issues with accessing and using technology (b) and clearly differentiate with teachers between learning targets for student technology skills and learning targets for student thinking and content quality (d).

45. B: School leaders who form data inquiry teams of teachers should direct these teams to develop action plans based on their analyses of student assessment data. They should assign the teams to implement these plans; supporting their implementation (b) is the school leader's job. School leaders should direct teams to analyze data from both formative and summative assessments (c) by classes, student subgroups, and individual students (d).

46. A: Research conducted over recent decades finds that although socioeconomic status (SES) correlates strongly with student academic achievement, both available school resources and school curriculum correlate even more strongly with student achievement than SES. Researchers say these findings should motivate school leaders and schools to reduce achievement gaps rather than blame them on family or community SES.

47. D: Experts recommend that school leaders not simply complete a checklist for classroom visits (a) but further student success through improving teacher instructional quality by applying their observations of classroom instructional practices. School leaders should give both individual teachers feedback, through conversations and written communications, and collective teacher feedback (b), through providing statistics (d). They can produce formative feedback through making walk-throughs (c) and both formative and summative feedback through making formal observations.

48. A: Expert recommendations for school leaders in the best use of school-wide student achievement data include instituting supports for developing a data-driven school culture (a); instructing students to understand and use their own data (b) to set learning goals; developing and maintaining data systems on a district-wide basis (c); and incorporating data as an essential component of a cycle of continuous instructional improvement (d).

Copyright © Mometrix Media. You have been licensed one copy of this document for personal use only. Any other reproduction or redistribution is strictly prohibited. All rights reserved.

49. C: School-wide data teams should not hold school staff accountable for using data (a), supervise staff data activities (b), or assume the role of giving expert advice to school staff (d) about using data. Rather they should lead the school staff by example through modeling the effective use of data (c) for improving instruction and meeting school goals.

50. D: To collaborate effectively with teachers regarding assessment, school leaders must know classroom assessment principles, including that no assessment instrument is error free (a)—that is, all assessment involves some error; that authors and users of assessments typically underestimate testing error (b); that reliability, that is, getting consistent results across repeated administrations, applies to test scores and not the tests themselves (c); and that good assessment is not only valid (tests what it means or claims to test) and reliable but also ethical and fair (d).

51. B: In recent decades, environmental quality issues have emerged that affect school facility operations management. These include asbestos, radon, and other hazardous materials control; energy conservation; and improvement of water, indoor air quality, and acoustics, which may involve district support in hiring expert facility consultants. School leaders have government guidelines for food services (a); transportation (c) and custodial (d) services have existed longer than environmental awareness, have school policies and procedures in place, and are less likely to require expert consultation.

52. B: School leaders are directly responsible for allocating budget for school maintenance and inspections. They should assign experienced maintenance supervisors to develop specific inspection and maintenance procedures (a) and schedules (c) and should oversee the implementation of preventive maintenance procedures, which they cannot directly implement by themselves (d).

53. C: Among school principals' roles in leading the implementation of school-wide technology adoption, prioritizing change and supporting and encouraging faculty (a) are responsibilities associated with the role of motivator and cheerleader. Assuring teachers have what they need to meet change goals (b) is associated with the role of resource provider. Establishing conditions for change by setting standards for learning and collaboration (c) is associated with the role of learning organization leader. Leading change initiatives, resolving problems, and providing learning opportunities for faculty (d) are associated with the role of facilitator.

54. A: The National Education Association (NEA) identifies essential components of any school Acceptable Use Policy (AUP), including a preamble and definition section; an acceptable uses section (b), defining appropriate student internet use; an unacceptable uses section (c), defining prohibited uses, behaviors, and Web sites; a policy statement (d) identifying covered services and student use conditions; and a violation and sanctions section (a) informing students how to question policy applications and report violations, which may conform to the general school disciplinary code.

55. D: School district personnel and school leaders can predict employee salaries more easily than benefits (a), particularly health-care benefits, which have been changing recently due to both new federal legislation and health-care provider practices. Estimating the next school year's budget expenses must include reserving funds for unexpected emergencies (b) like unplanned facility repairs. Districts issue school budgets for school

Copyright © Mometrix Media. You have been licensed one copy of this document for personal use only. Any other reproduction or redistribution is strictly prohibited. All rights reserved.

leaders that display revenue allocation figures side by side with enrollment figures (c) for easier reference. Transportation expenses can be among the most necessary and costly yet are not reflected in school budgets (d).

56. D: Researchers have found that more effective schools can fill vacancies by recruiting and hiring more effective teachers from other schools (a); they assign new teachers among students using more equitable methods (b); teachers improve faster after hiring in more effective schools than in less effective schools (c); and more effective schools have greater ability to retain higher-quality teachers than less effective schools do (d).

57. B: These are activities that school leaders can ask staff to participate in to increase their skill and knowledge bases. The (a) activities are ways school leaders can get staff involved in school leadership to develop these skills. The (c) activities are ways school leaders can offer staff opportunities for observation and reflection to develop leadership skills. The (d) activities are ways school leaders can support staff participation in professional development to promote leadership skills.

58. A: Goals for school leaders related to their school safety plans include leading school needs assessments, safety plan development, and implementation monitoring; developing a system to track, report, and give feedback on school incidents and crime and communicating this information to stakeholders (b); designing safe traffic patterns to, from, and within the school rather than appointing others to do this (c); and not only adopting emergency evacuation procedures but also adopting crisis management procedures for the school rather than delegating this (d).

59. C: Developing a school safety plan requires participation by the entire community because schools with the most numerous and severe violence and crime incidents are in communities with the same characteristics. School leaders and staff are not the only ones (a) because addressing community issues reflected in schools requires collaboration among resources contributing varied expertise and because schools are for learning, not controlling (b) violence or crime. Not only law enforcement and mental health personnel (d) but also parents, community leaders, business leaders, and other community professionals serving youth should participate as well as students, teachers, and administrators.

60. A: That No Child Left Behind's stress on accountability has shifted school counselors' responsibilities away from mental health (MH) toward academic performance, reducing professional support services, represents limited resources. That students are routinely diagnosed with serious disorders and prescribed costly treatments, despite the fact that prevention and MH promotion can address most issues (b), represents inadequate research. That MH resources are not proportionate or equitable (c) represents uneven resource distribution. That cultural traditions marginalize school MH priority (d) represents stigmatizing MH issues.

61. D: External stressors (a) can exist in the home, community, and/or school. Educational problems (b) can originate within the individual student (e.g., learning disabilities [LD] and attention deficit hyperactivity disorder [ADHD]), family, community, and/or school. Psychosocial problems (c) can often be prevented or addressed in schools. However, psychological disorders (d) are LEAST likely to be caused or treated in schools, typically requiring psychotherapeutic treatment and often therapy plus medication.

Copyright © Mometrix Media. You have been licensed one copy of this document for personal use only. Any other reproduction or redistribution is strictly prohibited. All rights reserved.

62. C: Whereas the National Association of Secondary School Principals (NASSP) recommends staff training in all these areas, strategies promoting school-wide positive environments are most related to Response to Intervention (RtI). RtI involves instituting school-wide positive learning and behavioral supports with three tiers of progressively more intensive intervention. Whereas the first tier includes universal screening, which relates to early identification (a), all three tiers benefit from school-wide positive supports, including students in Tiers 2 and 3, who receive additional interventions. Referrals (b) are only made for students not responding in Tier 3 and/or responding but needing additional services. Cooperative school models (d) are beneficial irrespective of using or not using RtI.

63. A: Conducting drills prepares school staff for responding in a timely, organized, efficient manner in the event of an actual emergency. Drills do not prevent (b) emergencies but prepare people for them. Though response (c) is prominently featured in the question description as the focus of drills, staff are not actually responding during drills but preparing to respond if or when the need should arise. Recovery (d) follows response; neither occurs without an actual emergency.

64. D: The Incident Command System (ICS) planning (a) function collects and evaluates data, identifies issues, develops action plans, and recommends future actions. The logistics (b) function identifies services and resources needed to support incident response needs. The command (c) function is responsible for overall incident management, public safety, information, and community agency liaisons. The operations (d) function develops objectives, organizes resources, and directs resources and actions to incident response. (The other ICS function is finance.)

65. B: School leaders must not only communicate feedback from monitoring safety plan implementation to school staff and students; they must also document this feedback (a). They must document their observations from monitoring safety plan implementation (b). They must document not only school incidents disrupting safety but also related feedback they give to stakeholders (c). School leaders are responsible for documenting safety management procedures they adopt, but they may designate others to document these (d).

66. B: In many American states and communities, schools are the only, or main, mental health (MH) service providers for children (a). Because services like clinical psychiatric care are unfeasible and inappropriate in schools (b), school and community MH services must be integrated within the care continuum. Students and parents are more comfortable getting MH help with familiar school settings and staff (c). Research studies show students are more likely to seek counseling services in schools (d).

67. C: Researchers have found segregated services more likely to cause isolated skill development and fragmentation, whereas integrated comprehensive services require cross-disciplinary sharing of specific educator expertise, benefiting students (a) and colleagues alike. Although its staff design must be student based, a principle underlying integrated comprehensive services is that the source of student failure is the system, not the student (b). School leaders and other educators integrating services should design curriculum and instruction beginning with differentiation (c) rather than adapt it afterward (d).

68. B: School leaders and other educators should involve families in collaborative educational design as they are their children's primary advocates (a). Families can advocate

Copyright © Mometrix Media. You have been licensed one copy of this document for personal use only. Any other reproduction or redistribution is strictly prohibited. All rights reserved.

for other families within school-based dialogues (c), and they can offer service and support to schools in developing learning communities (d). However, when family participation is limited to an elite minority who volunteer, other families are more likely to feel intimidated against participating than inspired to participate (b).

69. C: Some successful school leaders find sharing real estate data with the business community shows how better schools raise property values and local consumer spending (a). More local families attend schools when leaders share improved student test scores with them (b). Whereas significantly improved test scores for students in minority groups that typically experience achievement gaps are best shared within the first year (c) to encourage and attract minority families, school leaders find it better to share overall school academic gains over several years, when these gains are more substantial (d).

70. A: Community partners can establish relationships that afford students greater social capital, which empowers their successful interactions beyond the community. Community partners also can expedite student and family access to services (b), which meet their physical, mental, and social needs more than contributing to global competency; give students safe contexts for experimentation and leadership (c); and offer adult guidance and positive role models (d), contributing to physical, intellectual, emotional, and social development and academic and nonacademic skills overall more than to specific, real-world, interactional success.

71. D: Researchers find that public engagement in education strengthens local safety and security (a), improves public perceptions of school reform efforts (b), revitalizes communities as well as helping schools (c), and increases the participation of citizens and students in both school service and community service (d).

72. B: Using a constructivist model to incorporate multiple stakeholder perspectives, school leaders first identify who stakeholders are then discover their concerns; supply a method and frame of reference for obtaining and analyzing stakeholders' input; and bring stakeholder groups to consensus. If consensus building hits an impasse, leaders should have an agenda for negotiations; procure and disseminate information for negotiating with disagreeing stakeholders; and establish a forum for negotiations. Once negotiations are concluded, school leaders make and deliver a report to the stakeholders and then review any unresolved stakeholder issues.

73. A: Measures of how school community engagement strategies affect students include their greater academic achievement and fewer school behavior problems (a); increased school attendance and increased school enrollment (b); higher school enrollment and achievement (c); and increased satisfaction along with achievement (d).

74. C: School leaders who have engaged communities and families in school reform initiatives have found that their efforts resulted in more parent attendance not only to school events and meetings but also to school seminars, workshops, and other trainings (a). School leaders' outreach to families also resulted in more family-to-school outreach (b). More parents became advocates and organizers for school improvement (c). And both community members and parents responded by serving on school or advisory councils (d), actively participating in creating school policies, programs, and practices.

Copyright © Mometrix Media. You have been licensed one copy of this document for personal use only. Any other reproduction or redistribution is strictly prohibited. All rights reserved.

75. B: Improving the resources and methods available for collecting data is one way that state education departments can support school leaders in their jobs by facilitating their analyses of school strengths, needs, progress, trends, and so on. Another way state education departments can support school leaders in their jobs is by creating more learning opportunities for them (a), (c), (d).

76. D: Having multilingual staff interpret (a) addresses language differences. Suggesting parents ask children about assignments instead of helping with homework (b) addresses limited parental literacy and/or education by helping parents support children in nonliterate ways. Designating parent or community rooms where parents and other community members can meet with other parents and teachers and access information (c) addresses needs for linguistically, culturally, economically, and educationally diverse stakeholders; those with hectic schedules; and everybody else. Hiring community liaisons to help staff understand diverse parental beliefs about education (d), for example, that educators are authority figures they should never question, addresses cultural differences.

77. C: School-community interagency collaborations enable participants to develop shared visions and missions for education and service (a); pool their resources and funds for common purposes (b); offer multiple services, all within the same school setting (c); and exchange student and family information: although privacy laws like HIPAA, FERPA, parts of IDEA, and so on keep health-care or education agencies from disclosing health or education records, parents can give written informed consent; regardless, collaborators can still exchange much information about students and families without involving official records (d).

78. A: Effective school leaders must clarify what they need, what stakeholders want, and how these can coincide to communicate and determine partnership feasibility. They must adjust language for businesspeople. For example, business executives use more proactive than reactive language (b). School leaders should determine whether their visions and/or missions match other's, but these need not match exactly (c): they can overlap—and school leaders must identify these overlaps. Though a few rare businesspeople are altruistically motivated by school benefits, most must hear what they will get from partnership (d).

79. B: Through experience, school leaders have found that simply asking prospective community partners to listen to what they have to say (a) can often communicate their school's needs. Some have found sharing the story of their school communicated what their schools needed (c). Clearly identifying their school's assets and greatest needs (d) helps school leaders and community partners both define their expectations. Asking community leaders how their own experiences with education influenced who they are now (b) motivates their engagement and assistance by enabling meaningful connections between personal experience and school partnership.

80. A: "Build out" refers to building upon successful initiatives by sharing the results and supporting extended endeavors. "Spell out" (b) refers to defining the purposes and terms of a partnership, including each individual's duties and deadlines. "Work out" (c) refers to addressing problems as they occur and modifying approaches as needed. "Reach out" (d) refers to offering prospective community partners by offering them specific help in their own territories.

Copyright © Mometrix Media. You have been licensed one copy of this document for personal use only. Any other reproduction or redistribution is strictly prohibited. All rights reserved.

81. C: Obeying federal, state, and local laws and regulations (II) and implementing the local board of education's administrative regulations and policies (V) could both conflict with acting to change laws and regulations that are against valid education goals (IV), or vice versa, as obeying and implementing laws, regulations, and policies can be countermanded by acting to change laws, regulations, or policies.

82. D: Choices (a), (b), and (c) are almost identical word for word between the American Association of School Administrators (AASA) Code of Ethics for Educational Leaders and the National Association of Secondary School Principals (NASSP) recommendations for a code of ethical conduct, as are most of their other items. However, the AASA Code of Ethics additionally includes two statements of standards for school leaders to accept responsibility and accountability for their own actions and to commit to serving others above self (d). These are not included in the NASSP recommendations.

83. B: The Civil Rights Act of 1964 (a) protects everyone, including students, against discrimination for multiple reasons. The Americans with Disabilities Act (ADA, 1973) protects individuals against discrimination for disabilities; Title II of the ADA Amendments Act of 2008 (c) protects students with disabilities from discrimination by requiring equal opportunities to benefit from government programs, services, and activities, including education. Section 504 of the Rehabilitation Act of 1973, amended 2003 (d), also protects students with disabilities against discrimination. The 1974 Family Educational Rights and Privacy Act (FERPA) protects student education records privacy; the Individuals with Disabilities Act (IDEA) does this for students with disabilities (b).

84. A: The Individuals with Disabilities Education Act (IDEA) and Family Rights and Privacy Act (FERPA) both define the same document types as educational records (b). FERPA determines conditions for educational records destruction based on state laws (c). IDEA amendments regarding educational records collection, maintenance, confidentiality, disclosure (d), and destruction (c) are based on FERPA. However, the IDEA requires designating special education records custodians to ensure the instruction and training of all educators collecting confidential information, but FERPA does not (a).

85. C: Effective school leaders involve all students in developing systems for collecting, analyzing, applying, incorporating, and sharing data rather than only identifying some students to involve (a); involve all staff members in participating in developing assessment plans rather than designating certain members (b); involve students closely in knowing and monitoring their own data (c); and basing individual student goals on each student's specific data measures, not just on overall school data (d).

86. D: School leaders should not analyze only ethical implications of decisions for the school community (a) but habituate every member to such analysis to guide their approaches. Because total experience and learning contribute to their development, ethical frameworks should grow throughout school leaders' careers, not remain constant (b). Ethical school leaders never accept funding from donors requiring less effective methods (c). By regularly engaging staff and stakeholders in conversations helping them self-examine assumptions and develop ethical understanding (d), school leaders integrate ethical discussion into school culture.

87. B: The Council of Chief State School Officers (CCSSO) standards include developing school cultures and instructional programs promoting student learning and staff

Copyright © Mometrix Media. You have been licensed one copy of this document for personal use only. Any other reproduction or redistribution is strictly prohibited. All rights reserved.

professional growth (a); assuring safe, effective learning environments through efficient management of school resources, organization, and operations (c); and responding to needs and interests of diverse community members (d), among others. However, they do not include having students monitor their own data (b), which is otherwise an exemplary school leader policy but not part of these standards for respecting individual worth and dignity.

88. C: Research from the Council for Exceptional Children has found that of elementary school leaders surveyed, only 20 percent had positive attitudes toward inclusion (a) of students with disabilities. That minority of school leaders with such positive attitudes had more exposure to special education concepts (b) and more positive experiences with students having disabilities, making them more likely to place them into less restrictive settings (c). School leaders also had different experiences and made different placements depending on different student disability categories (d).

89. A: School leaders can change not only school board policies if they find these lacking racial or cultural sensitivity but also board composition to represent the student population. They should train students in mediation and conflict resolutions skills for settling disputes (b). When minority students are overrepresented in special education, they can do something by administering culturally fair tests and revisiting eligibility determinations based on results (c). They should not only make official policies against tolerating racism but also clearly define consequences (d) for racist behaviors.

90. B: To evaluate curriculum for cultural and racial equity and improve it as needed, school leaders can instruct teachers to view curriculum as pluralistic and constantly changing to meet changing student populations and needs (a); include multicultural education in the school's curriculum goals (b); not only make sure books contain diversity but also have teachers examine books for prejudiced or discriminatory content (c); and include multicultural education in books, other media, and learning experiences rather than focus it on only foods, festivals, and fun activities (d).

91. D: The best way to get teachers to model for students is for school leaders to model for teachers rather than only talking about it (a). If teaching practices conflict with student cultural beliefs, values, or practices, leaders must instruct teachers to replace or change these, not simply be aware of the conflict (b). Having all teachers know a few words or phrases in each student's first language (L1) makes classrooms welcoming, psychologically safe learning environments (c). Similarly, leaders should ensure all staff members learn to pronounce students' names correctly (d).

92. B: Research by state education departments finds the public believes school leaders improve schools by recruiting and retaining better teachers more than by requiring standardized tests for grade promotion (a), applying strategies to decrease class sizes (c), or getting state education departments to give local schools more control (d). This shows public perceptions of the importance of the school leader's role in teacher qualification and professional development.

93. A: Studies comparing school investments have found that investing in expanding teacher education (a) increases student achievement more than expanding teacher experience (b), increasing teacher salaries (c), or decreasing class size (d). This is significant considering how many critics have blamed lack of student achievement on new or inexperienced

Copyright © Mometrix Media. You have been licensed one copy of this document for personal use only. Any other reproduction or redistribution is strictly prohibited. All rights reserved.

teachers, inadequate teacher payment, and excessive class sizes more than on lack of teacher professional development.

94. C: Researchers have found that among family involvement and support (a), family socioeconomic status (b), qualifications of teachers (c), and the sizes of classes (d), 44 percent of the impact on student learning is attributed to teacher qualifications. This means that the other 56 percent of the impact is divided among the other three factors; so of these four factors, teacher qualifications have the most impact on student learning.

95. A: School leaders surveyed by state education department researchers believed that creating a supportive environment for teaching and learning was their most important role, superseding their roles of supporting parental involvement in education (b), managing school budgets and obtaining more funds (c), or maintaining school safety and discipline (d).

96. D: School leaders must combine enough knowledge and understanding of policies to follow and administer them (a) with good enough communication skills to explain them to the school community (b). Regarding school safety policies and procedures in particular, experts from the National Association of School Psychologists (NASP) recommend school leaders write letters to parents for their reference. Parents cannot remember or review this information from speeches (c). NASP also recommends school leaders conduct formal reviews of safety policies and procedures (d) to assure they address all potential issues.

97. B: Telling already agitated parents that their complaint is outside the school leader's control (a) will only exacerbate their frustration, as will putting them off by referring them to someone else (d). Answering each parental complaint as it occurs (c) interrupts the parent, who will perceive this as defensiveness and/or disinterest in getting to the root of the problem. Experienced school leaders report many parents simply want them to listen to everything they say; others add that communicating understanding (b), which shows compassion and concern, is critical.

98. C: Experts recommend that school leaders establish support networks for harassed students as part of creating safe, welcoming school environments that make all students feel valued. School leaders have far more knowledge and means for creating such networks than students (a). Rather than talk with staff periodically, experts say school leaders should model equity beliefs for them through daily interactions (b). They should also clarify misconceptions related to equity, like deficit theories (c), and encourage staff to be comfortable discussing diversity issues (d), values, and social justice.

99. A: From their direct involvement with schools and school districts, school leaders are most knowledgeable about educational issues; therefore, lawmakers need to hear from them about these issues to inform the bill they get passed. School leaders can lobby for their schools as individuals (b), or through community contacts (e.g., local businesses, community leaders, and local politicians), or through their professional organizations (c). The largest professional organizations for school administrators have their own registered lobbying staffs. School leaders need not be professional lobbyists (d) to influence legislators.

100. D: Researchers report that to advocate for excellence and equity in education, successful education leaders follow and recommend giving staff, colleagues, and other

Copyright © Mometrix Media. You have been licensed one copy of this document for personal use only. Any other reproduction or redistribution is strictly prohibited. All rights reserved.

learning community members opportunities to develop equity skills. Developing their own equity skills will not automatically spread these through the learning community (a). Successful school leaders study system inequities to discover how they are part of the problems (b) and study equitable leadership characteristics to discover solutions to the problems (c). Additionally, they advise others to develop collaborative approaches across systems (d), enabling exploration of varying perspectives on leadership practices.

Copyright © Mometrix Media. You have been licensed one copy of this document for personal use only. Any other reproduction or redistribution is strictly prohibited. All rights reserved.

Secret Key #1 - Time is Your Greatest Enemy

Pace Yourself

Wear a watch. At the beginning of the test, check the time (or start a chronometer on your watch to count the minutes), and check the time after every few questions to make sure you are "on schedule."

If you are forced to speed up, do it efficiently. Usually one or more answer choices can be eliminated without too much difficulty. Above all, don't panic. Don't speed up and just begin guessing at random choices. By pacing yourself, and continually monitoring your progress against your watch, you will always know exactly how far ahead or behind you are with your available time. If you find that you are one minute behind on the test, don't skip one question without spending any time on it, just to catch back up. Take 15 fewer seconds on the next four questions, and after four questions you'll have caught back up. Once you catch back up, you can continue working each problem at your normal pace.

Furthermore, don't dwell on the problems that you were rushed on. If a problem was taking up too much time and you made a hurried guess, it must be difficult. The difficult questions are the ones you are most likely to miss anyway, so it isn't a big loss. It is better to end with more time than you need than to run out of time.

Lastly, sometimes it is beneficial to slow down if you are constantly getting ahead of time. You are always more likely to catch a careless mistake by working more slowly than quickly, and among very high-scoring test takers (those who are likely to have lots of time left over), careless errors affect the score more than mastery of material.

Copyright © Mometrix Media. You have been licensed one copy of this document for personal use only. Any other reproduction or redistribution is strictly prohibited. All rights reserved.

Secret Key #2 - Guessing is not Guesswork

You probably know that guessing is a good idea. Unlike other standardized tests, there is no penalty for getting a wrong answer. Even if you have no idea about a question, you still have a 20-25% chance of getting it right.

Most test takers do not understand the impact that proper guessing can have on their score. Unless you score extremely high, guessing will significantly contribute to your final score.

Monkeys Take the Test

What most test takers don't realize is that to insure that 20-25% chance, you have to guess randomly. If you put 20 monkeys in a room to take this test, assuming they answered once per question and behaved themselves, on average they would get 20-25% of the questions correct. Put 20 test takers in the room, and the average will be much lower among guessed questions. Why?
1. The test writers intentionally write deceptive answer choices that "look" right. A test taker has no idea about a question, so he picks the "best looking" answer, which is often wrong. The monkey has no idea what looks good and what doesn't, so it will consistently be right about 20-25% of the time.
2. Test takers will eliminate answer choices from the guessing pool based on a hunch or intuition. Simple but correct answers often get excluded, leaving a 0% chance of being correct. The monkey has no clue, and often gets lucky with the best choice.

This is why the process of elimination endorsed by most test courses is flawed and detrimental to your performance. Test takers don't guess; they make an ignorant stab in the dark that is usually worse than random.

$5 Challenge

Let me introduce one of the most valuable ideas of this course—the $5 challenge:

You only mark your "best guess" if you are willing to bet $5 on it.
You only eliminate choices from guessing if you are willing to bet $5 on it.

Why $5? Five dollars is an amount of money that is small yet not insignificant, and can really add up fast (20 questions could cost you $100). Likewise, each answer choice on one question of the test will have a small impact on your overall score, but it can really add up to a lot of points in the end.

The process of elimination IS valuable. The following shows your chance of guessing it right:

If you eliminate wrong answer choices until only this many remain:	Chance of getting it correct:

Copyright © Mometrix Media. You have been licensed one copy of this document for personal use only. Any other reproduction or redistribution is strictly prohibited. All rights reserved.

1	100%
2	50%
3	33%

However, if you accidentally eliminate the right answer or go on a hunch for an incorrect answer, your chances drop dramatically—to 0%. By guessing among all the answer choices, you are GUARANTEED to have a shot at the right answer.

That's why the $5 test is so valuable. If you give up the advantage and safety of a pure guess, it had better be worth the risk.

What we still haven't covered is how to be sure that whatever guess you make is truly random. Here's the easiest way:

Always pick the first answer choice among those remaining.

Such a technique means that you have decided, **before you see a single test question**, exactly how you are going to guess, and since the order of choices tells you nothing about which one is correct, this guessing technique is perfectly random.

This section is not meant to scare you away from making educated guesses or eliminating choices; you just need to define when a choice is worth eliminating. The $5 test, along with a pre-defined random guessing strategy, is the best way to make sure you reap all of the benefits of guessing.

Copyright © Mometrix Media. You have been licensed one copy of this document for personal use only. Any other reproduction or redistribution is strictly prohibited. All rights reserved.

Secret Key #3 - Practice Smarter, Not Harder

Many test takers delay the test preparation process because they dread the awful amounts of practice time they think necessary to succeed on the test. We have refined an effective method that will take you only a fraction of the time.

There are a number of "obstacles" in the path to success. Among these are answering questions, finishing in time, and mastering test-taking strategies. All must be executed on the day of the test at peak performance, or your score will suffer. The test is a mental marathon that has a large impact on your future.

Just like a marathon runner, it is important to work your way up to the full challenge. So first you just worry about questions, and then time, and finally strategy:

Success Strategy

1. Find a good source for practice tests.
2. If you are willing to make a larger time investment, consider using more than one study guide. Often the different approaches of multiple authors will help you "get" difficult concepts.
3. Take a practice test with no time constraints, with all study helps, "open book." Take your time with questions and focus on applying strategies.
4. Take a practice test with time constraints, with all guides, "open book."
5. Take a final practice test without open material and with time limits.

If you have time to take more practice tests, just repeat step 5. By gradually exposing yourself to the full rigors of the test environment, you will condition your mind to the stress of test day and maximize your success.

Copyright © Mometrix Media. You have been licensed one copy of this document for personal use only. Any other reproduction or redistribution is strictly prohibited. All rights reserved.

Secret Key #4 - Prepare, Don't Procrastinate

Let me state an obvious fact: if you take the test three times, you will probably get three different scores. This is due to the way you feel on test day, the level of preparedness you have, and the version of the test you see. Despite the test writers' claims to the contrary, some versions of the test WILL be easier for you than others.

Since your future depends so much on your score, you should maximize your chances of success. In order to maximize the likelihood of success, you've got to prepare in advance. This means taking practice tests and spending time learning the information and test taking strategies you will need to succeed.

Never go take the actual test as a "practice" test, expecting that you can just take it again if you need to. Take all the practice tests you can on your own, but when you go to take the official test, be prepared, be focused, and do your best the first time!

Copyright © Mometrix Media. You have been licensed one copy of this document for personal use only. Any other reproduction or redistribution is strictly prohibited. All rights reserved.

Secret Key #5 - Test Yourself

Everyone knows that time is money. There is no need to spend too much of your time or too little of your time preparing for the test. You should only spend as much of your precious time preparing as is necessary for you to get the score you need.

Once you have taken a practice test under real conditions of time constraints, then you will know if you are ready for the test or not.

If you have scored extremely high the first time that you take the practice test, then there is not much point in spending countless hours studying. You are already there.

Benchmark your abilities by retaking practice tests and seeing how much you have improved. Once you consistently score high enough to guarantee success, then you are ready.

If you have scored well below where you need, then knuckle down and begin studying in earnest. Check your improvement regularly through the use of practice tests under real conditions. Above all, don't worry, panic, or give up. The key is perseverance!

Then, when you go to take the test, remain confident and remember how well you did on the practice tests. If you can score high enough on a practice test, then you can do the same on the real thing.

Copyright © Mometrix Media. You have been licensed one copy of this document for personal use only. Any other reproduction or redistribution is strictly prohibited. All rights reserved.

General Strategies

The most important thing you can do is to ignore your fears and jump into the test immediately. Do not be overwhelmed by any strange-sounding terms. You have to jump into the test like jumping into a pool—all at once is the easiest way.

Make Predictions

As you read and understand the question, try to guess what the answer will be. Remember that several of the answer choices are wrong, and once you begin reading them, your mind will immediately become cluttered with answer choices designed to throw you off. Your mind is typically the most focused immediately after you have read the question and digested its contents. If you can, try to predict what the correct answer will be. You may be surprised at what you can predict.

Quickly scan the choices and see if your prediction is in the listed answer choices. If it is, then you can be quite confident that you have the right answer. It still won't hurt to check the other answer choices, but most of the time, you've got it!

Answer the Question

It may seem obvious to only pick answer choices that answer the question, but the test writers can create some excellent answer choices that are wrong. Don't pick an answer just because it sounds right, or you believe it to be true. It MUST answer the question. Once you've made your selection, always go back and check it against the question and make sure that you didn't misread the question and that the answer choice does answer the question posed.

Benchmark

After you read the first answer choice, decide if you think it sounds correct or not. If it doesn't, move on to the next answer choice. If it does, mentally mark that answer choice. This doesn't mean that you've definitely selected it as your answer choice, it just means that it's the best you've seen thus far. Go ahead and read the next choice. If the next choice is worse than the one you've already selected, keep going to the next answer choice. If the next choice is better than the choice you've already selected, mentally mark the new answer choice as your best guess.

The first answer choice that you select becomes your standard. Every other answer choice must be benchmarked against that standard. That choice is correct until proven otherwise by another answer choice beating it out. Once you've decided that no other answer choice seems as good, do one final check to ensure that your answer choice answers the question posed.

Valid Information

Don't discount any of the information provided in the question. Every piece of information may be necessary to determine the correct answer. None of the information in the question is there to throw you off (while the answer choices will certainly have information to throw you off). If two seemingly unrelated topics are discussed, don't ignore either. You can be confident there is a relationship, or it wouldn't be included in the question, and you are probably going to have to determine what is that relationship to find the answer.

Copyright © Mometrix Media. You have been licensed one copy of this document for personal use only. Any other reproduction or redistribution is strictly prohibited. All rights reserved.

Avoid "Fact Traps"

Don't get distracted by a choice that is factually true. Your search is for the answer that answers the question. Stay focused and don't fall for an answer that is true but irrelevant. Always go back to the question and make sure you're choosing an answer that actually answers the question and is not just a true statement. An answer can be factually correct, but it MUST answer the question asked. Additionally, two answers can both be seemingly correct, so be sure to read all of the answer choices, and make sure that you get the one that BEST answers the question.

Milk the Question

Some of the questions may throw you completely off. They might deal with a subject you have not been exposed to, or one that you haven't reviewed in years. While your lack of knowledge about the subject will be a hindrance, the question itself can give you many clues that will help you find the correct answer. Read the question carefully and look for clues. Watch particularly for adjectives and nouns describing difficult terms or words that you don't recognize. Regardless of whether you completely understand a word or not, replacing it with a synonym, either provided or one you more familiar with, may help you to understand what the questions are asking. Rather than wracking your mind about specific detailed information concerning a difficult term or word, try to use mental substitutes that are easier to understand.

The Trap of Familiarity

Don't just choose a word because you recognize it. On difficult questions, you may not recognize a number of words in the answer choices. The test writers don't put "make-believe" words on the test, so don't think that just because you only recognize all the words in one answer choice that that answer choice must be correct. If you only recognize words in one answer choice, then focus on that one. Is it correct? Try your best to determine if it is correct. If it is, that's great. If not, eliminate it. Each word and answer choice you eliminate increases your chances of getting the question correct, even if you then have to guess among the unfamiliar choices.

Eliminate Answers

Eliminate choices as soon as you realize they are wrong. But be careful! Make sure you consider all of the possible answer choices. Just because one appears right, doesn't mean that the next one won't be even better! The test writers will usually put more than one good answer choice for every question, so read all of them. Don't worry if you are stuck between two that seem right. By getting down to just two remaining possible choices, your odds are now 50/50. Rather than wasting too much time, play the odds. You are guessing, but guessing wisely because you've been able to knock out some of the answer choices that you know are wrong. If you are eliminating choices and realize that the last answer choice you are left with is also obviously wrong, don't panic. Start over and consider each choice again. There may easily be something that you missed the first time and will realize on the second pass.

Tough Questions

If you are stumped on a problem or it appears too hard or too difficult, don't waste time. Move on! Remember though, if you can quickly check for obviously incorrect answer choices, your chances of guessing correctly are greatly improved. Before you completely give up, at least try to knock out a couple of possible answers. Eliminate what you can and

Copyright © Mometrix Media. You have been licensed one copy of this document for personal use only. Any other reproduction or redistribution is strictly prohibited. All rights reserved.

then guess at the remaining answer choices before moving on.

Brainstorm

If you get stuck on a difficult question, spend a few seconds quickly brainstorming. Run through the complete list of possible answer choices. Look at each choice and ask yourself, "Could this answer the question satisfactorily?" Go through each answer choice and consider it independently of the others. By systematically going through all possibilities, you may find something that you would otherwise overlook. Remember though that when you get stuck, it's important to try to keep moving.

Read Carefully

Understand the problem. Read the question and answer choices carefully. Don't miss the question because you misread the terms. You have plenty of time to read each question thoroughly and make sure you understand what is being asked. Yet a happy medium must be attained, so don't waste too much time. You must read carefully, but efficiently.

Face Value

When in doubt, use common sense. Always accept the situation in the problem at face value. Don't read too much into it. These problems will not require you to make huge leaps of logic. The test writers aren't trying to throw you off with a cheap trick. If you have to go beyond creativity and make a leap of logic in order to have an answer choice answer the question, then you should look at the other answer choices. Don't overcomplicate the problem by creating theoretical relationships or explanations that will warp time or space. These are normal problems rooted in reality. It's just that the applicable relationship or explanation may not be readily apparent and you have to figure things out. Use your common sense to interpret anything that isn't clear.

Prefixes

If you're having trouble with a word in the question or answer choices, try dissecting it. Take advantage of every clue that the word might include. Prefixes and suffixes can be a huge help. Usually they allow you to determine a basic meaning. Pre- means before, post-means after, pro - is positive, de- is negative. From these prefixes and suffixes, you can get an idea of the general meaning of the word and try to put it into context. Beware though of any traps. Just because con- is the opposite of pro-, doesn't necessarily mean congress is the opposite of progress!

Hedge Phrases

Watch out for critical hedge phrases, led off with words such as "likely," "may," "can," "sometimes," "often," "almost," "mostly," "usually," "generally," "rarely," and "sometimes." Question writers insert these hedge phrases to cover every possibility. Often an answer choice will be wrong simply because it leaves no room for exception. Unless the situation calls for them, avoid answer choices that have definitive words like "exactly," and "always."

Switchback Words

Stay alert for "switchbacks." These are the words and phrases frequently used to alert you to shifts in thought. The most common switchback word is "but." Others include "although," "however," "nevertheless," "on the other hand," "even though," "while," "in spite of," "despite," and "regardless of."

Copyright © Mometrix Media. You have been licensed one copy of this document for personal use only. Any other reproduction or redistribution is strictly prohibited. All rights reserved.

New Information

Correct answer choices will rarely have completely new information included. Answer choices typically are straightforward reflections of the material asked about and will directly relate to the question. If a new piece of information is included in an answer choice that doesn't even seem to relate to the topic being asked about, then that answer choice is likely incorrect. All of the information needed to answer the question is usually provided for you in the question. You should not have to make guesses that are unsupported or choose answer choices that require unknown information that cannot be reasoned from what is given.

Time Management

On technical questions, don't get lost on the technical terms. Don't spend too much time on any one question. If you don't know what a term means, then odds are you aren't going to get much further since you don't have a dictionary. You should be able to immediately recognize whether or not you know a term. If you don't, work with the other clues that you have—the other answer choices and terms provided—but don't waste too much time trying to figure out a difficult term that you don't know.

Contextual Clues

Look for contextual clues. An answer can be right but not the correct answer. The contextual clues will help you find the answer that is most right and is correct. Understand the context in which a phrase or statement is made. This will help you make important distinctions.

Don't Panic

Panicking will not answer any questions for you; therefore, it isn't helpful. When you first see the question, if your mind goes blank, take a deep breath. Force yourself to mechanically go through the steps of solving the problem using the strategies you've learned.

Pace Yourself

Don't get clock fever. It's easy to be overwhelmed when you're looking at a page full of questions, your mind is full of random thoughts and feeling confused, and the clock is ticking down faster than you would like. Calm down and maintain the pace that you have set for yourself. As long as you are on track by monitoring your pace, you are guaranteed to have enough time for yourself. When you get to the last few minutes of the test, it may seem like you won't have enough time left, but if you only have as many questions as you should have left at that point, then you're right on track!

Answer Selection

The best way to pick an answer choice is to eliminate all of those that are wrong, until only one is left and confirm that is the correct answer. Sometimes though, an answer choice may immediately look right. Be careful! Take a second to make sure that the other choices are not equally obvious. Don't make a hasty mistake. There are only two times that you should stop before checking other answers. First is when you are positive that the answer choice you have selected is correct. Second is when time is almost out and you have to make a quick guess!

Check Your Work

Copyright © Mometrix Media. You have been licensed one copy of this document for personal use only. Any other reproduction or redistribution is strictly prohibited. All rights reserved.

Since you will probably not know every term listed and the answer to every question, it is important that you get credit for the ones that you do know. Don't miss any questions through careless mistakes. If at all possible, try to take a second to look back over your answer selection and make sure you've selected the correct answer choice and haven't made a costly careless mistake (such as marking an answer choice that you didn't mean to mark). The time it takes for this quick double check should more than pay for itself in caught mistakes.

Beware of Directly Quoted Answers

Sometimes an answer choice will repeat word for word a portion of the question or reference section. However, beware of such exact duplication. It may be a trap! More than likely, the correct choice will paraphrase or summarize a point, rather than being exactly the same wording.

Slang

Scientific sounding answers are better than slang ones. An answer choice that begins "To compare the outcomes..." is much more likely to be correct than one that begins "Because some people insisted..."

Extreme Statements

Avoid wild answers that throw out highly controversial ideas that are proclaimed as established fact. An answer choice that states the "process should used in certain situations, if..." is much more likely to be correct than one that states the "process should be discontinued completely." The first is a calm rational statement and doesn't even make a definitive, uncompromising stance, using a hedge word "if" to provide wiggle room, whereas the second choice is a radical idea and far more extreme.

Answer Choice Families

When you have two or more answer choices that are direct opposites or parallels, one of them is usually the correct answer. For instance, if one answer choice states "x increases" and another answer choice states "x decreases" or "y increases," then those two or three answer choices are very similar in construction and fall into the same family of answer choices. A family of answer choices consists of two or three answer choices, very similar in construction, but often with directly opposite meanings. Usually the correct answer choice will be in that family of answer choices. The "odd man out" or answer choice that doesn't seem to fit the parallel construction of the other answer choices is more likely to be incorrect.

Copyright © Mometrix Media. You have been licensed one copy of this document for personal use only. Any other reproduction or redistribution is strictly prohibited. All rights reserved.

Special Report: How to Overcome Test Anxiety

The very nature of tests caters to some level of anxiety, nervousness, or tension, just as we feel for any important event that occurs in our lives. A little bit of anxiety or nervousness can be a good thing. It helps us with motivation, and makes achievement just that much sweeter. However, too much anxiety can be a problem, especially if it hinders our ability to function and perform.

"Test anxiety," is the term that refers to the emotional reactions that some test-takers experience when faced with a test or exam. Having a fear of testing and exams is based upon a rational fear, since the test-taker's performance can shape the course of an academic career. Nevertheless, experiencing excessive fear of examinations will only interfere with the test-taker's ability to perform and chance to be successful.

There are a large variety of causes that can contribute to the development and sensation of test anxiety. These include, but are not limited to, lack of preparation and worrying about issues surrounding the test.

Lack of Preparation

Lack of preparation can be identified by the following behaviors or situations:

Not scheduling enough time to study, and therefore cramming the night before the test or exam
Managing time poorly, to create the sensation that there is not enough time to do everything
Failing to organize the text information in advance, so that the study material consists of the entire text and not simply the pertinent information
Poor overall studying habits

Worrying, on the other hand, can be related to both the test taker, or many other factors around him/her that will be affected by the results of the test. These include worrying about:

Previous performances on similar exams, or exams in general
How friends and other students are achieving
The negative consequences that will result from a poor grade or failure

There are three primary elements to test anxiety. Physical components, which involve the same typical bodily reactions as those to acute anxiety (to be discussed below). Emotional factors have to do with fear or panic. Mental or cognitive issues concerning attention spans and memory abilities.

Copyright © Mometrix Media. You have been licensed one copy of this document for personal use only. Any other reproduction or redistribution is strictly prohibited. All rights reserved.

Physical Signals

There are many different symptoms of test anxiety, and these are not limited to mental and emotional strain. Frequently there are a range of physical signals that will let a test taker know that he/she is suffering from test anxiety. These bodily changes can include the following:

Perspiring
Sweaty palms
Wet, trembling hands
Nausea
Dry mouth
A knot in the stomach
Headache
Faintness
Muscle tension
Aching shoulders, back and neck
Rapid heart beat
Feeling too hot/cold

To recognize the sensation of test anxiety, a test-taker should monitor him/herself for the following sensations:

The physical distress symptoms as listed above
Emotional sensitivity, expressing emotional feelings such as the need to cry or laugh too much, or a sensation of anger or helplessness
A decreased ability to think, causing the test-taker to blank out or have racing thoughts that are hard to organize or control.

Though most students will feel some level of anxiety when faced with a test or exam, the majority can cope with that anxiety and maintain it at a manageable level. However, those who cannot are faced with a very real and very serious condition, which can and should be controlled for the immeasurable benefit of this sufferer.

Naturally, these sensations lead to negative results for the testing experience. The most common effects of test anxiety have to do with nervousness and mental blocking.

Nervousness

Nervousness can appear in several different levels:

The test-taker's difficulty, or even inability to read and understand the questions on the test
The difficulty or inability to organize thoughts to a coherent form
The difficulty or inability to recall key words and concepts relating to the testing questions (especially essays)
The receipt of poor grades on a test, though the test material was well known by the test taker

Copyright © Mometrix Media. You have been licensed one copy of this document for personal use only. Any other reproduction or redistribution is strictly prohibited. All rights reserved.

Conversely, a person may also experience mental blocking, which involves:

Blanking out on test questions
Only remembering the correct answers to the questions when the test has already finished.

Fortunately for test anxiety sufferers, beating these feelings, to a large degree, has to do with proper preparation. When a test taker has a feeling of preparedness, then anxiety will be dramatically lessened.

The first step to resolving anxiety issues is to distinguish which of the two types of anxiety are being suffered. If the anxiety is a direct result of a lack of preparation, this should be considered a normal reaction, and the anxiety level (as opposed to the test results) shouldn't be anything to worry about. However, if, when adequately prepared, the test-taker still panics, blanks out, or seems to overreact, this is not a fully rational reaction. While this can be considered normal too, there are many ways to combat and overcome these effects.

Remember that anxiety cannot be entirely eliminated, however, there are ways to minimize it, to make the anxiety easier to manage. Preparation is one of the best ways to minimize test anxiety. Therefore the following techniques are wise in order to best fight off any anxiety that may want to build.

To begin with, try to avoid cramming before a test, whenever it is possible. By trying to memorize an entire term's worth of information in one day, you'll be shocking your system, and not giving yourself a very good chance to absorb the information. This is an easy path to anxiety, so for those who suffer from test anxiety, cramming should not even be considered an option.

Instead of cramming, work throughout the semester to combine all of the material which is presented throughout the semester, and work on it gradually as the course goes by, making sure to master the main concepts first, leaving minor details for a week or so before the test.

To study for the upcoming exam, be sure to pose questions that may be on the examination, to gauge the ability to answer them by integrating the ideas from your texts, notes and lectures, as well as any supplementary readings.

If it is truly impossible to cover all of the information that was covered in that particular term, concentrate on the most important portions, that can be covered very well. Learn these concepts as best as possible, so that when the test comes, a goal can be made to use these concepts as presentations of your knowledge.

In addition to study habits, changes in attitude are critical to beating a struggle with test anxiety. In fact, an improvement of the perspective over the entire test-taking experience can actually help a test taker to enjoy studying and therefore improve the overall experience. Be certain not to overemphasize the significance of the grade - know that the result of the test is neither a reflection of self worth, nor is it a measure of intelligence; one grade will not predict a person's future success.

Copyright © Mometrix Media. You have been licensed one copy of this document for personal use only. Any other reproduction or redistribution is strictly prohibited. All rights reserved.

To improve an overall testing outlook, the following steps should be tried:

Keeping in mind that the most reasonable expectation for taking a test is to expect to try to demonstrate as much of what you know as you possibly can.
Reminding ourselves that a test is only one test; this is not the only one, and there will be others.
The thought of thinking of oneself in an irrational, all-or-nothing term should be avoided at all costs.
A reward should be designated for after the test, so there's something to look forward to. Whether it be going to a movie, going out to eat, or simply visiting friends, schedule it in advance, and do it no matter what result is expected on the exam.

Test-takers should also keep in mind that the basics are some of the most important things, even beyond anti-anxiety techniques and studying. Never neglect the basic social, emotional and biological needs, in order to try to absorb information. In order to best achieve, these three factors must be held as just as important as the studying itself.

Study Steps

Remember the following important steps for studying:

Maintain healthy nutrition and exercise habits. Continue both your recreational activities and social pass times. These both contribute to your physical and emotional well being.
Be certain to get a good amount of sleep, especially the night before the test, because when you're overtired you are not able to perform to the best of your best ability.
Keep the studying pace to a moderate level by taking breaks when they are needed, and varying the work whenever possible, to keep the mind fresh instead of getting bored.
When enough studying has been done that all the material that can be learned has been learned, and the test taker is prepared for the test, stop studying and do something relaxing such as listening to music, watching a movie, or taking a warm bubble bath.

There are also many other techniques to minimize the uneasiness or apprehension that is experienced along with test anxiety before, during, or even after the examination. In fact, there are a great deal of things that can be done to stop anxiety from interfering with lifestyle and performance. Again, remember that anxiety will not be eliminated entirely, and it shouldn't be. Otherwise that "up" feeling for exams would not exist, and most of us depend on that sensation to perform better than usual. However, this anxiety has to be at a level that is manageable.

Of course, as we have just discussed, being prepared for the exam is half the battle right away. Attending all classes, finding out what knowledge will be expected on the exam, and knowing the exam schedules are easy steps to lowering anxiety. Keeping up with work will remove the need to cram, and efficient study habits will eliminate wasted time. Studying should be done in an ideal location for concentration, so that it is simple to become interested in the material and give it complete attention. A method such as SQ3R (Survey, Question, Read, Recite, Review) is a wonderful key to follow to make sure that the study habits are as effective as possible, especially in the case of learning from a textbook. Flashcards are great techniques for memorization. Learning to take good notes will mean that notes will be full of useful information, so that less sifting will need to be done to seek out what is pertinent for studying. Reviewing notes after class and then again on occasion will keep the information fresh in the mind. From notes that have been taken summary sheets and outlines can be made for simpler reviewing.

A study group can also be a very motivational and helpful place to study, as there will be a sharing of ideas, all of the minds can work together, to make sure that everyone understands, and the studying will be made more interesting because it will be a social occasion.

Basically, though, as long as the test-taker remains organized and self confident, with efficient study habits, less time will need to be spent studying, and higher grades will be achieved.

To become self confident, there are many useful steps. The first of these is "self talk." It has been shown through extensive research, that self-talk for students who suffer from test anxiety, should be well monitored, in order to make sure that it contributes to self confidence as opposed to sinking the student. Frequently the self talk of test-anxious students is negative or self-defeating, thinking that everyone else is smarter and faster, that they always mess up, and that if they don't do well, they'll fail the entire course. It is important to decreasing anxiety that awareness is made of self talk. Try writing any negative self thoughts and then disputing them with a positive statement instead. Begin self-encouragement as though it was a friend speaking. Repeat positive statements to help reprogram the mind to believing in successes instead of failures.

Helpful Techniques

Other extremely helpful techniques include:

Self-visualization of doing well and reaching goals
While aiming for an "A" level of understanding, don't try to "overprotect" by setting your expectations lower. This will only convince the mind to stop studying in order to meet the lower expectations.
Don't make comparisons with the results or habits of other students. These are individual factors, and different things work for different people, causing different results.
Strive to become an expert in learning what works well, and what can be done in order to improve. Consider collecting this data in a journal.
Create rewards for after studying instead of doing things before studying that will only turn into avoidance behaviors.
Make a practice of relaxing - by using methods such as progressive relaxation, self-hypnosis, guided imagery, etc - in order to make relaxation an automatic sensation.
Work on creating a state of relaxed concentration so that concentrating will take on the focus of the mind, so that none will be wasted on worrying.
Take good care of the physical self by eating well and getting enough sleep.
Plan in time for exercise and stick to this plan.

Copyright © Mometrix Media. You have been licensed one copy of this document for personal use only. Any other reproduction or redistribution is strictly prohibited. All rights reserved.

Beyond these techniques, there are other methods to be used before, during and after the test that will help the test-taker perform well in addition to overcoming anxiety.

Before the exam comes the academic preparation. This involves establishing a study schedule and beginning at least one week before the actual date of the test. By doing this, the anxiety of not having enough time to study for the test will be automatically eliminated. Moreover, this will make the studying a much more effective experience, ensuring that the learning will be an easier process. This relieves much undue pressure on the test-taker.

Summary sheets, note cards, and flash cards with the main concepts and examples of these main concepts should be prepared in advance of the actual studying time. A topic should never be eliminated from this process. By omitting a topic because it isn't expected to be on the test is only setting up the test-taker for anxiety should it actually appear on the exam. Utilize the course syllabus for laying out the topics that should be studied. Carefully go over the notes that were made in class, paying special attention to any of the issues that the professor took special care to emphasize while lecturing in class. In the textbooks, use the chapter review, or if possible, the chapter tests, to begin your review.

It may even be possible to ask the instructor what information will be covered on the exam, or what the format of the exam will be (for example, multiple choice, essay, free form, true-false). Additionally, see if it is possible to find out how many questions will be on the test. If a review sheet or sample test has been offered by the professor, make good use of it, above anything else, for the preparation for the test. Another great resource for getting to know the examination is reviewing tests from previous semesters. Use these tests to review, and aim to achieve a 100% score on each of the possible topics. With a few exceptions, the goal that you set for yourself is the highest one that you will reach.

Take all of the questions that were assigned as homework, and rework them to any other possible course material. The more problems reworked, the more skill and confidence will form as a result. When forming the solution to a problem, write out each of the steps. Don't simply do head work. By doing as many steps on paper as possible, much clarification and therefore confidence will be formed. Do this with as many homework problems as possible, before checking the answers. By checking the answer after each problem, a reinforcement will exist, that will not be on the exam. Study situations should be as exam-like as possible, to prime the test-taker's system for the experience. By waiting to check the answers at the end, a psychological advantage will be formed, to decrease the stress factor.

Another fantastic reason for not cramming is the avoidance of confusion in concepts, especially when it comes to mathematics. 8-10 hours of study will become one hundred percent more effective if it is spread out over a week or at least several days, instead of doing it all in one sitting. Recognize that the human brain requires time in order to assimilate new material, so frequent breaks and a span of study time over several days will be much more beneficial.

Additionally, don't study right up until the point of the exam. Studying should stop a minimum of one hour before the exam begins. This allows the brain to rest and put

Copyright © Mometrix Media. You have been licensed one copy of this document for personal use only. Any other reproduction or redistribution is strictly prohibited. All rights reserved.

things in their proper order. This will also provide the time to become as relaxed as possible when going into the examination room. The test-taker will also have time to eat well and eat sensibly. Know that the brain needs food as much as the rest of the body. With enough food and enough sleep, as well as a relaxed attitude, the body and the mind are primed for success.

Avoid any anxious classmates who are talking about the exam. These students only spread anxiety, and are not worth sharing the anxious sentimentalities.

Before the test also involves creating a positive attitude, so mental preparation should also be a point of concentration. There are many keys to creating a positive attitude. Should fears become rushing in, make a visualization of taking the exam, doing well, and seeing an A written on the paper. Write out a list of affirmations that will bring a feeling of confidence, such as "I am doing well in my English class," "I studied well and know my material," "I enjoy this class." Even if the affirmations aren't believed at first, it sends a positive message to the subconscious which will result in an alteration of the overall belief system, which is the system that creates reality.

If a sensation of panic begins, work with the fear and imagine the very worst! Work through the entire scenario of not passing the test, failing the entire course, and dropping out of school, followed by not getting a job, and pushing a shopping cart through the dark alley where you'll live. This will place things into perspective! Then, practice deep breathing and create a visualization of the opposite situation - achieving an "A" on the exam, passing the entire course, receiving the degree at a graduation ceremony.

On the day of the test, there are many things to be done to ensure the best results, as well as the most calm outlook. The following stages are suggested in order to maximize test-taking potential:

Begin the examination day with a moderate breakfast, and avoid any coffee or beverages with caffeine if the test taker is prone to jitters. Even people who are used to managing caffeine can feel jittery or light-headed when it is taken on a test day.
Attempt to do something that is relaxing before the examination begins. As last minute cramming clouds the mastering of overall concepts, it is better to use this time to create a calming outlook.
Be certain to arrive at the test location well in advance, in order to provide time to select a location that is away from doors, windows and other distractions, as well as giving enough time to relax before the test begins.
Keep away from anxiety generating classmates who will upset the sensation of stability and relaxation that is being attempted before the exam.
Should the waiting period before the exam begins cause anxiety, create a self-distraction by reading a light magazine or something else that is relaxing and simple.

During the exam itself, read the entire exam from beginning to end, and find out how much time should be allotted to each individual problem. Once writing the exam, should more time be taken for a problem, it should be abandoned, in order to begin another problem. If there is time at the end, the unfinished problem can always be returned to and completed.

Copyright © Mometrix Media. You have been licensed one copy of this document for personal use only. Any other reproduction or redistribution is strictly prohibited. All rights reserved.

Read the instructions very carefully - twice - so that unpleasant surprises won't follow during or after the exam has ended.

When writing the exam, pretend that the situation is actually simply the completion of homework within a library, or at home. This will assist in forming a relaxed atmosphere, and will allow the brain extra focus for the complex thinking function.

Begin the exam with all of the questions with which the most confidence is felt. This will build the confidence level regarding the entire exam and will begin a quality momentum. This will also create encouragement for trying the problems where uncertainty resides.

Going with the "gut instinct" is always the way to go when solving a problem. Second guessing should be avoided at all costs. Have confidence in the ability to do well.

For essay questions, create an outline in advance that will keep the mind organized and make certain that all of the points are remembered. For multiple choice, read every answer, even if the correct one has been spotted - a better one may exist.

Continue at a pace that is reasonable and not rushed, in order to be able to work carefully. Provide enough time to go over the answers at the end, to check for small errors that can be corrected.

Should a feeling of panic begin, breathe deeply, and think of the feeling of the body releasing sand through its pores. Visualize a calm, peaceful place, and include all of the sights, sounds and sensations of this image. Continue the deep breathing, and take a few minutes to continue this with closed eyes. When all is well again, return to the test.

If a "blanking" occurs for a certain question, skip it and move on to the next question. There will be time to return to the other question later. Get everything done that can be done, first, to guarantee all the grades that can be compiled, and to build all of the confidence possible. Then return to the weaker questions to build the marks from there.

Remember, one's own reality can be created, so as long as the belief is there, success will follow. And remember: anxiety can happen later, right now, there's an exam to be written!

After the examination is complete, whether there is a feeling for a good grade or a bad grade, don't dwell on the exam, and be certain to follow through on the reward that was promised…and enjoy it! Don't dwell on any mistakes that have been made, as there is nothing that can be done at this point anyway.

Additionally, don't begin to study for the next test right away. Do something relaxing for a while, and let the mind relax and prepare itself to begin absorbing information again.

From the results of the exam - both the grade and the entire experience, be certain to learn from what has gone on. Perfect studying habits and work some more on confidence in order to make the next examination experience even better than the last one.

Copyright © Mometrix Media. You have been licensed one copy of this document for personal use only. Any other reproduction or redistribution is strictly prohibited. All rights reserved.

Learn to avoid places where openings occurred for laziness, procrastination and day dreaming.

Use the time between this exam and the next one to better learn to relax, even learning to relax on cue, so that any anxiety can be controlled during the next exam. Learn how to relax the body. Slouch in your chair if that helps. Tighten and then relax all of the different muscle groups, one group at a time, beginning with the feet and then working all the way up to the neck and face. This will ultimately relax the muscles more than they were to begin with. Learn how to breathe deeply and comfortably, and focus on this breathing going in and out as a relaxing thought. With every exhale, repeat the word "relax."

As common as test anxiety is, it is very possible to overcome it. Make yourself one of the test-takers who overcome this frustrating hindrance.

Copyright © Mometrix Media. You have been licensed one copy of this document for personal use only. Any other reproduction or redistribution is strictly prohibited. All rights reserved.

Copyright © Mometrix Media. You have been licensed one copy of this document for personal use only. Any other reproduction or redistribution is strictly prohibited. All rights reserved.

Additional Bonus Material

Due to our efforts to try to keep this book to a manageable length, we've created a link that will give you access to all of your additional bonus material.

Please visit http://www.mometrix.com/bonus948/slla to access the information.

Copyright © Mometrix Media. You have been licensed one copy of this document for personal use only. Any other reproduction or redistribution is strictly prohibited. All rights reserved.

87194863R00102

Made in the USA
Middletown, DE
02 September 2018